WINGNUTS

WINGNUTS

Extremism in the Age of Obama

JOHN AVLON

New York

Books published by Beast Books are available at special discounts for bulk purchases in the United States by corporations, institutions, and other organizations. For more information, please contact the Special Markets Department at the Perseus Books Group, 2300 Chestnut Street, Suite 200, Philadelphia, PA 19103, or call (800) 810-4145, ext. 5000, or e-mail special .markets@perseusbooks.com.

Some material in the book was previously published in *The Telegraph* (UK) and *The Daily Beast*.

Design by Jack Lenzo
Text set in 12-point Apollo

Library of Congress Cataloging-in-Publication Data
Avlon, John P.
Wingnuts : extremism in the age of Obama / John Avlon.
pages cm
Includes bibliographical references and index.
ISBN 978-0-9912476-0-8 (paperback)—ISBN 978-0-9912476-1-5 (e-book) 1. United States—Politics and government—2009-. 2. Political culture—United States. 3. Right and left (Political science) 4. Radicals—United States. 5. Political parties—United States. 6. Polarization (Social sciences)—United States. 7. Mass media—Political aspects—United States. 8. Hate—Political aspects—United States. 9. Fear—Political aspects—United States. I. Title. II. Title: Wingnuts.
E907.A923 2014
320.97309′051—dc23
2014015546

10 9 8 7 6 5 4 3 2 1

For my bride, Margaret

I didn't vote for him, but he's my president, and I hope he does a good job.

—**John Wayne,**
after the 1960 election of John F. Kennedy

I hope he fails.

—**Rush Limbaugh,**
after the 2008 election of Barack Obama

CONTENTS

PREFACE

Wingnuts chronicles the outburst of extremism at the outset of the Obama administration. This new edition, published in the run-up to the 2014 midterm election, seems needed because so many of the characters and conflicts introduced in the book have migrated from the freakish sideshow of American politics to center stage while others have, mercifully, flamed out. Their stories need an update to give a sense of the arc of our politics— after all, politics is history in the present tense.

Beneath the gonzo fun of covering the extremes is a serious concern for the future of our country. Hyperpartisans are playing with forces that can easily get out of control and threaten to destabilize our democracy. And though *The Daily Beast* founding editor, Tina Brown, originally intended this inaugural publication from Beast Books in 2010 to present reporting in e-book form while it was still white-hot and relevant, my secret aim was to present the hate-fueled protests in historic perspective.

Wingnuts remains in many ways my modest attempt to update Richard Hofstadter's classic *The Paranoid Style in American Politics* for our era. We see so many variations of the old themes—"the heated exaggeration, suspiciousness, and conspiratorial fantasy"[1]—now sold to enthusiastic new dupes via partisan media and online echo chambers. Their reach and influence stretch farther than ever before.

The word *wingnut* has entered the lexicon largely because we keep being confronted with unhinged examples of how the fringe is blurring with the base. These are the wages of polarization: a

2010 Pew poll found that one-third of Republicans believed that Barack Obama is Muslim—*double* the number of those expressing the same belief during the 2008 election—and 45 percent of Republicans believed that President Obama was not born in the United States and therefore is not constitutionally eligible to be president.[2] On the flip side, a 2006 Scripps poll found that 50 percent of Democrats believed that it was "very likely" or "somewhat likely" President Bush was complicit in the 9/11 terror attacks.[3]

Faced with such statistics, it is tempting to throw up your hands and renounce politics entirely. As the Irish satirist Jonathan Swift once quipped, "It is useless to attempt to reason a man out of a thing which he was never reasoned into."[4]

But the larger stakes are civic, not just political, and they cut to the heart of our country. The late New York senator Daniel Patrick Moynihan famously said, "Everyone is entitled to their own opinion, but not their own facts."[5] The problem is that today hyperpartisans enter debates armed with their own facts provided by partisan media performers. Not so long ago, party leaders fired off talking points to talk-radio show hosts. Now, talk radio provides the talking points to politicians who are terrified of being attacked by the base for seeming too responsible and willing to compromise with folks on the other side of the aisle.

We are self-segregating ourselves into separate political realities, and the rise of the Wingnuts is one powerful expression of that fact. It was sad but not surprising that when I interviewed one of Michele Bachmann's staffers, he explained that the congresswoman—who serves on the House Intelligence Committee—got most of her information from the conservative conspiracy theory website *WorldNetDaily* (*WND*).

An online poll by Harris Interactive inspired by Wingnuts and conducted at the height of the health-care debate drew a lot of attention and some criticism at the time.[6] Among the findings from Republicans polled: 67 percent thought President Obama was a "socialist"; 61 percent said he wanted to take away their right to own guns; 51 percent said he "wants to turn over the sovereignty of the United States to a one world government"; 45 percent agreed with the "Birthers" that he was "not born in the United States and so is not eligible to be president"; 42 percent said he was racist; 38 percent said that Obama is "doing many of the things Hitler did"; and 24 percent said that he "may be the Anti-Christ." And so on.

It's ugly stuff and I understand why professional partisans and their apologists would feel uncomfortable with the results. But subsequent polls have validated the data. A 2012 Fox News–Washington Times poll found that 89 percent of Republicans believed Obama is moving the nation toward socialism,[7] and a 2010 Democracy Corps poll found that 55 percent of all Americans thought Obama was socialist.[8] A 2011 Public Policy Polling (PPP) poll found that 51 percent of Republican primary voters didn't think Obama was born in the United States.[9] After Obama's reelection, PPP even fired off a conspiracy theory poll and found that 22 percent of Romney voters thought Obama was the Antichrist.[10]

Add to those stats the fact that the number of militant militia groups grew from forty-two in 2008 to 321 in 2012, according to the Southern Poverty Law Center (SPLC)—not coincidentally, at a time when the face of the federal government is black—while the number of associated patriot groups exploded more than 800 percent over President Obama's first term, from 149 to 1,360.[11] Ignoring disturbing dynamics won't make them go away. As H. L. Mencken once wrote: "Such are the facts. I apologize for the Babylonian indecency of printing them."[12]

But *Wingnuts* also had its critics on the left, the chief complaint being "moral equivalence" because I was not content to simply criticize the right. That would have been easy but a bit of partisan hackery, and it undercut my goal of trying to define the considerable common ground that exists in America by playing offense against the extremes on both sides. Common sense and history tell us that neither political party has a monopoly on virtue or vice. This isn't moral equivalence as much as an attempt at moral clarity. And though the far right and far left can be equally insane, there is no question that the far right has been far crazier in the opening years of the Obama administration. In their excellent book *It's Even Worse Than It Looks,* political scientists Thomas Mann and Norman Ornstein call this dynamic "asymmetric polarization"—a state of affairs backed up by congressional voting patterns. So why didn't I train my fire entirely in that direction? Because it would have ignored the larger cycle of incitement that has taken our political debates so off-center in recent decades. One other liberal gripe I might as well address—their complaint that the far left should properly be called "Moonbats" rather than "Wingnuts." But this distinction has a wispy, self-congratulatory tone and I still believe that a common term should be used. One other common misconception: Wingnuts are not conservatives—they are radicals. Overall, I back Cass Sunstein's recent dictionary-ready definition: "A Wingnut is someone who has a dogmatic commitment to an extreme view ('wing') that is false and at least a little bit crazy."[13]

Although some of the trends described in *Wingnuts* have gotten worse, there are some hopeful signs. After all, the three polarizing figures who were put on the first edition cover of *Wingnuts*—Glenn Beck, Sarah Palin, and Keith Olbermann—have gone from peak influence to near irrelevance. And responsible Republicans are beginning to realize that these extremes are ultimately their own side's worst enemy, an obstacle to winning national elections and governing effectively in the national interest. I wish those Republican reformers success going forward.

It's also important to recognize that some of America's political divides are not rooted in questions of left versus right as much as urban versus rural. These basic cultural differences have been the drivers of political debates since Alexander Hamilton squared off against Thomas Jefferson in George Washington's cabinet. They were reflected in the Civil War and Prohibition as well as in today's red-state-versus-blue-state debates.

This book is just a new chapter of an old story. President Theodore Roosevelt coined the term "lunatic fringe" to describe the Wingnuts of his day, and as I hope to show in a new section titled "A Brief History of Extremism in America," we have been battling these forces in some form since the beginning of our republic, many with strikingly similar themes and telltale rhetorical tricks. What's different now—and why the Wingnuts can't simply be dismissed as an irritant or curiosity—is the unprecedented polarization of the two parties along stark geographic and ideological lines, compounded by the rise of new technology that expands the reach of partisan media echo chambers to people who in the past would have been isolated by their absurdity.

In the end, what's fueling Wingnut conspiracies is hyperpartisanship—the pervasive team-ism that divides America into "us" against "them," my team versus your team. Hyperpartisanship pretends to be about differences of principle, but it is primarily about the pursuit of power. And it is hurting our ability to solve common problems while turning our politics into something like a cult—where conformity is confused with courage and dissent is seen as disloyalty. We can help break this fever by standing up to the forces of fear and ignorance, demanding something better for our democracy.

John Avlon, Editor-in-Chief, *The Daily Beast*
New York City, 2014

A WINGNUT GLOSSARY

9/11 Truthers: Conspiracy theorists from both the far right and far left who believe that the terrorist attacks of September 11, 2001, were an inside job.

Birthers: The term used to describe people who believe Barack Obama was born in Kenya and therefore is not constitutionally eligible to serve as president of the United States.

Bush Derangement Syndrome (BDS): Defined by conservative columnist Charles Krauthammer as "the acute onset of paranoia in otherwise normal people in reaction to the policies, the presidency—nay—the very existence of George W. Bush."

Code Pink: A left-wing feminist group formed to protest the invasion of Iraq. Code Pink specializes in performance-art protests against the federal government and military recruiting stations, with a fondness for screaming during congressional hearings.

Fright Wing: The paranoid politics of fearmongering and conspiracy theories that occurs on the outer limits of the political spectrum, where the far right and the far left start to echo and resemble each other.

Hatriots: Obama-era resurgence of the militia movements of the 1990s, motivated by antigovernment conspiracies and Revolutionary War imagery. These self-styled patriots fear the government and hate the president.

John Birch Society: Anti-Communist, paleoconservative group founded in 1958. The group's founder, Robert Welch, famously labeled President Dwight David Eisenhower a "dedicated, conscious agent of the Communist conspiracy." Despite drawing the rebuke of William F. Buckley Jr., founder of the *National Review,* and other prominent conservatives, the group persists in "End the Fed" and "US out of UN" efforts.

Know-Nothings: A Nativist political movement in the 1850s that opposed Irish Catholic immigration, it subsequently morphed into the short-lived American Party. Some later anti-immigrant movements have been dubbed the "new Know-Nothings."

League of the South: Founded in 1994, the League of the South advocates for the "independence of the Southern people" from the "American empire."

Lyndon LaRouche: A conspiracy theorist, quasi-cult leader, and frequent presidential candidate whose followers pushed Obama-as-Hitler posters and pamphlets during 2009's health-care debate.

Neo-Confederates: Contemporary pro-Confederate activists who advance the cause of Southern Civil War history, including putting Confederate flags on public lands. Under the banner of "Heritage, not Hate," many of these activists have a misty view of slavery and segregation—and some continue to advocate for secession.

Oath Keepers: An alliance of current and former military personnel and law-enforcement officers who pledge to abide by their oath to defend the Constitution. The group stands armed and ready, should another American revolution arise.

Obama Derangement Syndrome (ODS): Pathological hatred of President Obama, posing as patriotism.

RINO: Republican in Name Only, a label applied by absolutist conservative activists against any Republican who does not pass their fiscal and social conservative litmus test.

Rules for Radicals: A book by Chicago community organizer Saul Alinsky, which laid out a strategy for creating the conditions to achieve revolutionary social change. Conservative protesters have recently adopted its confrontational tactics.

Tenthers: Tenth Amendment advocates who believe that the federal government has exceeded its constitutional jurisdiction and that therefore states have a right to secede from the union. Supporters have recently passed "sovereignty" resolutions in eight states.

Three Percenters: A militia-inspired group that takes its name from the questionable statistic that only 3 percent of the American colonists actively fought for independence. It embraces the philosophy of the American Resistance Movement—a survivalist network that teaches its followers how to train for the fight against US government–led tyranny.

WorldNetDaily (WND): A right-wing website founded in 1997 that mixes reporting and opinion and reaches millions of people a month. It is often cited by conspiracy theorists as a prime news source.

INTRODUCING THE WINGNUTS

This is the story of how hope and change turned into hate and gridlock. It all happened as a bad craziness snaked through America in the first years of the Obama administration.

"Obama is raping America. Obama is raping our values. Obama is raping our democracy."[1] That's the considered judgment of Michael Savage, and it's the kind of talk that draws in millions of listeners, making him one of the top conservative radio hosts in the country.

On the left, MSNBC's Ed Schultz declares: "The Republicans lie. They want to see you dead. They'd rather make money off your dead corpse. They kind of like it when that woman has cancer and they don't have anything for us."[2]

Billy Glassberg believes President Obama is "a traitor and a tyrant." Glassberg doesn't have a talk show, but he is affiliated with the Oath Keepers, a group of armed law-enforcement officers, military men, and hangers-on who meet to reaffirm their oath to defend the Constitution against all enemies, foreign and domestic—a category that some of them believe includes President Barack Obama.

"The whole point of the Oath Keepers is to stop a dictatorship from ever happening here," says its founder, Stewart Rhodes, a Yale Law School graduate, former army paratrooper, and former aide to Congressman Ron Paul. "My focus is on the guys with the guns, because they can't do it without them . . . We say if the American people decide it's time for a revolution, we'll fight with you."[3]

Welcome to life on the freak beat. From the spring of 2009's Tea Party protests to the summer's health-care town hall hijackings, I've reported on the outbreak of hyperpartisanship in what was supposed to be the postpartisan Obama era. Policy debates are being overshadowed by apocalyptic accusations. The president is called both Hitler and a Communist by grassroots activists and members of Congress. The Wingnuts are on the attack.

What's a Wingnut? It's someone on the far-right wing or far-left wing of the political spectrum. They are the professional polarizers and the unhinged activists, the hard-core haters and the paranoid conspiracy theorists. One telltale sign: Wingnuts always confuse partisanship with patriotism. And they are on the rise.

Pumped up by the self-segregated echo chamber of talk radio, cable news, and the Internet, Wingnuts see politics as ideological blood sport, an all-or-nothing struggle for the nation's soul. They find purpose by dividing America into "us against them." And for those with a vested interest in stirring the crazy-pot, all this is good for business. Hate is a cheap and easy recruiting tool. But it can be murder on a democracy.

The Wingnuts took flight in the opening years of the Obama administration amid the anxieties of an economy in manic recession, double-digit unemployment, deep deficits, and a decade of war. Demagogues always rise when the economy goes south, offering a narcotic for the nervous and dispossessed, with occasionally violent side effects.

During the Great Depression, populist anger was directed at big business. When conservative populism reared its head in the late 1960s, anger shifted toward big government. Now we've got both—anger at big business *and* big government. It's a perfect political storm, primed for a return to pitchfork politics.

"If a country allows itself to get into deep economic trouble, that is going to unsettle the political system," explained Judge Richard Posner—a Reagan appointee—to the *New Yorker*'s Jeffrey Toobin. "That's what happened in the Thirties, with the Depression, and it's what's happening now. People get very upset, and they become vulnerable to extremist appeals. That's what's happened to the Republican Party in the House of Representatives."

Look—I'm not a Democrat and I'm not a Republican. I'm an American. I believe the far left and far right can be equally insane—but there's no question that in the first years of the Obama administration, the far right has been far crazier. After decades of work in DC, the political scientists Thomas Mann and Norman Ornstein assessed that "the GOP has become an insurgent outlier in American politics. It is ideologically extreme; scornful of compromise; unmoved by conventional understanding of facts, evidence and science; and dismissive of the legitimacy of its political opposition."

In many ways, this isn't a surprise. Parties out of power are often dominated by their most extreme voices. Without the responsibility of governing to ground them, ideological activists preach absolutism. They increasingly try to demonize and delegitimize a new president from day one—there is no constructive assumption of goodwill, only a permanent opposition campaign.

We saw this destructive dynamic at work during George W. Bush's administration, when far-left protests erupted into Bush Derangement Syndrome, comparing Bush to Hitler and calling for impeachment. Now the far right is out of power and, for some of them, losing an election feels like living under tyranny.

In the opening years of the Obama administration, Obama Derangement Syndrome proliferated: pathological hatred of the president posing as patriotism. The people afflicted believe there is a sinister socialist plot to undermine our constitutional republic. It's a hyperpartisan message hammered home on our airwaves and the Internet with apocalyptic urgency.

The presence of the first African American president is fueling another anxiety—the change from a traditionally white to a minority-led federal government. Race has been a core wound in America since the original sin of slavery, but I don't believe that the simple, stupid, old-school racism of the Bull Connor variety is motivating the majority of opposition to Obama. Instead, something more subtle is at work: the slumbering fear that our national heritage might be eclipsed by the rise of a nonwhite majority in America by midcentury. We are witnessing the birth of white-minority politics.

As I've traveled across the country interviewing the luminaries and low-lights among the Wingnuts, I've heard a consistent refrain: Armageddon days are here again.

On a Saturday morning in October 2009, I joined the Oath Keepers for their first annual meeting at the Texas Station Hotel and Casino, on the fringe of the Las Vegas strip. In a ballroom beside slot machines and frontier-town façades, nearly one hundred current and former military and law-enforcement officers met to reaffirm their constitutional oath.

On the display tables, there were images of a black-masked storm trooper standing behind the presidential podium with a skull imposed on the US Capitol dome. There was talk of an H1N1 vaccine conspiracy, false flag operations, and concentration camps—all part of a carefully planned descent into fascism and then communism.

Former Arizona sheriff Richard Mack—a militia hero in the 1990s and adviser to the Oath Keepers—felt that the anger in the room was justified. "The very people who promised us that they would protect our Constitution are the ones destroying it."

He believes President Obama violates his constitutional oath "on a daily basis—probably two or three times a day."

Billy Glassberg, a Nevada deli owner, counts Sheriff Mack among his heroes. He's sporting a bright yellow "Don't Tread on Me" T-shirt with a snakeskin cap pulled across his head and headphones around his neck and tells me earnestly: "There is a fascist takeover of America happening right now. They're trying to destroy the Constitution, enslave the American people and create a one-world government."

Garrett Lear, the self-styled "Patriot Pastor," earnestly nods his head. Dressed in navy-blue eighteenth-century regalia, complete with a tricornered hat, the frequent speaker at Tea Party protests believes that "Mr. Obama" is a "domestic enemy" as set forth by the US Constitution and should be impeached. "I have a hard time calling him president, though I do want to pay him respect as a human being," intones the six-foot-seven-inch *Mayflower* descendant, "but I don't personally believe that he's legitimately president of the United States."

The Oath Keepers' first meeting had been held just six months before at Lexington, Massachusetts, on the anniversary and site of the start of the American Revolution, on what is also the anniversary of the Oklahoma City bombing. By the time the group met in Vegas, it claimed more than 3,000 dues-paying members. They are far from the only folks singing from the same hymnal. There are other Hatriot groups such as the Three Percenters—who take their name from the questionable statistic that only 3 percent of the American population during the Revolutionary War participated as combatants—that are dedicated to staying armed and ready for the next civil war, whereas Tenth Amendment activists, known as Tenthers, make constitutional cases for taking another stab at secession.

This is not just a fringe festival. There are prominent figures fanning the flames. Former Republican House majority leader Dick Armey took a lead role organizing the Tea Party protests, and he rallies crowds by reaffirming their worst fears: "Nearly every important office in Washington, D.C., today is occupied by someone with an aggressive dislike for our heritage, our freedom, our history and our Constitution."[4]

Popular broadcasters amp up the outrage to increase their ratings. Glenn Beck is still telling the faithful that America is on the road to socialism, fascism, and communism—take your pick—with the kicker: "The country may not survive Barack Obama."[5] Conservative talk-radio show host Mark Levin, whose book *Liberty and Tyranny* topped the best-seller list, ups the ante by telling his audience, "Obama is literally at war with the American people."[6] Protest signs echo Rush Limbaugh's on-air riffs: "If al-Qaeda wants to demolish the America we know and love, they better hurry, because Obama's beating them to it."[7]

All this anger has an impact. At Camp Lejeune, North Carolina, twenty-year-old Lance Corporal Kody Brittingham of the US Marines wrote a letter explaining his intention to assassinate Barack Obama: "My vow was to protect against all enemies, both foreign and domestic. I have found, through much research, evidence to support my current state of mind. Having found said domestic enemy, it is my duty and honor to carry out by all means necessary to protect my nation and her people from this threat."[8] He called his plan Operation Patriot.

By pumping up hate in the service of hyperpartisanship, our country is playing with forces that can easily get out of control. We are giving cover—and sometimes a sense of purpose—to the crazies among us. We are encouraging a culture of extremism.

A BRIEF HISTORY OF EXTREMISM IN AMERICA

The good news is that we've overcome these forces before.

American political history has been marked by periodic eruptions of the "heated exaggeration, suspiciousness, and conspiratorial fantasy"[1] that Richard Hofstadter famously characterized as "the paranoid style in American politics." Wingnuts have masqueraded under different names and causes, but they have always been committed to "us against them" framing of domestic debates while enflaming group hatred in the name of politics and alleged principle. They prey on fear and ignorance. Survey Wingnut rhetoric through the ages and the usual suspects keep surfacing: appeals to religious suspicion; ethnic and racial divisions; foreign subversion of sovereignty; and perhaps the oldest conspiracy theory of them all: accusing the president of the United States of being a tyrant and a dictator hell-bent on destroying the Constitution.

Even our most beloved and broadly unifying figures were not immune from the Wingnuts' attack in their time. When George Washington served as the shaky young republic's first president, newspapers such as the *Aurora* (edited by Benjamin Franklin's grandson) obsessively attacked him, calling on Washington to resign the office while declaring that "the mask of political hypocrisy has been alike worn by Caesar, a Cromwell and a Washington."[2] Washington's onetime ally Thomas Paine turned on him in vicious fashion after the Jay Treaty of neutrality with Great Britain, writing, "The world will be puzzled

to decide whether you are an apostate or an imposter; whether
you have abandoned good principles or whether you ever had
any."[3] Pamphlets published by early partisan opponents such
as William Duane denounced Washington's "tyrannical act,"
"Machiavellian policy," and "monarchical privilege."[4] The former commander of the Continental Army was unaccustomed to
being attacked with such impunity, and he proved to be sur-
prisingly thin-skinned, complaining in his last letter to Thomas
Jefferson that he was being slandered "in such an exaggerated,
and indecent terms as scarcely be applied to a Nero; a notorious
defaulter; or even to a common pickpocket."[5]

Washington's presidential successor, John Adams, served amid
accelerated partisan attacks in the press that divided the parties
between alleged allegiances to England or to revolutionary-era
France. Overreaction predictably followed: in 1798, Congress
passed the Alien Act, which empowered the president to arrest
foreigners involved "in any treasonable or secret machinations
against the government."[6] Then came the infamous Sedition Act,
cracking down on freedom of the press and threatening to fine
or imprison individuals who "unlawfully combine or conspire
together, with intent to oppose any measure or measures of the
government. . . ." By the election of 1800, a backlash was in full
swing, with Thomas Jefferson and his Democratic-Republican
allies on the offense, claiming that "Mr. Adams and his Federal-
ists wish to sap the Republic by fraud, destroy it by force, and
elect an English monarchy in its place."[7]

In turn, Jefferson was accused of being a violent radical who
wanted to bring the French guillotine to America—an "infidel"
and a "howling atheist."[8] The *New England Palladium* newspaper proclaimed: "Should the infidel Jefferson be elected to the
Presidency, the seal of death is that moment set on our holy

religion, our churches will be prostrated, and some infamous prostitute, under the title of goddess of reason, will preside in the sanctuaries now devoted to the worship of the most High."[9] The Federalist *Gazette of the United States* framed the election this way: "The only question to be asked by every American, laying his hand on his heart, is 'shall I continue in allegiance to God—and a religious president; or impiously declare for Jefferson—and no God!'"[10] After Jefferson's inauguration—in which he declared "every difference of opinion is not a difference of principle"—opponents pushed for impeachment, arguing that the "self exalted tyrant shall be hurled head long from his political zenith to dwell with Jacobins and devils in the pit."[11]

Conspiracy theories would make their initial mark with such targets as the Freemasons, inspiring an early third party. But the obsession with religious difference that first attached itself to the freethinking Jefferson would manifest itself more thoroughly when combined with fears over early Catholic immigration.

In 1852, anti-Catholic anxieties gave rise to the Know-Nothing movement—so named because members were supposed to deny all knowledge of the secret society when asked by saying, "I know nothing." Their apparent embrace of ignorance did not appear ironic until decades later. Instead, the Know-Nothings were briefly a force to be reckoned with. Their mission was not subtle: the movement's newspaper, the *American Organ*, explained that the group's goal was "to resist the insidious policy of the Church of Rome and other foreign influences against the institutions of our country, by placing [in] all offices . . . none but native-born Protestant citizens."[12] Transforming into a Nativist political party called the American Party, it quickly gained influence by filling the void left by the implosion of the Whigs. Within two years, the American Party was ascendant, successfully electing governors in nine states, eight senators, and 104 members of the House.[13]

The rapid rise of flag-waving bigotry to political prominence provoked an anguished letter from Abraham Lincoln to his friend Joshua Speed: "'How can any one who abhors the oppression of Negroes be in favor of degrading classes of white people? . . . As a nation, we began by declaring that 'All men are created equal.' We now practically read it: 'All men are created equal except Negroes.' When the Know-Nothings gain control, it will read: 'All men are created equal except Negroes, foreigners, and Catholics! . . .'"[14]

Lincoln's election in 1860 as the first Republican president provoked even more furor. Southern Democrats took the outcome of the election as their cue to spark secession, with the president of the Confederacy, Jefferson Davis, claiming, "We are upholding the true doctrines of the Federal Constitution,"[15] while allies similarly twisted the Bible by conjuring up faith-based defenses of slavery.

The now near-sainted figure we see as America's greatest president was hated by many contemporaries, called a dictator and worse. "Confederates called Lincoln a 'tyrant,' a 'fiend,' and a 'monster'," recounts Don E. Fehrenbacher in his essay "The Anti-Lincoln Tradition." "In speeches, sermons, and songs, in books, magazines, newspapers, pamphlets, and broadsides, they also portrayed him as a simpleton, a buffoon, a drunkard, a libertine, a physical coward, and a pornographic story-teller."[16] Another attack on Lincoln was telling in light of future national evolutions—accusations that our sixteenth president was an advocate of "miscegenation," reflecting his own alleged heritage as "King Abraham Africanus the First."

Abuse of Lincoln was not limited to the Southern side of the Mason-Dixon Line. In a drunken speech on the Senate floor, Delaware's Democratic senator Willard Saulsbury declared, "I never did see or converse with such a weak and imbecile a man; the weakest man I ever knew in high place. If I wanted to paint a despot, a man perfectly regardless of every constitutional right of the people, I would paint the hideous ape-like form of Abraham Lincoln."[17] A copperhead Wisconsin newspaper editor named Marcus M. Pomeroy wrote that Lincoln was "but the fungus from the corrupt womb of bigotry and fanaticism" and a "worse tyrant and more inhuman butcher than has existed since the days of Nero."[18] With the election of 1864 looming, Pomeroy wrote, "The man who votes for Lincoln now is a traitor and murderer. . . . And if he is elected to misgovern for another four years, we trust some bold hand will pierce his heart with dagger point for the public good."[19]

Months later, John Wilkes Booth did just that, albeit with a pistol, while shouting, "*Sic semper tyrannis*"—the Virginia state motto, "Thus always to tyrants."

In the backlash to Reconstruction after the Civil War, the Knights of the Ku Klux Klan were born. Formed by Confederate veterans, members of the terrorist organization fancied themselves as noble defenders of a Southern way of life under siege by occupying forces. But the KKK actually reached its apex of influence during the 1920s. Parading under the American flag in marches on Washington and preaching law and order against a backdrop of foreign-associated anarchist bombings that claimed dozens of lives, they also boasted of "100 percent Americanism" in contrast to the unprecedented wave of immigration from Eastern and Southern Europe. This twentieth-century incarnation of the Klan attracted several million members, and its reach extended far beyond the borders of the former Confederacy, with some of its largest klaverns in Indiana, Illinois, Texas, Ohio, Pennsylvania, and California.[20] As always, its leaders paid lip service to lofty ideals to obscure the ugly base alloys. The KKK's imperial wizard, William Joseph Simmons, declared his faith in "the Fatherhood of God and the Brotherhood of Man," while simultaneously circulating a statement proclaiming: "We exclude Jews because they do not believe in the Christian religion. We exclude Catholics because they owe allegiance to an institution that is foreign to the Government of the United States. To assure the supremacy of the white race, we believe in the exclusion of the yellow race and in the disenfranchisement of the Negro."[21]

Later in the decade, another imperial wizard named Hiram W. Evans took a less strictly racial view of the Klan's mission, instead pitting "the great mass of Americans of the old pioneer stock" against "intellectually mongrelized 'Liberals.'"[22] "We are a movement," Evans wrote, "of the plain people, very weak in the matter of culture, intellectual support, and trained leadership. We are demanding, and we expect to win, a return of power into the hands of the everyday, not highly cultured, not overly intellectualized, but entirely unspoiled and not de-Americanized, average citizen of the old stock."[23] It was a message of rural "real Americans" against liberal urban interlopers that repeatedly resurfaces in our politics.

The Roaring Twenties also saw heated debates over evolution, most infamously the 1925 Scopes Monkey Trial, which pitted William Jennings Bryan against Clarence Darrow in a Tennessee courtroom, a drama captured in *Inherit the Wind* and H. L. Mencken's courtroom dispatches. Bryan, a three-time populist Democrat presidential candidate and Woodrow Wilson's secretary of state, was the era's premier spokesman for religious fundamentalism. In 1924, Bryan declared, "All the ills from which America suffers can be traced back to the teaching of evolution. It would be better to destroy every other book ever written, and save just the first three verses of Genesis."[24] The basic debate between creationism and evolution remains in play decades later.

Demagogues always do well during economic downturns and the Great Depression was a workers' paradise for Wingnuts on all sides. Louisiana populist Huey Long grabbed power across his home state in the name of making "every man a king" and was planning to run for president against Franklin D. Roosevelt from the left before being gunned down at the mammoth state capitol building he had constructed. One of Long's disciples and a founder of the "Share Our Wealth Society" was a preacher named Gerald L. K. Smith. He swung from the left to the right, first forming the isolationist America First Party and then the Christian Nationalist ticket to run for president while proclaiming the virtues of anti-Semitism in the pages of his newspaper, *The Cross and the Flag*.

At the same time, domestic Communist Party members tried to present their ideology as "20th Century Americanism"[25] even while genocide was systematically carried out in the Soviet Union. Father Charles Coughlin, the radio priest, drew massive audiences with his attacks on the always popular targets of plutocrats and international bankers ("the sands of intrigue and of evil machinations have filtered through the hour glass of their control"),[26] while stridently advocating isolationism in the face of Nazi expansion. Coughlin called for "100 percent for Americanism . . . an America that still stands by the traditions of our forefathers—traditions of liberty, traditions of godliness, traditions upon which we must establish a sane Christian nationalism."[27]

The New Deal and its excesses proved to be a flashpoint for ideological debates that occasionally came unhinged. Newspaper magnate William Randolph Hearst directed his papers nationwide to print exposés on the radicalism of the New Deal and its alleged infiltration by Communists. When pressed by FDR's White House for an apology, Hearst offered only this front-page editorial: "Let me say that I have not stated at any time whether the President willingly or unwillingly received the support of the Karl Marx Socialists, the Frankfurter radicals, communists and anarchists . . . which constitute the bulk of his following," Hearst wrote. "I have simply said and shown that he does receive the support of these enemies of the American system of government, and that he has done his best to deserve the support of all such disturbing and destructive elements."[28]

After World War II, anxiety turned more toward the Cold War threat of communism. Heated opposition to the establishment of the United Nations echoed the opposition to the League of Nations a generation earlier ("it seeks to destroy Nationalism, Patriotism, and Christianity"), this time unsuccessfully. While the left wing tried to extend wartime alliances with misty hymns to "Uncle Joe" Stalin and backed the labor-fueled Progressive Party candidacy of onetime FDR vice president Henry Wallace, anti-Communist Democrats blasted their dangerous naïveté, most memorably Arthur Schlesinger Jr., who wrote that Progressives "cannot believe that ugly facts underlie fair words. However they look at it, the USSR keeps coming through as a kind of enlarged Brook Farm community, complete with folk dancing in native costumes, joyous work in the fields and progressive kindergartens. Nothing in their system has prepared them for Stalin."[29] Meanwhile, the right-wing hunt for the "enemy within" took on new urgency in Washington.

Wisconsin senator Joseph McCarthy's Communist witchhunts offered a textbook look at Wingnut logic, laid out in this June 1951 speech accusing Harry Truman's secretary of state, George Marshall, of consciously aiding and abetting Communist gains globally:

> How can we account for our present situation unless we believe that men high in this Government are concerting to deliver us to disaster? This must be the product of a great conspiracy, a conspiracy on a scale so immense as to dwarf any previous such venture in the history of man. A conspiracy of infamy so black that, when it is finally exposed, its principals shall be forever deserving of the maledictions of all honest men. Who constitutes the highest circles of this conspiracy? About that we cannot be sure . . . What is the objective of the great conspiracy? I think it is clear from what has occurred and is now occurring: to diminish the United States in world affairs, to weaken us militarily, to confuse our spirit with talk of surrender in the Far East and to impair our will to resist evil. To what end? To the end that we shall be contained, frustrated and finally: fall victim to Soviet intrigue from within and Russian military might from without.[30]

This epic rant boasts all the Wingnut heraldry—the unveiling of a great conspiracy by evil imposters to weaken America from within, diluting our stock, sapping our resolve, and making us vulnerable to enemies who are determined to destroy our way of life. And of course the sinister conspiracy goes straight to the top of the opposing party in power, in this case George

C. Marshall, the general who did more than any other to prepare America to win World War II and subsequently secure the
peace. Because McCarthy eventually imploded (as all Wingnuts
do), it is tempting to dismiss him as a grubby, loudmouthed
bully whose bark was worse than his bite. But in his heyday,
no public poll showed him with less than 34 percent support
among the American public.[31]

McCarthy's mantle was picked up by groups such as the John
Birch Society, whose founder, Robert Welch, fully embraced the
Communist conspiracies and attacked President Eisenhower as
"a dedicated, conscious agent of the Communist conspiracy."[32]
Arguing that "Moscow and Washington are, and for many
years have been, but two hands of one body controlled by one
brain,"[33] Welch warned of a secret plan to create a worldwide
police state controlled by the Kremlin and built out his network
through such policy initiatives as "Get the US out of the UN,"
and "No to Gun Control," as well as such satellite single-issue
groups as the Movement to Restore Decency.[34] Anyone considered insufficiently anti-Communist was deemed a "comsymp"—
short for Communist sympathizer. The godfather of modern
conservatism, William F. Buckley Jr., denounced the Birchers
as "damaging to the cause of anti-communism" in the pages of
his *National Review* magazine.[35] Conservative author Russell
Kirk noted: "Cry wolf often enough and everyone takes you for
an imbecile or a knave, when after all there *are* wolves in this
world."[36] Bob Dylan even took the Birchers to task in his folk
tune "Talkin' John Birch Paranoid Blues." The discredited organization still endures today, having moved its headquarters to
Joe McCarthy's hometown of Appleton, Wisconsin.

Old anti-Catholic riffs reemerged during the 1960 campaign
as John F. Kennedy aimed for the presidency. In Texas, the

Baptist convention passed a resolution "cautioning members against voting for a Roman Catholic candidate"[37]—buoyed by the old argument that a Catholic president would put loyalty to the pope ahead of loyalty to the United States. Just weeks after his election, a virulently anti-Catholic retired postal worker tried to assassinate JFK in Florida.[38]

Kennedy's tentative embrace of civil rights caused him to be hated by some in the South. When James Meredith integrated the University of Mississippi, he was escorted by three hundred federal troops, while more than 2,000 students protested, chanting, "Two, four, one, three, we hate Kennedy." A movie theater in Georgia showing the film *PT 109* decorated its marquee with this message: "See how the Japs almost got Kennedy." The once-brilliant newspaper columnist turned bitter Bircher, Westbrook Pegler, openly fantasized about Robert F. Kennedy's assassination in 1965, writing, "Some white patriot of the Southern tier will spatter his spoonful of brains in public premises before the snow flies."[39]

Throughout the civil rights era, the twin accusations of communism and anti-constitutionalism were used to delay progress and discredit activists—including Martin Luther King Jr. The FBI director, J. Edgar Hoover, called King "the most notorious liar in the country."[40] In *At Canaan's Edge: America in the King Years, 1965–1968*, Taylor Branch details how Hoover "cultivated King as the fearsome dark symbol of the latest 20th century threat to tranquility on Main Street America—succeeding immigrants, Depression gangsters, Nazis and communists."[41]

While Southern society rallied against King under the auspices of the White Citizens Councils, there were roadside billboards scattered throughout the South purporting to show King at a Communist training camp. Alabama governor George

Wallace told the *New York Times* in 1963 that "President [Kennedy] wants us to surrender this state to Martin Luther King and his group of pro-Communists who have instituted these demonstrations."[42] But even an avowed segregationist like Wallace indignantly denied that he was racist, saying, "I never made a statement in my political career that reflects on a man's race . . . My only interest is in the restoration of local government."[43]

States' rights were the rationale, defense of the Constitution the ennobling ideal. And so when South Carolina senator Strom Thurmond (the 1948 presidential candidate for the pro-segregation Dixiecrat ticket) argued against the Voting Rights Act on behalf of a caucus of Southern senators who called themselves "Constitutional Democrats," he pulled out all the rationalizing rhetoric, arguing that "the Negro is almost a favored class of citizen in America" and making the case that the Fourteenth Amendment had questionable legitimacy because it was passed during Reconstruction. After the Civil Rights Act passed, Thurmond declared that the day marked the "final resting place of the Constitution and the rule of the law, for it is here that we will have been buried with shovels of emotion under piles of expediency in the year of our Lord, 1965."[44]

The late 1960s proved to be the most civically unstable since the 1860s. Culture wars erupted as nonviolent protests were replaced by race riots, and antiwar peace activists were eclipsed by hundreds of shootings, arsons, and bombings attributed to left-wing radical groups like the Weather Underground and the Black Panthers.[45] The backlash brought Richard Nixon and the Republicans into the White House on a message of law and order that would twist into the ugly abuse of power scandals surrounding Watergate, further decreasing trust in government. The scars of the era's excesses would be carried forward by the baby boomers' fractious political debates—pitting crew cuts against the longhairs—well into the opening years of the twenty-first century.

In the long journey from frontier expansion to landing on the moon, there are clear common undercurrents to the paranoid politics advanced by the Wingnuts of different eras in America. There is always the divisive drumbeat of "us against them"— the demagogue's favorite formula. There is always an emotional appeal to an idealized past, targeted to people who feel besieged by cultural change, paired with the promise of a well-deserved return to power after years of cultivating resentment. And there is always the sale of special knowledge, pulling the curtain back on a monstrous conspiracy that will prove once and for all that your political opponents are not just misguided, but evil. The result is not only vindication, but the self-serving sense that only you can save the republic.

Against this backdrop it's easier to see the patterns in our recent history, where the angry impulse to delegitimize the last three duly elected presidents of the United States has distorted our political debates beyond reason.

The Clinton-Hating Cottage Industry

The first baby-boomer president was always bound to run into a buzz saw of criticism. But political thoroughbred Bill Clinton seemed to personify all his generation's ambition and indiscipline, turning him into a lightning rod for the culture wars.

Almost as soon as he was elected governor of Arkansas at age thirty-two, resentments and rumors started piling high. And it didn't help matters that in the 1992 presidential election, the onetime bushy-haired draft dodger squared off against a patrician World War II veteran who was the virtual poster boy of the Greatest Generation, President George H. W. Bush.

Republicans had basically owned the White House since 1968, with a one-term break by the not-much-lamented Jimmy Carter. The GOP had won each of the previous three elections by more than forty states. They never believed they could lose to a man they saw as an amoral, opportunistic yuppie whom they repeatedly called the "failed governor of a small southern state."[46]

Bill Clinton's baggage included more than just his periodic Bimbo eruptions—there were also unsettled national debates about feminism, symbolized by his wife, Hillary Clinton, who seemed to disdain traditional roles ("I suppose I could have stayed home and baked cookies")[47] in favor of political and professional ambition. The couple's half-joking "two for the price of one" promise made even some allies wince at the presumption of an unelected political spouse wielding real power in the West Wing. According to the *New York Times,* at least twenty articles written during the presidential election compared Hillary Clinton to Lady Macbeth.[48] There were whispers about Communist sympathies dating back to her time at Yale Law School. During the GOP convention, the future senator and secretary of state was derided as a "radical feminist" and in a pointed pushback, Marilyn Quayle, wife of Vice President Dan Quayle, said, "Most women do not wish to be liberated from their essential natures as women."[49] A cover story in *U.S. News and World Report* summed up the situation with this opening paragraph: "For some, she's an inspiring mother-attorney. Others see in her the overbearing yuppie wife from hell."[50]

But after what felt like 1,000 near-death experiences on the campaign trail that tracked along cultural more than policy lines—sex, drugs, rock 'n' roll and post-collegiate trips to the USSR—Bill Clinton seemed to be closing in on victory in the fall of 1992 as the country struggled to pull itself out of a recession.

The weekend before the election, the anti-abortion group Operation Rescue set the tone for opposition to come by taking out full-page ads in *USA Today* and 157 other newspapers, posing this prominent question: "The Bible warns us not to follow another man in his sin—lest God chasten us. How then can we vote for Bill Clinton?"[51] A pamphlet distributed by the same organization put it more bluntly: "To vote for Bill Clinton is to sin against God."[52]

Clinton's centrist New Democrat strategy won the day anyway with 370 electoral votes—but only 43 percent of the popular vote in a three-way race. For reasons that were moral, political, and now statistical, Clinton would be seen as an illegitimate president by increasingly frustrated opponents.

In Congress, conservative revolutionaries of a new generation, led by Newt Gingrich, were determined to embrace the role of total opposition and run against what they characterized as corruption in Congress and the unchecked power of the new president. Their Contract with America hammered home talking points such as "anti-flag," "anti-family," "radical," and "traitors" to characterize the Democrats. Newt Gingrich called the Clintons "Stalinist,"[53] "the enemy of normal people,"[54] and "counter-culture elitists."[55]

But red-meat Republicans were not fueled by Clinton-hatred in a vacuum. They would receive huge support from the seedlings of modern conservative media as well. Right-wing talk radio, just then coming into its own as a nakedly partisan cultural force, thrived with a polarizing target in the White House. New conservative publishing imprints—their new books flacked shamelessly on those talk-radio stations—seemed to pop up every week, and in common cause with such muckraking magazines as the *American Spectator*, they obsessively dug for dirt on the Clintons. Hillary Clinton would later be mocked for describing "a vast right-wing conspiracy" dedicated to attacking them by any means necessary, but just because you're paranoid doesn't mean you're crazy.

In fact, as early as 1992, conservative activists were busy trolling around Arkansas trying to find smoking guns that would help them discredit the Clintons. Some of their names would become notorious.

Floyd Brown was the author of the infamous race-baiting Willie Horton ad in 1988 that accused Democratic nominee Michael Dukakis of releasing a murderer on furlough who subsequently raped a woman and committed armed robbery. (Brown would later be denounced by the Bush-Quayle campaign as "one of the lowest forms of life" in an official complaint to the Federal Elections Commission.)[56]

During the 1992 campaign, Brown was pursuing a new partisan venture named Citizens United and scrambling to finish a book with a young deputy investigator, David Bossie, titled *Slick Willie: Why America Cannot Trust Bill Clinton*. This effort was described by liberal journalists Joe Conason and Gene Lyons in their book *The Hunting of the President* as "an unwieldy farrago of fact, exaggeration, and sheer invention, the book charged Clinton with dodging the draft, raising taxes, coddling blacks, chasing women, corrupting state agencies, flip-flopping on abortion, awarding special privileges to gays, promoting secularism (and witchcraft!), wrecking the school system, flirting with socialism, and, in its stirring final chapter, blaspheming the Lord with his campaign slogan of a 'New Covenant' between citizens and government."[57]

But the election proved only the beginning. Soon after Clinton's 1993 inauguration, a loose affiliation of old Arkansas enemies, conservative journalists, activist catalysts, leaders of the religious right, and big money donors redoubled their effort to demonize the new president.

When Deputy White House Counsel Vincent Foster killed himself in June 1993, he left a note agonizing over the negative public attention he had come under as one of the Clintons' closest Arkansas associates from the Rose Law Firm. "WSJ editors lie without consequence," he wrote, referring to a series of personal attacks published in the editorial pages of the *Wall Street Journal*. "I was not meant for the job or the spotlight of public life in Washington. Here ruining people is considered sport."[58]

The suicide was a tragedy, but the Clinton Haters smelled a conspiracy. Brown and Bossie took up the issue, pushing it on background to reporters. Rush Limbaugh spouted rumors that "Vince Foster was murdered in an apartment owned by Hillary Clinton,"[59] rather than Fort Marcy Park, where his body was found with gun in hand.

In Pittsburgh, the conservative owner of the *Tribune Review*, Richard Mellon Scaife, ordered reporter Christopher Ruddy (now the publisher of *Newsmax*) to investigate the conspiracy claims in an extended series of articles. Scaife was also the multi-million-dollar funder of what became known as "The Arkansas Project" within the *American Spectator*, which broke the news of Clinton's Little Rock dalliances in what became known as Troopergate (in an article written by David Brock, who would later go on to write *Blinded by the Right: The Conscience of an Ex-Conservative* and found the liberal watchdog group Media Matters for America) and printed the first mention of sex suit accuser Paula Jones.

Scaife likewise funded the conservative nonprofit Western Journalism Center, founded by Joseph Farah, the former publisher of Scaife's shuttered *Sacramento Union* (and now best known as the publisher of the for-profit *WorldNetDaily* website). In a money-go-round, the Western Journalism Center paid for Ruddy's series on Foster to be reprinted in other papers and publicized a pamphlet collecting the articles in full-page ads, raising half a million dollars from donors. Among the right-wing luminaries on the WJC board were a then-conservative Arianna Huffington and conservative professor Marvin Olasky, both of whom also worked as senior fellows at the Newt Gingrich–associated Progress and Freedom Foundation.[60] Scaife's generosity came at a cost—when the *American Spectator* ran a critical review of Ruddy's book, its funding stream was cut off.[61] But in the meantime, the money train was rolling for the obsessively anti-Clinton crowd.

A flurry of further allegations followed, pushed out in those pre-Internet days by magazines, talk radio, and videotape. Tiny Jeremiah Films had previously produced videos for the evangelical circuit with titles such as *The Evolution Conspiracy* and *Gay Rights, Special Rights*. Now a group with the lofty name Citizens for Honest Government was looking for anti-Clinton video, and Jeremiah Films' Pat Matrisciana worked with veteran Arkansas Clinton antagonist Larry Nichols to produce a series. Their first video, *Circle of Power,* was distributed by the Reverend Jerry Falwell's Liberty Alliance. It began with Vince Foster's death and went on from there to include thirty-four people who were allegedly killed at Bill Clinton's behest. Former congressman William Dannemeyer sent a list of the body count and demanded a congressional investigation.[62]

Their follow-up, *The Clinton Chronicles,* cast an even wider net. Opening with the allegation that Clinton "achieved absolute control over the political, legal and financial systems of

Arkansas—as president he would attempt to do the same with the nation," the hourlong video expanded to include allegations of Clinton overseeing millions of dollars of cocaine smuggling from the tiny Mena, Arkansas, airport and then laundering the money through foreign banks. There were voice-over testimonies from Arkansas associates who claimed that the twenty-something Bill Clinton "went to Moscow and did business with them against the United States government." "His sexual partners numbered over one hundred," the video's narrator intoned, going on to allege that one talkative paramour was confronted by Clinton's goons, who told her she could have "a federal job— or break her legs—whichever one was best . . . you see, that's illegal." The video ended with a list of witnesses' mysterious deaths and harassment, including Larry Nichols, who said he'd narrowly survived three attempts on his life. "Clinton can be a very dangerous individual," the video explained.[63]

Viewers of Jerry Falwell's *Old Time Gospel Hour* were repeatedly treated to excerpts of the videos in the spring of 1994 and a half-hour infomercial offering them for purchase at the low, low price of $40 plus $3 for shipping and handling. It was a classic success story for conspiracy entrepreneurs. Citizens for Honest Government claimed sales of more than 150,000 videotapes and copies were sent to every member of Congress.

In the fall of 1994, Republicans took control of the House of Representatives for the first time in forty years. Bill Clinton was down but not out. He would fight back to win reelection in 1996. But his second term would prove even bumpier than the first, as federal investigations set in motion over Whitewater, Troopergate, and other Arkansas scandals eventually culminated in revelations about the president's affair with White House intern Monica Lewinsky, which in turn led to impeachment. The president who proclaimed, "I have less and less control over my reputation but I still have full control over my character,"[64] had made himself vulnerable to his enemies.

Long before Clinton left the White House, Newt Gingrich's Republican Revolution wore out its welcome, seeming increasingly ideological and dogmatic, and leading to his resignation from the Speakership after a loss of congressional seats in 1998 and his own affair with an office aide. The intensity of the Clinton animus on the right ended up spurring a backlash that helped propel Hillary Clinton to the US Senate and let Bill Clinton leave the oval office with a 66 percent approval rating.

But as the country looked to the 2000 election, the time seemed ripe for a brand-name, born-again Republican presidential candidate who promised to represent "compassionate conservatism" and "restore honor and decency to the Oval Office."

Bush Derangement Syndrome

In my interviews with the more unhinged sign-wavers at anti-Obama protests, they always eventually say the same thing: "They started it." In other words, the prevalence of Bush Derangement Syndrome on the left gave the right the green light to escalate. Coinage credit goes to conservative columnist and trained psychiatrist Charles Krauthammer, who in 2003 had diagnosed the condition as "the acute onset of paranoia in otherwise normal people in reaction to the policies, the presidency—nay—the very existence of George W. Bush."[65]

It began with the left's belief that Bush was an illegitimate president, inspired by the bitterly contested results of the 2000 election. He'd lost the popular vote and won with an assist from the Supreme Court. Fresh from the Florida recount—where

97,000 leftist protest votes for Ralph Nader helped deliver the Sunshine State to George W. Bush by a 537-vote margin[66]— Inauguration Day protesters wielded "Hail to the Thief" signs and chanted, "Racist, sexist, anti-gay, Bush and Cheney go away!" "We want Bush out of DC" and "You're not our president."

Bush Derangement Syndrome, though, was slower to boil than Obama Derangement Syndrome. In the wake of 9/11, the far left's insatiable appetite for moral equivalency made little impact, but, of course, the blame-America-first crowd did its best. Two weeks after the attacks, nearly 10,000 assembled for a protest in Washington, inevitably titled the Anti-War and Anti-Racist Rally, to imbibe Wingnut wisdom from such as the Reverend Graylan Hagler, senior minister of the Plymouth Congregational United Church of Christ in Washington, DC ("Today we do not stand with any terrorists, whether it is the United States or foreign terrorists"),[67] or Stephanie Simard from the Women's Fight Back Union ("Millions of women and children around the world wake up to this kind of terror every single day. And this terror is made in the United States . . . Bush's program is anti-women, anti-gay, and anti a lot of us").[68] I wonder how she would have liked the Taliban by comparison.

The Iraq War proved a potent recruitment tool. Michael Moore's 2004 film *Fahrenheit 9/11* sought to document a case of blood for oil by mixing provocative footage of Bush's missteps and malapropisms along with a full range of conspiracy theories revolving around the Bush family's ties to the Saudi royal family and the bin Laden family, documenting a case of blood for oil. It won the Palme d'Or at the Cannes Film Festival. In 2006, the movie *Death of a President,* a mockumentary of sorts, purported to follow the investigation of the unsolved assassination of George W. Bush and the subsequent expansion of the Patriot Act by President Dick Cheney. It won the International Critics Prize at the Toronto Film Festival.

The left-Wingnut netroots paraded their Bush hate in volleys typified by this post at the leading left-wing political blog *Daily Kos:* "I know hate is a strong word. But I do hate the man. I hate him."[69] Groups such as Code Pink staged "die-ins," screamed during congressional hearings, protested military recruitment stations, and attempted citizen's arrests of administration officials. A collection of memorable signs from the anti-Bush protests gives you a sense of the derangement: "Bush = Satan," "Save Mother Earth, Kill Bush," "Hang Bush for War Crimes," "End the Illegal Occupation in the White House," "Bush is the Disease, Death is the Cure," "Bush is the only Dope worth Shooting," "Death to Extremist Christian Terrorist Pig Bush," and "Kill Terrorists, Bomb There [*sic*] House, Kill Bush, Bomb His F—in House." The "s" in Bush's name was routinely turned into a swastika on protest posters and the telltale tiny mustache drawn upon his image.

But Bush-as-Hitler comparisons did not just gain currency on protest placards—this was Café Society stuff. The 2005 winner of the Nobel Prize in Literature, British playwright Harold Pinter, penned a statement saying, "The Bush administration is the most dangerous force that has ever existed. It is more dangerous than Nazi Germany because of the range and depth of its activities and intentions worldwide."[70] Liberal author and onetime Al Gore clothing consultant Naomi Wolf offered comparisons of the Bush administration to the Nazi regime in her book *The End of America* (an assertion benignly recounted in an interview on National Public Radio titled "Naomi Wolf Likens Bush to Hitler").[71] MSNBC *Countdown* host Keith Olbermann called Bush a fascist on air,[72] and MoveOn.org took heat for an online advertising contest in which two contributors offered Bush = Hitler comparisons.[73]

Legendary singer, civil rights leader, and Hollywood elder statesman Harry Belafonte visited Venezuela's leftist dictator Hugo Chávez and announced: "No matter what the greatest tyrant in the world, the greatest terrorist in the world, George W. Bush says, we're here to tell you: Not hundreds, not thousands, but millions of the American people . . . support your revolution."[74] Cindy Sheehan, an antiwar protester and the mother of a fallen soldier, became a brief media sensation for camping out near Bush's Crawford ranch—a status not considerably diminished when she followed Belafonte's lead by calling President Bush "a bigger terrorist than Osama bin Laden."[75]

When Nobel Peace Prize–winner Betty Williams of Northern Ireland gave the keynote speech to the International Women's Peace Conference in Dallas, she said, "Right now, I could kill George Bush, no problem. No, I don't mean that. I mean—how could you nonviolently kill somebody? I would love to be able to do that."[76] She chuckled a bit in her confessional Irish brogue, and members of the audience laughed. Not that Dallas has any history with presidential assassinations.

Democrats didn't seem allergic to these outbursts, they seemed instead subtly to encourage them for partisan gain—just as they accuse Republicans of doing now. Bush Derangement Syndrome was so widespread on the left—and Bush so broadly unpopular by the end of his term—that it failed to inspire much mainstream media outrage. It wasn't considered news.

But after one Bush-bashing protest in September 2005, Fox News host Sean Hannity had a rare moment of clarity: "The president was called every name in the book—from a terrorist to the Führer," he said, shaking his head, and then turned his attention to one of the protest's liberal organizers. "If you really believe what you're saying, you need to distance yourself from the extremists that are running this thing."[77]

It was good advice—then and now.

We are caught in a pendulum swing of hyperpartisanship. The extremes echo and incite each other, confirming their side's worst stereotypes while providing the most potent recruitment poster for the other party. Politics follows the lines of physics— every action creates an equal and opposite reaction.

Wingnuts on the right are intimidating responsible Republicans into silence. The hunt for heretics has become a hobby for right-wing activists in an effort to drive all centrists out of the GOP. They are burning down the big tent. The roots of this new radicalism can be found in the anger of an increasingly regional party facing a deep diversity deficit, reflecting a historic irony: Republicans are now captive to the Southern conservatives their party was founded to oppose. The Party of Lincoln is in danger of becoming the Party of Limbaugh.

But Democrats have their own polarizing forces to contend with, a far less influential but increasingly resurgent wing of activist liberals in Congress and the netroots.

As the two parties have become more polarized, the ranks of independent voters have rocketed to a historic high—reaching more than 40 percent[78]—while Democrats and Republicans have declined dramatically. Independents are now the largest and fastest-growing segment of the electorate. Independents tend to be fiscal conservatives but social progressives. They more accurately reflect centrist national attitudes than either party's base:

the 11 percent of Americans who describe themselves as liberal Democrats or the 15 percent who call themselves conservative Republicans.[79]

Our politics are being hijacked by a comparatively small number of people who seek to dominate the debate by screaming the loudest. They see the world as an urgent struggle between true believers and nonbelievers. They attempt to impose strict litmus tests and insist on conformity. They demonize dissent and too often consider political opponents their personal enemies. Fear is their favorite tactic as they try to divide and conquer.

At a time when our country is still fighting a war against extremism abroad, we are confronting extremism at home. We should know the dangers of demagogues, politicized religion, and ideological absolutists by now. The cultivation of rage and resentment for political gain or personal profit has real costs that can affect us all.

The attack of the Wingnuts is ultimately an assault on the idea that what unites us is greater than what divides us as Americans, which the Founding Fathers enshrined in our national motto, E Pluribus Unum—out of many, one. The moderate majority needs to stand up to the extremes before they spark a season of violence. We have done this before and we can do it again, remembering what the old warrior President Eisenhower once said: "The middle of the road is all the usable surface. The extremes, left and right, are in the gutters."[80]

THE RISE OF THE TEA PARTY

It started with the rant heard 'round the world.

CNBC's Rick Santelli was railing against President Obama's mortgage bailout plan from the floor of the Chicago Mercantile Exchange. It was February 19, 2009—one day short of the president's first month in office. And Santelli was pissed.

"This is America!" Santelli screamed. "How many of you people want to pay for your neighbor's mortgage that has an extra bathroom and can't pay their bills? Raise your hand." The question was met with a motley chorus of boos from the traders, kicking Santelli into high-gear capitalist evangelist mode: "President Obama," Santelli shouted straight into the camera, "Are you listening?"[1] There was a roar of recognition from the floor.

"This is like mob rule, I'm getting scared," blow-dried co-host Joe Kernen joked nervously. He hadn't seen nothin' yet.

"We're thinking of having a Chicago Tea Party in July," yelled Santelli. "All you capitalists that want to show up to Lake Michigan, I'm going to start organizing."

Within twelve hours, ChicagoTeaParty.com was live.

There had been Tea Party protests as part of libertarian Republican Ron Paul's 2008 presidential campaign. And a protest over "Porkulus" (a Rush Limbaugh–coined word combining "pork" and "stimulus") had been held a few days before in Seattle at the suggestion of a blogger who went by the name Liberty Belle. But the call for a Tea Party on live television, with all its

American Revolution imagery, was immediately resonant.*

On February 27, some three hundred people gathered in Chicago's Daley Plaza to protest the stimulus bill and government spending, with gatherings in forty other cities. People in parkas stood alongside protesters dressed in Revolutionary-era garb wielding "Don't Tread on Me" flags. There was also the first post-election protest sighting of an Obama poster with a Hitler mustache added on. The word "change" now read "chaos."[2] A spark had been lit.

Congressional Democrats unwittingly fanned the flames, voting to spend an unprecedented $1.2 trillion in taxpayer money in the first one hundred days of the Obama administration as part of a stimulus package. Their plans promised to double the public debt in five years, equivalent to all the debt accumulated by every US president from George Washington to George W. Bush combined.[3]

It seemed to validate every slumbering "socialist" accusation leveled at Obama during the campaign, but liberal House Democrats didn't care—they hadn't enjoyed unified control of congress for fifteen years. This was their chance to run the table with a long-delayed wish list of pork-barrel projects. The economic crisis and Bush's backing of the first bailout round gave

---

* There was a more recent antecedent to the Tea Party protests than the Revolutionary War. In 1936, a group that dubbed itself the "Minute Women" gathered at the Old South Church where the Boston Tea Party was planned 162 years before to protest what its members called "President Roosevelt's wealth redistribution program." Revolutionary-era speeches were read by activist actors in colonial garb who then signed a petition that read in part: "We view with concern the unwarranted waste of the savings of the thrifty upon unsound experiments, which are not bringing relief or prosperity to the nation, but which are breaking down the moral fiber of the American people and piling up debts it will take generations to pay."

them perfect political cover. Keynesianism was suddenly cool again, and with it they could justify a smorgasbord of spending. It would all pay for itself, after all.

They had forgotten that hypocrisy is the unforgivable sin in politics. Obama had campaigned on a commitment to be a postpartisan president and restore fiscal responsibility. But the $787-billion stimulus bill passed along narrow partisan lines, with Republicans shut out of the negotiating process. Despite the president's hopes of gaining Republican support by putting one-third of the funds into tax cuts, the House bill received no GOP votes at the urging of party leadership determined to show party discipline and lost the support of eleven centrist Democrats.[4] Weeks later, when an additional $410-billion supplemental spending bill was passed along partisan lines with 9,000 earmarks,[5] Obama's campaign promise of transparency seemed abandoned as well.

Bailout backlash was in full effect. It didn't matter that the bailouts had started under Bush—the man left holding the bag got the blame. The economy had been in free fall for four months when Obama was inaugurated. Then it got worse, with the stock market hitting a twelve-year low on his fiftieth day in office, March 9. With unemployment rising, 401(k)s decimated, but billions of taxpayer dollars going to banks and Wall Street bonuses, Americans began to have a collective Howard Beale moment—they were mad as hell and not going to take it anymore.

The deep deficit spending seemed only to add insult to injury. After watching the jet-set excesses of the Bernie Madoff class from afar, middle-class families were left with less and still asked to clean up the mess. While they were struggling to pay their bills, big government and big business had their debts forgiven through billion-dollar backroom deals on the taxpayers' backs.

Big mistake. Back in 1992, independents protested the bipartisan deficit spending they considered generational theft by backing the independent presidential candidacy of Ross Perot. By March 2009, independents began to break decisively with Obama, surpassing Democrats as the largest segment of the electorate.

On Tax Day, April 15, Tea Party protests were held in 346 towns and cities, drawing more than 300,000 people.[6] The largest gathering was in Atlanta, where 15,000 showed up. Liberal columnists and MSNBC hosts joined with Speaker of the House Nancy Pelosi in trying to downplay the events, dismissing them as artificial "Astroturf" protests rather than a genuine grassroots movement. True, well-funded activist groups such as Americans for Prosperity and FreedomWorks paid for many organizational costs,[7] while Fox News helped make the protests a national conservative happening by airing more than one hundred commercial promotions for the protests in the ten days before Tax Day,[8] but these were the equivalent of conservative public-service announcements. For all the "Astroturf" asides, the crowds were homegrown. They may have been pumped up by partisan interests, but they were not purchased.

I went to the New York City Tea Party rally, where, given the city's Democratic dominance, I expected to see a few hundred people clustered under a gray sky. Instead, 3,500 people, a kaleidoscope of the modern conservative movement, lined both sides of Broadway beside City Hall Park, a few blocks from Wall Street. There were libertarians, traditionalists, free-marketers, middle-class tax protesters, the more-patriotic-than-thou crowd, conservative shock jocks, frat boys, suit-and-tie Buckley-ites, and more than a couple of requisite residents of Crazytown.

The Tax Day Tea Parties offered a perfect confluence for conservative populism: a Founding Fathers–sanctioned rebellion against big government combined with the age-old frustration of paying taxes, especially during a recession. And compared with the average G-20 or World Trade Organization protests, the New York rally was a model of civil disobedience. Instead of anarcho-punks leaving broken windows in their wake, there were American flags, country music, and repeated reminders to pick up trash before leaving the site. There were whole families on parade, such as the father carrying the American flag with an image of John Wayne emblazoned on it, followed by three children with pint-size "Don't Tread on Me" flags (a patriotic sentiment that also doubled as a crowd-control notice).

The founder of the New York Tea Party Patriots chapter was a soft-spoken twenty-seven-year-old aspiring architect named Kellen Giuda. A New Hampshire native, he'd never been active in politics before, but the spending spurred him into action and he coordinated the initial rally over Facebook. Kellen defined the overall Tea Party message as "fiscal responsibility and government accountability," adding, "In New York, we're strictly fiscal responsibility but if the Morristown, New Jersey, Tea Party wants to be anti-abortion then that's their prerogative." He stressed that "there is no Tea Party leader" and that both parties have failed when it comes to fighting for the taxpayer. "That's why a lot of Tea Parties around the country have considered starting a political party."

But even though speaker after speaker hammered home the apparently poll-tested line that these rallies were not about Republicans or Democrats, their appeal was self-evidently partisan and strenuously anti-Obama.

"What's the Difference Between Obama and Chavez?" asked one sign, referring to Hugo Chávez, the leftist president of

Venezuela (Answer: "Nothing"). Others went after "Ali Obama and the 40 Thieves," "Free Markets not Free-Loaders," and "Hitler was a Socialist Too." Some messages stood out, such as one carried by a Ron Paul acolyte that read "Obama = Bush lite." When I asked about the underlying logic, he explained, "Obama was elected with the promise of change and then pursued the same failed policies of Bush's fiscal irresponsibility."

When speakers extolled the virtue of "individual responsibility," the crowd roared—the billion-dollar bailouts blocked any memory of the president's call for a "new era of responsibility" in his inaugural address. Democratic stereotypes about being an overspending party of the welfare state had reasserted themselves. Old scripts felt fresh again, even when they were straw men. When one local radio host asserted, "We are told that if the few prosper, the many will suffer," he was reflexively riffing off old anti-Communist playbooks, not anything said by Obama. And when Christian conservative-radio personality Jordan Sekulow decried "cutting funding for our troops," he apparently hadn't bothered to read the budget he was busy attacking.

For all the invocations of American history at the protest, there was a striking lack of perspective. However disenfranchised conservatives felt, we are a world away from "taxation without representation"—the closer truth might be found in one woman's hand-painted sign: "taxation with crappy representation."

In fact, the federal taxes due on the day of the Tea protests—April 15, 2009—were the lowest they had been since Harry Truman was president, back in 1950.[9] For all the populist anger, 98.6 percent of all tax-filers saw a tax *reduction*—albeit temporary, due to the stimulus many were protesting—during the first year of the Obama administration.[10] The larger, looming debate about rolling back the Bush tax cuts to Clinton-era rates—however unwise in a recession—does not put us inexorably on the road to socialism, let alone communism. It reminded me of a Stephen Colbert line: "I love the truth; it's facts I'm not a fan of."

Conservatives were playing the mirror image of the liberals they mocked after 2000, portraying a popular election as an unconstitutional usurpation of power. But liberals who wanted to dismiss the Tea Parties did so at their peril: never forget that America was founded in part by a tax revolt.

And this was only the eighty-sixth day of Barack Obama's presidency.

Right-Wing Rules for Radicals

By summer, politics had gotten even more heated over President Obama's proposed health-care plan—simultaneously the Holy Grail and third rail of Democratic presidents since Harry Truman.

The Tea Party protesters now focused their energies on the town halls hosted by congressmen every August for their constituents. Normally, these were sleepy affairs, but by the end of the summer they looked more like a collective crystal-meth binge than a Norman Rockwell painting.

The roots of the town hall protests were the same as those of the Tea Parties—anger at the growth of government and the unprecedented spending amid economic anxiety. The fact that the president had called for the health-care legislation to pass before the August recess felt to many citizens like liberal arrogance and overreach. When liberal Democratic leaders such as House Judiciary Committee chairman John Conyers mocked the idea of actually reading the health-care bill—telling the National Press Club, "What good is reading the bill when it's a thousand pages? And you don't have two days and two lawyers to find out what it means after you've read the bill?"[11]—protesters went ballistic.

"Obama was elected to unify the nation," a plaid-shirted baby boomer named Dan Cochran told me at a town hall in Windsor, Colorado. "And what we've got with health care is the most divisive debate I've seen since Vietnam. They attempted to cram it down our throat overnight with no consideration to We the Taxpayer."

When nervous aides told Dan and the rest of the Colorado crowd that local Democratic congresswoman Betsy Markey would not be appearing at the town hall as advertised (because of a death threat, her press officer quietly told me on the side), the natives went from restless to revolt—they were going to have their hearing with or without the congresswoman. One local farmer rose out of the crowd and offered a laundry list of grievances written out on a pad of paper: "Loss of individual rights; the Deficit; Health Care Cost/Limitation of Choice; Stimulus Plan; Government Bailouts that were not read but passed; Card Check; Fairness Doctrine; CIA investigation; Cap & Trade. Stop the spending. Listen to the people."

These citizens were angry, but they were not uninformed— they had just gotten their highly questionable information from partisan sources, professional polarizers like Rush Limbaugh and Glenn Beck, who pump up outrage to pump up ratings. Policy debates now felt like referendums on the future of the republic, with nothing short of tyranny and genocide ahead. But with Democrats in control of Congress and the White House, they felt unheard. And so the screaming started.

Maryland congressman Frank Kratovil was hanged in effigy outside his office. New York congressman Tim Bishop had to be escorted to his car by police after one town hall to protect him from the protesters. North Carolina congressman Brad Miller decided to cancel his August town halls after receiving a death threat. "They're inciting people to riot with just total distortions of facts," said freshman Virginia representative Gerry Connolly. "They think we're going to euthanize Grandma and the government is going to take over."[12]

The fringe was starting to blur with the base. The curtain was pulled back on this shift in the form of a memo titled "Rocking the Town Halls—Best Practices." Written by a Connecticut grassroots conservative activist named Bob MacGuffie under the banner of his group, Right Principles, the memo tried to teach people how to disrupt the town halls held in support of what was called "the socialist agenda of the Democrat leadership in Washington." In a perfect Wingnut irony, the memo counseled conservatives to "Use the [Saul] Alinsky playbook of which the left is so proud: freeze it, attack it, personalize it and polarize it."

Saul Alinsky was a Chicago community organizer and the author of *Rules for Radicals,* a bible for post-1960s leftist protesters. The book laid out a strategy for creating the conditions to achieve revolutionary social change. As Alinsky explained in the first chapter, "*The Prince* was written by Machiavelli for the Haves on how to hold power. *Rules for Radicals* is written for the Have-Nots on how to take it away." His rules included such aphorisms as "In war the end justifies almost any means." He advised adherents to obscure their ultimate goals in general and unobjectionable terms, for example, "Liberty, Equality, Fraternity," "Of the Common Welfare," and "Pursuit of Happiness."[13]

Vilified by conservatives and idolized by liberals, Alinsky's impact endured after his death in 1972. Hillary Clinton wrote her ninety-two-page undergraduate thesis at Wellesley on Alinsky, earnestly titled "'There Is Only the Fight . . . ': An Analysis of the Alinsky Model." As a young Chicago community organizer, Barack Obama reportedly studied and taught Alinsky's techniques, seeding conservative distrust of his centrist rhetoric. MacGuffie's memo was a minor screed, but it applied the liberal protesters' confrontational approach to conservative goals: "The objective is to put the Rep on the defensive . . . you need to rock the boat early. Watch for an opportunity to yell out and challenge the Rep's statements early. If he blames Bush for something or offers other excuses—call him on it, yell back and have someone else follow up with a shout-out . . . Look for these opportunities even before he takes questions."

Beyond barraging members of Congress, the goal was to intimidate the undecided: "We want the independent thinkers to leave the hall with some doubts about the Democrat solutions continually proposed by the national leadership."[14]

This was the decisive shift in conservative opposition tactics in 2009—a decision to mimic the confrontational street theater of the far left they had spent decades despising. Extremes always end up resembling each other. Now conservative activists were manning the ramparts, seeing themselves as patriots protesting the president. Civility was the first calculated casualty.

In Connecticut, protesters against Senator Chris Dodd suggested that he commit suicide with whiskey and painkillers as a treatment for his newly diagnosed prostate cancer.[15] One sign summed up their unhinged sentiments: "universal health care = medical genocide." Screaming matches became a regular feature of Senator Arlen Specter's town hall meetings in Pennsylvania after he switched parties and became a Democrat in April 2009. Choice cuts include: "You are trampling on our Constitution" and "This is the Soviet Union, this is Maoist China. The people in this room want their country back."[16] In Missouri, Senator Claire McCaskill was shouted down repeatedly at a health-care town hall attended by 1,500 people. "I don't understand this rudeness," McCaskill told the crowd. "I honestly don't get it."[17] In Washington State, a retired US Marine Corps veteran accused Representative Brian Baird of trying to "indoctrinate" his children and said that Nazis also took over finance and health care: "I've kept my oath. Do you ever intend to keep yours?"

Doctored photos of President Obama as Hitler began popping up at town halls, courtesy of longtime political fringe magnet Lyndon LaRouche, alongside pamphlets offering details about "Obama's Nazi Health Plan."

Sarah Palin, newly resigned from her elected position as Alaska's governor, picked up the LaRouche-ite riff and doubled down on the crazy talk with a Facebook post: "The America I know and love is not one in which my parents or my baby with Down syndrome will have to stand in front of Obama's 'death panel' so his bureaucrats can decide, based on a subjective judgment of their 'level of productivity in society,' whether they are worthy of health care. Such a system is downright evil."[18]

Soon the talk of "death panels" and "killing granny" seemed to be everywhere. At a "Patients First" health-care protest in Pueblo, Colorado, the featured speaker expanded the death-panel argument to genocidal dictators. "Stalin in the 1920s issued about 20 million end of life orders for his fellow Russians. Pol Pot did it in the Vietnam War. He issued about 2 million end of life orders. It's being done in Africa today. Mugabe is doing it every day. Adolf Hitler issued 6 million end of life orders.

He called his program the final solution. I kind of wonder what we're going to call ours."[19]

A swastika was spray-painted outside the office of Representative David Scott's office in Georgia. Arizona representative Gabrielle Giffords's aides called the cops after one town-hall attendee dropped a gun at the event.* After Washington representative Brian Baird was faxed a death threat addressed to President Obama, he declared, "What we're seeing right now is close to Brown Shirt tactics." At a Republican town hall, John McCain received a chorus of angry boos and jeers for simply stating that "Obama respects the Constitution of the United States."[20]

The Tea Party Express was also winding its way through the country. A thirty-four-city tour backed by the conservative political action committee (PAC) Our Country Deserves Better was one of several that sought to carry the banner of the Tea Parties forward, raising $1.9 million in the process.[21] The lead speakers at their rallies were former talk-radio show hosts Mark Williams and Deborah Johns. Williams's signature crowd-pleasing line was ripped from the National Rifle Association (NRA): "You can have our country when you pry it from our . . . cold . . . dead . . . fingers!"[22]

Johns aimed a little lower: "The men and women in our military didn't fight and die for this country for a communist in the White House!" The Louisville, Kentucky, crowd chanted its approval: "U-S-A, U-S-A!"[23]

---

* In January 2011, Congresswoman Giffords was shot along with eighteen other people at a constituent meeting outside a Tucson supermarket. Despite being shot through the head at point-blank range, she miraculously survived. Jared Lee Loughner, a twenty-two-year-old paranoid schizophrenic, pled guilty to the attack and is currently serving a sentence of life in prison.

Down in the crowd, two men in fatigues were trying to re-cruit new members for their militia, the Ohio Valley Freedom Fighters, by carrying signs that read: "AK-47s: today's pitch-fork" and "Quit worrying. Start your militia training today."[24]

With all the violent rhetoric, it was perhaps inevitable that ac-tual violence would start breaking out. There were fistfights in Florida town halls alongside senior-citizen scuffles.[25] In Missouri, a brawl between Tea Party activists and counter-protesting Ser-vice Employees International Union (SEIU) members got one man hospitalized and six arrested.[26] In California, health-care reform opponent Bill Rice had his finger bitten off at a rally sponsored by MoveOn.org. As Rice gamely recounted, "A scuffle ensued and he ate my finger in the process."[27] The weirdness had only just begun.

The 9/12 March on Washington

After Representative Joe Wilson screamed, "You lie!" at Presi-dent Obama during his health-care speech in front of a joint ses-sion of Congress, Wilson said he was just expressing the angry outbursts he'd been hearing at town halls back home in South Carolina. It was a feedback loop of anger and alienation.

Wilson was censured by the House for his outburst, becoming the first congressman in 221 years to earn the dishonor, but in return he became an overnight folk hero on the far right. Soon he was raising more than $1 million by playing the victim card online: "Joe Wilson is Under Attack," the ads read. "Help him fight back." His opponent also raised $1 million. The cycle of in-citement is good for the business of politics, if not the country.

Five days after his scream, I saw signs of support dotting the Washington Mall—"Joe Wilson told the Truth," "Joe Wilson speaks for me," and "Palin/Wilson 2012."

The posters were all part of the latest Wingnut Woodstock—
the 9/12 march on Washington. The date had been selected by
the guru of the growing Tea Party movement, Fox News host
Glenn Beck. He pitched it as a day to return to the unity, patriotism, and sense of national purpose we felt the day after the
attacks of September 11, 2001.

What emerged was something precisely the opposite: a protest
that celebrated the deepest domestic political divisions we've
seen since 9/11, with unhinged accusations of traitors and des-
pots in the White House and talk of resistance and revolution.

As I walked out of Union Station that morning, I folded into
the waves of white people who descended on the Washington
Mall. As more than one T-shirt put it, they were exercising
their First Amendment rights so they didn't have to exercise
their Second Amendment rights—yet.

They had the giddy glow of those who feel they are speaking
truth to power, a reversal of fortune that had left conservatives
recycling some of the Dems' favorite lines from the Bush era:
"Obama is a domestic terrorist," "Dissent is patriotic," and the
ever-proliferating Obama-as-Hitler.

"It's wonderful to see so many patriots here!" shouted one
speaker from the podium on the steps of Capitol Hill to a chorus
of cheers—and he started to list US battles from Guadalcanal
on, won by courageous patriots, not the government, to defend
a freedom that he said was now under threat from inside the
White House. South Carolina senator Jim DeMint and Indiana
congressman Mike Pence were among the few elected officials
who addressed the crowd.

But the homemade signs on the ground spoke more clearly
than many of the speakers. There were appropriations of
Obama's red, white, and blue "O" symbol inserted into the

words "Treason" and "Destroyer." A man dressed as George Washington approvingly nodded at a collage featuring Obama's "best friends"—Karl Marx, Hugo Chávez, and Mohammed.

Here is a selection of signs, chosen more or less at random:

- "Don't Make the U.S. a Third World Country—Go Back to Kenya"
- "We Came Unarmed (This Time)"
- "Christians Unite"
- "Muslim Marxist"
- "Mugabe-Pelosi in '12"
- "If you are a liberal or progressive Democrat or Republican you are a communist. Impeach Obama!"
- "Obama the Exterminator: Killing Our Jobs, Killing Our Future, Killing Our Freedom"
- "Radical Socialists are Damaged Hate-Filled Power Hungry Destroyers"
- "Bury ObamaCare with Kennedy"
- "King George Didn't Listen Either"
- "God Bless Glenn Beck and Fox News"
- "Preserve Mom, Apple Pie and the American Way"
- "Barack Obama Supports Abortion, Sodomy, Socialism and the New World Order"
- "An Obamanation of Taxation! The Lifeblood of Tyranny!"
- "Obama Lied, Granny Died"
- "NObama Healthcare is America's Nightmare"

And finally, inevitably, seriously,

- "Don't Touch My Medicare"

One man sat with his family on the rim of a reflecting pool, brandishing a homemade red Soviet-style flag complete with hammer and sickle, with the words "United States Socialist Republic" on it. He was a Vietnam vet from the Shenandoah Valley who gave his name only as Bob. "I was always afraid of my country being attacked from the outside by bombs and rockets and missiles," Bob told me. "Now I'm watching it being destroyed from right here. I'm scared for my country." But did he think Obama is a Communist? "I think he's a direct threat to my country, but it's not just him. It's the Congress. I think this is all part of a plan. I don't know what he is. I do believe he has socialist tendencies."

Among the crowd were a few scattered Confederate flags flapping in the wind. I went up to one auburn-haired middle-aged woman named Becky and asked why she was carrying the Stars and Bars to the rally. "Because I'm from the South," Becky said. "It has nothing to do with slavery. People think it means slavery. That's not what it stood for. It stood for the Union."

Somewhere, Lincoln just threw up.

A guy named Norm decided to step in and help her out: "I don't think it's so much that anybody would advocate any secession-like movement, or that anybody wants to remove a star from the flag. I think if anything, the Confederate flag serves to remind me of where we've been and where we would not like to go again."

There is a "Don't make me shoot this dog" aspect to this logic: an angry, divisive protest designed to stop the divisions they feel erupting from Washington's policies. It echoed what one young man at the Tea Party Express stop in Jackson, Michigan, told a reporter who asked why he was carrying a loaded AK-47 and two loaded handguns. "I don't want a revolution. I don't want a civil war," he said. "But it is a possibility. It's there as an option, as a last resort."[28]

This is the tragedy of the Tea Party: what began as fiscal-conservative protests against the generational theft of deficits and debt soon became infected by a serious strain of Obama Derangement Syndrome. But the right only recognized the principled fiscal-conservative protests, while the left could only see the fever of Obama Derangement Syndrome—and constructive civic conversation became almost impossible across that divide.

Liberals who want to ignore the populist anger of the Tea Parties and town halls do so at their political peril—the frustration at Washington overspending is real, a reflection of bailout backlash. People are angry because they are expected to pay their bills and balance their budgets, but both big business and big government seem arrogantly exempt while passing the buck to the next generation.

But Republicans are playing a dangerous game. They are benefiting from all this anger in the short term, but they have tapped into something they can't control. Calling the president a Nazi or Communist is something far beyond simple incivility or street theater—it is an accusation that intentionally stirs the crazy-pot.

OBAMA DERANGEMENT SYNDROME

Obama is Hitler. Obama is a Communist. Obama is Muslim. Obama is not a citizen. Obama is the Antichrist.

If you agree with any or all of these statements, you might be suffering from Obama Derangement Syndrome—pathological hatred of the president often mistaken for healthy patriotism.

It's a hydra-headed hysteria—cut off one accusation and another emerges in its place. The condition is apparently contagious, communicable through a steady diet of hyperpartisan talk radio and Wingnut websites. Its ugliest manifestation has led some to call—and even pray—for the death of the president. And the fury of Obama Derangement Syndrome's emergence shocked even the most jaded political observers.

The day after Election 2008 ended, the Obama resistance began. The *Drudge Report* had been featuring ominous black-and-white photos of candidate Obama on its popular home page for days. Now banner ads on the site announced the beginning of an organized "Patriotic, Resilient, Conservative Resistance" to the president-elect at the *Grassfire Nation* website, bridging the ugliest rhetoric of the campaign with what would erupt in the Tea Party protests and town halls.

Wealth redistribution and higher taxes? We Resist! Government takeover of more and more of our lives? We Resist! Open borders, amnesty and undermining of our uniquely American culture? We Resist! Taxpayer-funded abortions and a radical anti-life agenda? We Resist! The weakening of our military and retreat in the war on Terror? We Resist! Socialized health care? We Resist! The end of marriage and the exaltation of LGBT rights? We Resist! International taxation and submitting our nation to the ideals of "global citizenship"? We Resist! The Courts stacked with leftist judges who betray our Constitution? We Resist![1]

Obama's opponents were already invested in a nightmare vision of the future, a far-left socialist dystopia opposed only by a small band of militant patriots. This fear-based appeal drew 500,000 visitors in its first month online and succeeded in registering 250,000 people before Inauguration Day.

Whether the site's organizers knew it or not, the word *resistance* is loaded with history: it was invoked by white opposition to Reconstruction after the Civil War, it was reborn as an organized policy of "massive resistance" during the Southern desegregation battles a century later, and more recent militia movements proclaim the virtues of armed "leaderless resistance." But this call to arms was relatively civil compared to the raw expressions of hate incubated down at the netroots.

Only minutes after the election, a threat was posted to *Fox-Forum* on the Fox News website: "Let's have a huge parade . . . How about Nov 22 . . . in Dallas . . . Barack can ride in the back of a convertible with his wife . . . they could drive by the School Book Depository."[2]

Over at fringe website *American Sentinel*, an unhinged culture warrior named Michael Eden fired off his own welcome to the White House: "Barack Hussein Obama and his Democratic lackeys get to wear the bull's-eyes on their foreheads for the duration of the next election cycle. . . . don't let a bunch of appallingly blatant hypocrites tell you that you owe Obama one more iota of respect than they gave Bush . . . It's time to start burning down their houses and salting their fields."[3]

A white supremacist website, *Stormfront*, founded by a former grand dragon of the Ku Klux Klan, reported 2,800 new users in the first twenty-four hours after the election.[4] One poster on the site—identified as Dalderian Germanicus of North Las Vegas—wrote, "I want the SOB laid out in a box to see how 'messiahs' come to rest. God has abandoned us, this country is doomed."[5]

The craziness extended right into the halls of Congress. It was a Republican from Georgia named Paul Broun who got first dibs on the post-election comparisons of Obama to Hitler and Soviet dictators. In an interview with the Associated Press, Broun referenced Obama's proposal for a civilian reserve corps—an idea endorsed by the Bush administration to handle postwar reconstruction efforts, but which had become a fearful talking point on the far right with Obama in power. "That's exactly what Hitler did in Nazi Germany and it's exactly what the Soviet Union did," Broun said. "When he's proposing to have a national security force that's answering to him, that is as strong as the U.S. military, he's showing me signs of being Marxist." Broun clarified his statement by saying, "We can't be lulled into complacency. You have to remember that Adolf Hitler was elected in a democratic Germany."[6] Broun's office refused to issue an apology.

Even churches couldn't offer safe harbor. The Sunday after the election, the Reverend Jay Scott Newman told his South Carolina parishioners they should not take communion if they voted for "Barack Hussein Obama" because "our nation has chosen for its chief executive the most radical pro-abortion politician ever to serve in the United States Senate or to run for president," and that "constitutes material cooperation with intrinsic evil."[7]

It might be tempting to dismiss these statements as the work of a few well-placed cranks, congressmen, and clergy. But the Secret Service reported more threats against Obama than any other president-elect.[8] The politics of hate has a trickle-down effect, as the residents of Madison County, Idaho—which voted 85 percent for McCain-Palin—found out days after the election when a school bus full of second- and third-graders chanted "assassinate Obama."[9]

All these incidents occurred in the week after the election. So much for a presidential honeymoon.

Praying for the President's Death

"I hate Barack Obama. You say, well, you just mean you don't like what he stands for. No, I hate the person. Oh, you mean you just don't like his policies. No, I hate him . . . I am not going to pray for his good. I am going to pray that he dies and goes to hell."[10]

Here endeth the lesson at the Faithful Word Baptist Church in Tempe, Arizona. That's where Pastor Steven L. Anderson fired off a straight-to-the-point sermon on Sunday, August 16, 2009, titled, "Why I Hate Barack Obama."

"Obama is overturning the U.S. Constitution, overturning everything we believe as a country, overturning some 200 years of history," Anderson thundered from the pulpit. "He is the revolutionary and it's a socialist/communist revolution. We are the counter-revolutionaries saying no, we don't want a change." He even offered parishioners a view into his own private Obama prayer: "Break his teeth, oh God, in his mouth; as a snail which

melteth, let him pass away; like an untimely birth of a woman—
that he thinks—he calls it a woman's right to choose, you know,
he thinks it's so wonderful, he ought to be aborted. It ought to
be, 'Abort Obama,' that ought to be the motto."[11]

Anderson can be dismissed as a deranged fringe figure, Elmer
Gantry on a hate bender. Pastor Wiley Drake over in Orange
County, California, is a more troubling phenomenon. He served
as a second vice president of the Southern Baptist Convention
in 2006 and 2007. In 2008, he received 47,000 votes as the vice
presidential nominee of the American Independent Party, alongside conservative activist Alan Keyes. But that's not what he's
best known for these days.

Pastor Drake first surfaced on the national political radar
when he declared that the death of Kansas abortionist George
Tiller—murdered in church on May 31, 2009—occurred because he had prayed for it. "George Tiller was far greater in his
atrocities than Adolf Hitler," Drake told Fox's Alan Colmes, "so
I am happy. I am glad that he is dead." Then he took a deeper
leap into infamy by calmly announcing that he was also offering
imprecatory prayers for the death of "the usurper that is in the
White House . . . B. Hussein Obama."[12]

I wanted to see what a man who prays for the president's
death is like in person, so I arranged to meet him on his home
turf. The encounter provided a surprising portrait of someone
living with a full-blown case of Obama Derangement Syndrome.

Drake's First Southern Baptist Church stands less than a mile
from an amusement park, Knott's Berry Farm, in Orange County.
It's a beige cinderblock building constructed in the 1950s. In its
front yard, a broken wooden set of Ten Commandments juts out
of a rock. A sign reading "ETERNITY" hangs over a flickering
Coke machine.

Out back, a genial gray-haired man greets me, looking every inch the Western grandfather of five. He's wearing a red shirt with black suspenders and a senior-citizen-friendly big-buttoned cell phone hung on a string around his neck. This is the man who is praying for President Obama's death.

Wiley ushers me back into the empty church, past a sign saying "God Bless America," and we sit in the front pew. Hard-core haters are rarely friendly, their lives tending instead toward bitter isolation. But Wiley Drake's life story, it turns out, has a fascinating Forrest Gump quality.

Wiley at thirteen, shouting as nine African American students are escorted by armed US soldiers into a Little Rock, Arkansas, school: "2-4-6-8 we're not gonna integrate!" ("I grew up with the prejudice like everybody else did and thought I was right for a number of years," he says regretfully.) Wiley at eighteen, on the USS *Kitty Hawk* when the captain said on the loudspeaker, "We've been ordered to go to the South China Sea and to furnish air support for what's going on in a place called Indochina."

The late 1960s found Wiley married and ministering to the poor at the Union Rescue Mission in downtown Los Angeles and to Jesus Freak hippies on Huntington Beach. Incongruously, he also joined the John Birch Society and got a degree in communications from the University of Southern California. A brief stint in the private sector working for global manufacturing conglomerate Ingersoll Rand found Wiley at the US embassy in Iran days before the gates were stormed and hostages taken. He was already souring on his fellow Southern Baptist in the White House. "Carter began to have cocktails in the White House, and that to me was a dead giveaway," Wiley sniffs. "He wasn't as strict as he thought he was."

Back in Arkansas and back in the church, Wiley was part of a group of pastors approached by Bill Clinton as he tried to regain the governor's mansion in 1982. "He said, 'I lost because I didn't have the support of the church,' and he said, 'I want to put morality back in the governor's mansion.' . . . I said, 'Hey, this guy sounds good.' So I literally helped Bill Clinton get re-elected as the Comeback Kid. I very quickly found out that I had been flimflammed and sold a bill of goods; so then it was my desire to come back to Southern California."

Like many a fundamentalist, Wiley is a biblical literalist with a fondness for the Old Testament: "Just because man changed the law doesn't mean God's law is changed," he explains. "The Bible says that if a man lays down with a man, or a woman with a woman, it deserves death—and that's why the average homosexual only lives about less than fifty years of age on either side, man or woman. And now we're being told that we can't preach the Bible and that if we do it's a hate crime." This is a Wingnut vision of Big Brother—a liberal oppressor in conflict with God's law.

But strict readings of the Old Testament have been used to justify slavery and segregation from pulpits in the past. Where would Wiley draw the line today? "Do you believe then that disobedient children should be stoned, like it says in the Old Testament?" I asked. Wiley hesitated and chose his words carefully. "Yes, I believe that if a child is continuing to be totally disobedient, totally reprobate, then stoning would be biblically correct and legally correct."

As Wiley sees it, his devotion to speaking the word of God is what's caused all this controversy.

I'm known as a Birther, you know. I don't believe Obama was born in this country. He's an illegal alien and so forth. And so I

began to pray what the Bible teaches us to pray and that is imprecatory prayer.

An imprecatory prayer is very strong. Imprecatory prayer in
Psalms 109, for example, says if you have an evil leader above
you, you pray that Satan will stand by his side and you ask God
to make his children fatherless and his wife a widow and that
his time in office be short . . . Other psalms say when they speak
evil, God will break out their teeth and when they run to do
destruction, God will break their legs.

To those offended by the idea of praying for death, Wiley
shrugs. "I'm praying the word of God. I didn't write it. Don't
get mad at me." But threatening the president's life is a felony,
and when word got out about Wiley's imprecatory prayers, he
says the feds came over for a visit. "Within a week I had Secret Service people knocking on my door at the house saying
we want to talk to you. And I said no; I'm not talking to you. I
don't have to talk to you. I have freedom of speech. You want to
talk to me, see my attorney."

After the election, Wiley became one of the first to file a lawsuit alleging that Obama was constitutionally ineligible for office because he was born not in the United States but in Kenya.
Drake says that Obama had been on his radar even before the
campaign. "When he was still in Chicago, I had heard that the
Communist Party had chosen him to be the one that they would
bring about in this nation. I heard a testimony of a businessman
who had been at a meeting overseas where they said, 'We're
gonna bring a man to America that's going to be the next president and he's gonna be coming from Africa,' and so forth. They
said, 'In fact, we even know his name—Barack.' So I had heard
early on that he was the proverbial Manchurian candidate."

And what do you think will happen to America if Barack Obama is in office for a full two terms?

"I think most preachers like me are going to be in jail," says Wiley. "I don't know if you're familiar with H.R. 645, but it is the bill to set up at least a half a dozen encampments around the country, and one of the reasons . . . is to have a place to intern those that are faith-based organizations."

"Where do you get your information?" I ask.

"Well, the Internet, of course . . . *WorldNetDaily* is one of my favorite websites."

Having hit the Manchurian candidate and government plans for concentration camps in short order, I decided to go down the Obama Derangement Syndrome checklist with Wiley.

"Do you believe Obama's a Muslim?"

"Oh, absolutely. No doubt about it. No doubt in my mind he's a Muslim . . . he sort of likes Christianity, but he is primarily a Muslim." Check.

Next. "Some people call him Hitler or call him a Communist. They use words like 'treason' or 'traitor.'"

"Well, those are all terms in my opinion that fit," says Wiley. "If you look at how Hitler used children, he came up with the whole idea of kindergarten to brainwash the children. And Obama has come up with this whole concept of getting the children to chant and to literally worship him. He's followed Alinsky and others. He's very much following their pattern: to take over the country, to take us down economically. He knows that if he can take us down economically, then when the people are poor, the people will follow almost anyone, anyone that holds out any hope."

One final question: "Do you think that Barack Obama is the Antichrist?"

Wiley sighed and furrowed his brow. "In my opinion, and my theological understanding of the Scripture, there will be one Last Days, and in the Last Days there will be one Antichrist, but there will be several that lead up to the Antichrist, and I'm of the opinion that Barack Hussein Obama is the Antichrist."

"How exactly?"

"Well, you know, in reference to the fact that the Antichrist will be the one that's going to want to be the savior of the world, not through Jesus or God, but being the savior [himself]. We have to have medical care for everybody. We have to have all of these bailouts—control and own and operate. He has come as close to an Antichrist as anybody ever has in this country because, you know, it's not General Motors anymore. It's Government Motors. And he's taken over the banks and he's taken over everything."

So, to be clear, you believe that President Obama is going to bring about the end of the world?

"Absolutely, yeah. I don't have any idea how and when. But I think there's going to be some resistance . . . We're just seeing a resistance movement. We're seeing a group of people that are saying, 'Enough is enough. We're not going to let Congress do this.'"

The prospect of a cleansing Armageddon is pleasing to this grandfather of five. "People are finally waking up. One of the things that the Bible indicates about the Antichrist is that he will force the issues so much so that there will indeed be one last big war. And I think we're headed for that war."

How Obama Became Hitler, a Communist, and the Antichrist

You never forget your first Obama-is-the-Antichrist e-mail. Mine came in July 2008, with the subject header, "This Should

Open Our Eyes." What opened my eyes most was that it was sent sincerely by a generally sane local attorney and family friend. We've had presidents called Hitler, a Communist, and even the Antichrist in the past, but no president before Obama has hit the full insanity trifecta so fast—even before his election. Which got me wondering: How did this happen?

In search of answers, I wandered through the Wingnutsphere and found out how these contradictory conspiracy theories took flight from the fringe to mainstream consciousness—from e-mails and talk radio to cable news and then a protest near you. It shows the evolution of an idea, a genealogy of hate and hyperpartisanship in our time.

Obama as Hitler

Godwin's Law states that the longer any online debate goes on, the likelier it is that someone will play the Nazi card. It's the rhetorical equivalent of going nuclear and stupid at the same time. It used to be the reflexive attack of the campus politically correct crowd on conservatives, but in Obama's first year, a political role reversal was pulled off—Hitler was now a liberal.

This was a neat trick, inspired in part by a popular and thoughtful anti–big government treatise by *National Review* editor-at-large Jonah Goldberg (and son of Clinton nemesis Lucianne Goldberg), titled "Liberal Fascism." It allowed conservatives to de-link the right with fascism by pointing out that Nazis got their name because they were National Socialists. Goldberg himself pointed to an overlap in Obama's utopian rhetoric on Glenn Beck's show during the spring of 2008: "When Barack Obama campaigns, he's basically saying, 'I'm a silver bullet. I'm going to solve all your problems just by electing me.' FDR, Hitler, all these guys, they basically said, 'All your problems can be solved.'"[13]

The initial point of departure wasn't dictatorship or genocide but the ugliest imaginable partisan spin on Obama's oratorical talents. It's an interesting move: you turn inspiration into adulation and then you call it a cult of personality—next stop, Hitler.

The first known Obama-Hitler comparison occurred in February 2008, when Fox News radio host Tom Sullivan offered side-by-side airings of Obama's speech at the Iowa Jefferson-Jackson Dinner and a Hitler speech.[14] After Obama's address in Germany outside the Brandenburg Gate, conservative columnist Charles Krauthammer drily made the same point: "Standing in front of 200,000 Germans at a rally who are chanting your name—bad vibes sometimes, historically."[15] "Seventy-five thousand people at an outdoor sports palace, well, that's something the Führer would have done," concurred conservative economist (and sometime actor, most famous for droning, " . . . Bueller? Bueller?" in the iconic 1980s teen comedy *Ferris Bueller's Day Off*) Ben Stein after Obama's August nomination acceptance speech at Denver's Invesco Field at Mile High.[16] Ann Coulter lock-jawed another form of literary comparison, casting "B. Hussein's" memoir *Dreams from My Father* as "a dime store *Mein Kampf.*"[17]

Soon the comparison started gaining currency at the grass-roots. A sign drawn up by a volunteer in one of the McCain campaign's Florida field offices compared "Barack Hussein Obama" to a litany of dictators from Hitler to Stalin to Mussolini to Castro. "Who else called for change in this fashion?" the sign asked. "Each and every one called on youth movements. And you want Obama for President? Are you nuts!"[18]

The designer of the sign, a self-identified "twelfth-generation" American named Robert E. J. Driscoll, was dismissed from volunteering for the campaign but refused to apologize. He said he had been offended by the way activists on the left had compared Bush to Hitler without mainstream media criticism. In any case, he told the *Sun-Sentinel*, "Clinically and morally there is nothing wrong with the poster . . . If I compare the oration ability of Senator Obama with that of Adolf Hitler (both quite good in communicating), does that mean I am suggesting Obama will be a mass murderer? Of course not."[19]

Congressman Paul Broun's post-election outburst comparing Obama to Hitler offered a similar qualification: "I'm not comparing him to Adolf Hitler. What I'm saying is there is the potential of going down that road."[20]

The delicate politics of this differentiation was explained in fuller detail by the master of political-attack-as-entertainment, Rush Limbaugh: "When you're dealing with a guy like Obama and the Democrat Party, who are going to impose Nazi-like socialism policies on this country, you've got to say it. And the same time you say it, you have to go out and point we're not talking about the genocide—that's at the tail end of Hitler."[21]

Right. So the Wingnut argument is that they are not comparing Obama to Hitler the genocidal dictator, but they're comparing Obama to Hitler the political leader—those 6 million Jews murdered in the Holocaust are just a detail people keep getting hung up on.

In April 2009, as the Republican Party's officials tried to regroup, Michigan party chair Saul Anuzis—an ambitious if unsuccessful aspirant for national Republican National Committee (RNC) chair—advanced the ball by advising the GOP to characterize Obama's policies as "economic fascism." "We've so overused the word 'socialism' that it no longer has the negative connotation it had 20 years ago, or even 10 years ago," Anuzis reasoned. "Fascism—everybody still thinks that's a bad thing."[22]

Later that month, Glenn Beck obligingly picked up the talking point: "They're marching us to a non-violent fascism. Or to put it another way, they're marching us to 1984. Big Brother. Like it or not, fascism is on the rise."[23] Fox producers partnered the commentary with a minute's worth of goose-stepping Nazi b-roll.

The message was received loud and clear. In June, the president of the Republican Women of Anne Arundel County, Maryland, fired off this e-mail, complete with the requisite paranoid capital letters: "Obama and Hitler have a great deal in common in my view. Obama and Hitler use the 'blitzkrieg' method to overwhelm their enemies. FAST, CARPET BOMBING intent on destruction. Hitler's blitzkrieg bombing destroyed many European cities—quickly and effectively. Obama is systematically destroying the American economy and with it AMERICA."[24]

Prefab Obama-as-Hitler signs began to pop up at August health-care town halls, featuring the president with a narrow mustache, bearing the slogan: "I've changed." They were the product of the conspiracy theory cult of Lyndon LaRouche. It was a LaRouche aide named Anton Chaitkin who started the Obama-as-Hitler attack on health care in response to what he called "a propaganda movement for euthanasia." Soon, pamphlets were produced: "Act Now to Stop Obama's Nazi Health Plan!"

In Massachusetts, Congressman Barney Frank's town hall was disrupted by a glassy-eyed young LaRouche-ite who asked, "Why are you supporting this Nazi policy, as Obama has?" (Frank deserves bipartisan props for his response: "On what planet do you spend most of your time?")

In Nevada, at a Las Vegas town hall, an Israeli American was defending Israel's national health care to reporters when a woman named Pamela Pigler shouted, "Heil Hitler!" and then proceeded to make whining sounds mocking him when he took offense. Pigler later explained, "I'm a conservative and I just believe in biblical values."[25] It remains unclear how shouting "Heil Hitler" is consistent with biblical values.

In Iowa, a World War II vet named Tom Eisenhower (presumably no relation to the late president) proclaimed to the crowd at Senator Chuck Grassley's town hall, "The president of the United States, that's who you should be concerned about. Because he's acting like a little Hitler . . . I'd take a gun to Washington if enough of you would go with me."[26]

By the 9/12 march on Washington, dozens of homemade Obama-as-Hitler signs were a prominent part of the scenery. I saw side-by-side portraits of the president next to Hitler and Lenin, with the tag, "In troubled times the fearful and naïve are always drawn to charismatic radicals. We will never allow this Change to happen." There was iconic Nazi-era imagery with President Obama pasted in as "the new face of national socialism."

The seeds of the association had blossomed into full-fledged acceptance by some people on Main Street. An Ohio couple didn't understand why they were denied a permit to drive through the annual Fredricktown Tomato Show Parade on a float that showed President Obama with a swastika armband beside a Nazi flag.[27] Richard and Jacqueline Ruhl said they found "strong parallels between what President Obama is doing and Adolf Hitler" and proposed the float as a way to get their neighbors to "wake up."

"It was the swastikas that seemed to be turning off most people," reflected Jackie. "We are not extremists and we have not done anything like this before . . . He denied us our First

Amendment right. He is an extremist," Jackie said, referring to President Obama. "If anyone thinks I like pulling a swastika around, they are crazy," said Richard. "I hated it just as much as anybody."[28]

With the growing use of the Obama-as-Hitler comparison, a few more GOP leaders started indulging as well.

Former Bush administration official Ellen Sauerbrey—who served as assistant secretary of state and was a two-time GOP nominee for governor in Maryland—reportedly told a September Lincoln-Reagan Dinner audience that the president was surrounded by "a cult-like following edging toward those of past dictators like Juan Perón and even Adolf Hitler."[29] When subsequently asked to clarify her comments by the *County Times*, Sauerbrey denied having dropped the H-bomb but acknowledged: "I think that we have a government that is following policies that are socialistic and fascist."[30]

Georgia congressman John Linder, a member of the powerful House Ways and Means Committee, decided to make his Hitler comparisons in op-ed form, penning a condemnation of progressivism for *Politico* that tied together Robespierre, Woodrow Wilson, Hitler, Mussolini, and Obama: "All believed in the minimum wage, state control of private property for the public good, unionization and environmentalism. And they believed in eugenics to purify the gene pool."[31]

Ask a Nazi

All these Nazi comparisons made me wonder what actual Nazis thought of the hype—it must be bittersweet for them to have the first African American president compared to Hitler, a curious mix of pride and prejudice. I hunted down the phone number of the Northeast Nazi chapter (apparently, they are fussy about being called the American National Socialist Party) and got someone who called himself SS Corporal Schneider on the line.

"The people who are referring to him as a Nazi know very little or nothing about authentic Nazism," Schneider stiffly said. "I'd laugh if it wasn't so ludicrous. The last thing in the world I would ever call President Obama—and I hesitate to call him president—is a Nazi. I most certainly would not refer to him as a Nazi. It seems to me that if he was successful at what he was doing, he'd be more of a Communist than a Nazi. A Nazi is completely at the opposite end of the spectrum where he is concerned . . . and his is not a Nazi health plan, not by any stretch of the imagination." So we've got that creepily cleared up.

I couldn't resist pressing Schneider on how self-styled Aryans feel about the Obama comparisons: "Having the first African American president being the one who's been called Nazi the most—that's got to get under your skin."

"Well, you'll find no blacks among the ranks of the National Socialist movement, for obvious reasons," Schneider understated. "It gets under members' skin, not so much because of his color, but because of his ideas and some of the things that he's been saying . . . The concept of color in the movement here is not quite the issue that it was."

In Schneider's world, the Nazi Party is "comprised of tax-paying, law abiding, nine-to-five working people who are very devoted to their families, pay their taxes, stop for red lights, respect the police and the law, and basically are out to support their own country and save it from the ruination of the corrupt politicians that are destroying and undermining this entire system." But are there any politicians he likes? "Reagan. And if that man came back from the dead, I'd vote for him again. It's just a shame that the man passed away and it's just a shame that man couldn't have been president for life."

Perhaps the best response to all this Wingnut distortion of history came from one seventy-year-old man, a classically trained musician by the name of Henry Gasparian. His family had experienced real Nazis—not metaphorical ones—in Armenia during World War II.

They'd killed his uncles and sent a cousin to die in a concentration camp. When he saw the Obama-as-Hitler posters at a sidewalk protest near his home in Seattle, his reaction was "personal and emotional." A heated conversation turned into a shoving match, and the cops came and took Gasparian away. His son, who bailed him out of jail eight hours later, was shocked, saying his father had never received more than a speeding ticket. But Henry was unrepentant. "I saw Hitler's soldiers. I saw swastikas every day," he said. "To call Obama stupid, even criminal— okay, that's politics. But Hitler? It's hurting to anyone no matter who is president."[32]

Obama as Communist

"There is no doubt that he is a Marxist, but he is much more than that, much more dangerous than that—and this is the reality that should make all Americans very, very nervous and fearful."[33]

No, it's not Barack Obama they're referring to. It's Bill Clinton being called a Marxist Manchurian candidate back in the 1990s.

The same Wingnut website, *WorldNetDaily,* has been pushing the same paranoid argument against President Obama, complete with epic preelection screeds with titles like "Barack Obama Really Is a Manchurian Candidate."[34] (I love the "really"—in their italics. It's vaguely apologetic in a boy-who-cried-wolf sort of way—they might have been wrong about Bubba, but they've got the real Marxist Manchurian candidate this time.)

The slippery slope from socialist to Communist attacks on Obama began during the campaign. It focused first on economics. When Barack Obama met "Joe the Plumber" in Toledo, Ohio, and uttered the phrase "Spread the wealth," socialism became an omnipresent Hail Mary campaign tactic. Sarah Palin enthusiastically dove in, repeatedly saying, "Now is no time to experiment with socialism."[35]

Former Republican House majority leader Tom DeLay hammered home the theme a bit harder: "Unless he proves me wrong, he is a Marxist."[36] On CNN's *Larry King Live,* conservative-radio show host Lars Larson recommended that McCain needed "to tag Obama as the Marxist that he is."[37]

But for most conservatives, calling Obama an outright Communist seemed a stretch. The defamatory door was opened with examinations of his family history. Writing on *National Review Online,* former Dan Quayle speechwriter Lisa Schriffen[38] wondered whether Obama's parents had first met through a love of communism: "How had these two come together at a time when it was neither natural nor easy for such relationships to flourish? Always through politics. No, not the Young Republicans. Usually the Communist Youth League. Or maybe a different arm of the CPUSA. But, for a white woman to marry a black man in 1958, or '60, there was almost inevitably a connection to explicit Communist politics."[39]

Allegations of Obama's influence under "communist and socialist mentors" while growing up in Hawaii and later Chicago occupied a chapter in the best-selling *Obama Nation: Leftist Politics and the Cult of Personality.* Written by *WorldNetDaily* senior staff reporter Jerome R. Corsi, author of the anti–John Kerry tome *Unfit for Command,* the book concluded that Obama "is a likely communist sympathizer."

Down the stretch, Ohio-based conservative-radio host Bill Cunningham went into full Communist-revolution-is-coming mode, telling his 200,000 swing-state listeners, "Much like Castro took over Cuba, Mao Zedong took over Red China, and the Communists took over Russia, Obama now is poised—according to many of my good friends on the left . . . to seize power in America, and I hope [it will] be a bloodless coup."[40]

Shortly after the election, Michael Savage managed to tie the Communist and Birther craziness all together for his audience. "We're getting ready for the Communist takeover of America with a non-citizen at the helm—I love it."[41]

All this remained festering on the fringes, until Glenn Beck's new show debuted on Fox in January. Sixteen days into the new administration, Beck featured a graphic showing America galloping down the road from capitalism to socialism and then to communism—and then began offering a regular "Comrade Update."[42]

At the Tax Day Tea Party in 2009, Obama-as-Communist signs first started to pop up in the crowd, next to the protestations of patriotism and fidelity to the Founding Fathers. At the City Hall Park rally in New York, I went up to one guy impassively holding a giant placard that read "Hussein = Commie." He was wearing a hoodie and sunglasses and holding an iPod—a hipster irony outfit by way of the Unabomber—so I asked him if the sign was serious. Oh, yeah.

"Every time he opens his mouth he spouts textbook Marxism, communism, socialism," said the man who initially gave his name as "Barry Soetoro"—Obama's name when he lived in

Indonesia as a child. After some prodding, it turned out the protester was a Manhattan real estate executive with a degree in economics from Georgetown. This was a high-end kind of crazy.

Likewise, the African American politician Alan Keyes has a pedigree that would seem to counter off-the-rails accusations. But Keyes can be considered patient zero in the spread of Obama Derangement Syndrome. The one-time protégé of Reagan's United Nations ambassador, Jeane Kirkpatrick—and a three-time presidential candidate—was recruited to run against then–state senator Barack Obama in 2004 for the Illinois US Senate seat, despite the fact that Keyes lived in Maryland. (That the GOP could not find an African American candidate to run in all of Illinois, the Land of Lincoln, is its own evidence of the Party of Lincoln's problems.) In his 2006 book, *The Audacity of Hope,* Obama angrily recounts Keyes's campaign claim that "Christ would not vote for Barack Obama."

Keyes has only ratcheted up his rhetoric since then, both in his 2008 third-party campaign for the presidency alongside Wiley Drake and in comments outside a Nebraska anti-abortion fund-raiser in the spring of 2009. "Obama is a radical Communist, and I think it is becoming clear. That is what I told people in Illinois and now everybody realizes it's true," Keyes told a reporter from local station KHAS-TV. "He is going to destroy this country, and we are either going to stop him or the United States of America is going to cease to exist."[43]

By the summer of 2009, the Soviet hammer and sickle was being slapped on e-mails and T-shirts, advertised by smiling girls on conservative websites, purchasable on bumper stickers, tote bags, and mugs. Search online for "Obama" and "Communist" or "hammer and sickle" and hundreds of Internet images pop up. The proliferation of Obama-as-Communist gear is

presumably supposed to be sarcastic opposition or ironic commentary—the online retailer Noisebot.com actually labeled one
of its wares as a "funny Obama Communist T-shirt."

Twenty years after the end of the Cold War, I can appreciate
how easy it is to treat communism as a curiosity, like the last
Japanese soldier found wanting to fight for the emperor on a
Pacific island in 1974. But any ideology that managed to murder
100 million people in less than a century is not a joke. It's a con-
duit for evil.

At the 9/12 march on Washington, there were posters of
Obama as Che Guevara over the slogan "Obamunism." There
were signs telling America to "Wake Up" with pictures of
Obama alongside Lenin and Castro, with another featuring
Obama's face morphing into Stalin's. Obama was painted as
the Joker in whiteface and lipstick over the slogan "I lied" and
"Communism isn't funny." One veteran held a sign that read, "I
didn't serve in the military to live in a socialist country" and
"Obama's America looks a lot like the Soviet Union." Another
proclaimed "Red Dawn 2009: The Enemy is Within."

A glossy poster of Joe McCarthy holding a photo of Obama
caught my eye. "Vindicated," it read. Its creator was a twenty-
four-year-old from Pennsylvania named Brad. "When I was
younger, I always heard right-wing speech from my grandfather about Joseph McCarthy and the Communists," he said.
"But now you come to realize that there are a lot of socialists
not only in Hollywood but in the public school systems, and
they've taken over the media and sort of hijacked democracy, so
I figured this was good."

I went up to one woman dressed as a cross between Betsy
Ross and Mrs. Claus and asked her what message she was trying
to send.

"I was in Cuba at the age of twelve when Castro took over," she said. "He promised a change just like this president is promising us, and right after that he began to do certain things that I see very familiar now, the same steps toward total control. So I had no choice but to leave my country as a child without my parents . . . I never saw them again, and here I am fifty years later with concern that our children here might run into the same problems that we had."

So do you really think there are parallels between Castro and Obama? I asked. "Yes," she said. "Do some reading and you'll see. Go to the Communist Party USA."

So I did.

Ask a Communist

"Obama is certainly no Communist," Communist Party USA national board member Dan Margolis told me. "There's no way that you could say that he's gone anywhere close to being a Communist. The only similarity I can see is that Fidel Castro said the word *change* and Obama uses the word *change.* . . . The idea that Obama is somehow leading a socialist revolution in this country is just patently ridiculous. Actually, I don't even see any parallels."

"His policies aren't socialist," Comrade Margolis insisted. "You know, with the economic crisis, they wanted to prop up big finance. What we would have said is simply: 'We need to nationalize these banks.' . . . We're not happy with the idea of escalating troops in Afghanistan. We don't see a military victory there as really possible . . . And health care, of course, if it were up to us, we'd have socialized medicine."

But wait, isn't the whole debate over whether Obama's health-care plan constitutes socialized medicine? "It's clearly not socialized medicine," said Margolis. "An example of socialized medicine would be Cuba, where all doctors are employees of the government . . . We consider that a better system but that's not what Obama's proposing." It turns out that Obama wasn't even the Democratic candidate whom Communists saw as the closest thing to a fellow traveler in the 2008 campaign. The Communists liked Dennis Kucinich.

Obama as Antichrist

Twenty-five percent of Americans have heard the rumor that Obama is the Antichrist (the biblically predicted false messiah who will rule the world until the second coming of Christ), according to a Scripps-Howard poll.[44] This is courtesy of a widely circulated e-mail chain that began to hit critical mass in March 2008, when Obama was on the verge of clinching the nomination:

According to The Book of Revelations [sic] . . . the Anti-Christ will be a man, in his 40s, of MUSLIM descent, who will deceive the nations with persuasive language, and have a MASSIVE Christ-like appeal . . . the prophecy says that people will flock to him and he will promise false hope and world peace, and when he is in power, he will destroy everything.

And Now: For the award winning Act of Stupidity of all times the People of America want to elect, to the most Powerful position on the face of the Planet—The Presidency of the United States of America . . . A Muslim Male Extremist Between the ages of 17 and 40.

Have the American People completely lost their Minds, or just their Power of Reason ???

I'm sorry but I refuse to take a chance on the "unknown" candidate Obama.

The e-mail was a tiny classic in paranoid politics and character assassination, bringing together war-on-terror anxiety, the moral authority of religious imagery, and McCain campaign talking points about "the unknown Obama."

Among the folks who forwarded the e-mail was Mayor Danny Funderburk of Fort Mill, South Carolina, who explained to an inquiring reporter, "I was just curious if there was any validity to it . . . I was trying to get documentation if there was any Scripture to back it up."[45]

Former *Saturday Night Live* comedienne-turned-conservative-blogger Victoria Jackson also jumped in, writing that Obama "bears traits that resemble the anti-Christ."[46]

I met more believers in this theory in the summer of 2009, when Shirley Phelps-Roper decided to take her two young daughters on a field trip from Topeka, Kansas, to Manhattan. They were coming to celebrate—yes, celebrate—the death of Walter Cronkite outside his memorial service.

You might have heard of the Phelps-Roper family from the Westboro Baptist Church because of their practice of protesting at soldiers' funerals—where signs range from "God Hates Fags" to "God Hates America"—apparently because we don't hate quite enough for their taste. I ran into them on a bright Tuesday morning on the Upper West Side, where they were killing time in a pre-game protest outside a Jewish community center, stomping on American and Israeli flags. The daughters Megan and Grace were carrying signs that read, "Barack Obama is the anti-Christ" and "America is Doomed."

I asked twenty-two-year-old Megan what she thought of President Obama. Her eyes lit up. "Oh, he's the Antichrist," she said. I asked for a little more explanation. "Well, he's against Christ," she said.*

Liberty University Law School dean Matthew Staver felt he had to offer a word of caution to those who wanted to take the full step to crazy: though he did not personally believe Obama is the Antichrist, he could see how others might. "They are expressing a concern and a fear that is widely shared."[47] Depressingly, the journalistic accuracy website Snopes found it necessary to burst these hot-air balloons, pointing out that "nothing in the Bible—in Revelation or elsewhere—describes the anti-Christ as being 'a man, in his 40s, of Muslim descent.' In fact, since the book of Revelation was complete by the end of the second century, but the religion of Islam wasn't founded until about 400 years later, the notion that Revelation would have mentioned the word 'Muslim' at all is rather far-fetched."[48]

Despite the chronological absurdity, the McCain campaign put out a Web ad that seemed to play on Obama-as-Antichrist fears. Titled "The One," it began with the sarcastic humor that distinguished the campaign's communication style, mocking Obama supporters' adulation of their candidate, interspersed

---

* In March 2013, I spoke with Meagan and Grace Roper again for a column in *The Daily Beast*. They had taken the brave step of leaving their family and their church to see the world for themselves. "There was a disconnect between the way that I felt and the way I was taught," said Megan. "We were told a lot of things that weren't true, and we assumed they were true because we didn't see any evidence otherwise. But we weren't really looking . . . There's so much that we didn't know about the way people believe and how they live. And we thought we did. We thought we knew. And we did not have a clue."

with clips of Charlton Heston as Moses from Cecil B. DeMille's *The Ten Commandments.*

The ad careened off into scriptural wording—"And the world will receive his blessings"—and used imagery that recalled the cover of the 70-million-copy seller the *Left Behind* series, which chronicles the rise of the Antichrist in politics. The Reverend Tim LaHaye, co-author of *Left Behind,* said he recognized allusions to his work in the ad.[49]

It was the creation of McCain media adviser Fred Davis, a man familiar with evangelical code as the friend of former Christian Coalition leader Ralph Reed and the nephew of conservative Oklahoma senator James Inhofe. *Time* magazine editorialized, "It's not easy to make the infamous Willie Horton ad from the 1988 presidential campaign seem benign. But suggesting that Barack Obama is the Antichrist might just do it."[50]

The caricatures kept popping up, furthered by the mock humor-hysteria of partisan sites. *WorldNetDaily* repeatedly weighed in on the affirmative, while the conservative website *RedState.com* started selling T-shirts and mugs sporting a large "O" with horns and the words "The Anti-Christ" underneath.[51] Glenn Beck felt compelled to ask conservative evangelical leader the Reverend John Hagee what were the "odds that Obama is the Antichrist"? Hagee said simply and clearly, "No Chance."[52]

The weekend before the election, the *Salt Lake Tribune* published an article addressing the fears: "For eons, Christians have believed the world is hurling toward oblivion. But with the current economic downturn, the war in Iraq and the likely election of Barack Obama, many think it has picked up speed."[53]

The so-called Rapture Index—an evangelical website that keeps tabs on signs that the end of the world may be at hand—reached 50,000 hits a day in the run-up to Election Day, and the index hit new highs after Obama's election.[54]

And the Obama-as-Antichrist rumors didn't dissipate after the election; evangelicals were buzzing that the winning lottery numbers in Illinois the day after the election were 666, considered the biblical "mark of the beast." And in September 2009, Public Policy Polling found that 14 percent of New Jersey Republicans thought that Obama was the Antichrist, while 15 percent weren't sure.[55]

Opinion had only worsened by the time of Obama's second term. After the 2012 election, PPP polling found that 22 percent of Romney voters believed Obama was the Antichrist.[56]

The Obama Haters Book Club

By the end of President Obama's first term, no less than eighty-nine obsessively anti-Obama books had been published, as catalogued by *The Daily Beast*. We're not talking about cool statements of policy difference, but overheated and often unhinged screeds painting a picture of the president as a dangerous radical, hell-bent on undermining the republic by any means necessary.

Welcome to the Obama Haters Book Club—a parallel universe of fearmongering for fun and profit.

By their very nature, books offer the promise of education and enlightenment. These conspiracy entrepreneurs prey on the prejudices of their audience. This is high-priced hardcover bile, boasting such titles as the following:

The Communist; The Muslim Brotherhood in the Obama Administration; Where's the Birth Certificate?; The Manchurian President: Barack Obama's Ties to Communists, Socialists and Other

Anti-American Extremists; The Great Destroyer: Barack Obama's War on the Republic; Trickle Down Tyranny: Crushing Obama's Dream of the Social States of America; Gangster Government: Barack Obama and the New Washington Thugocracy; How Obama Embraces Islam's Sharia Agenda; The Post-American Presidency: The Obama Administration's War on America; To Save America: Stopping Obama's Secular Socialist Machine; The Blueprint: Obama's Plan to Subvert the Constitution and Build an Imperial Presidency; and what is still my personal favorite title: *Whiny Little Bitch: The Excuse Filled Presidency of Barack Obama.*

The titles themselves suggest palpable weirdness and un-wellness, a departure from reality commensurate with joining a cult. But the authors are not all fringe figures nervously typing up pamphlets in their basement. They include former elected officials, administration appointees, and at least one presidential candidate among the parade of professional polarizers and right-wing shock jocks.

They've been able to spread their message and make a lot of money in the process by hitting the hyperpartisan circuit with high-profile help. A stunning fifty-six of the authors in the Obama Haters Book Club had been featured on Fox News, giving them valuable mass media exposure, the opportunity to preach to the conservative choir and sell books by the boatload.

As a result, the cottage industry of hating Barack Obama is now big business. Hackish screeds such as *The Amateur* by Edward Klein outsell such well-written and thoroughly reported books as *Barack Obama: The Story,* by David Maraniss. Hate sells because it is simple and has a built-in constituency looking for confirmation bias.

Of course, President Obama isn't the first White House occupant to face unhinged hatred and conspiracy theories. It is in part a tradition going back to our earliest days, consistent with the First Amendment. But because of the pervasive nature of partisan media in the modern world, the problem has gotten demonstrably worse.

By the midterm elections of 2010, the number of anti-Obama titles was at forty-six. Compare that to the literature of Bush Derangement Syndrome, which totaled just five at the midterm elections of 2002 and rocketed up to forty-six by November 2004—by which time there were eighty-nine books boasting ODS appeal.

In other words, by the end of their respective first terms, there were twice as many Obama Derangement Syndrome books as specimens of Bush Derangement Syndrome in the same period of time. The cycle of incitement has gotten worse and more widespread because it's been semilegitimized. Some of the same folks who called BDS treasonous see ODS as part of a patriotic resistance. This is more insidious than simple hypocrisy.

Barack Obama is the first Democratic president who has truly had to contend with the full spectrum of partisan media machinery. Hating Bill Clinton was an essentially analog event. Talk radio was in its full glory, but Fox News was still in its infancy, as was the Internet. So stories about Bubba's alleged propensity for Marxism, murder, and drug dealing never really got beyond Moral Majority mailing lists. And as of 2014, Bill Clinton seems to be, hilariously, every Republican's favorite living Democrat (a status that will no doubt change if his wife runs for president in 2016). The core problem with Clinton for many conservatives seemed to be that they could not accept him as a legitimate president until he was out of office. The same is now true with Barack Obama, but on steroids, with the added alloy of race inserted into the mix.

We will look back on Birtherism and some of the other strange conspiracy theories that have clustered around Obama as, at the very least, vestigial remnants of racism. The sheer tonnage of hate and lies directed his way in the White House is stunning, and it will seem somewhere between stupid, silly, and sad in the future.

But for now, we are witnessing the harvest of that hate. Talk to otherwise decent, well-intentioned citizens on the campaign trail and these themes keep creeping up in conversation: "Obama is a socialist" and "He wants to make us more like Europe" are among the most benign; "Muslim" and "Marxist" are not uncommon.

In the final weeks of the 2012 campaign, I spoke with three tipsy middle-aged women who helped put on an Ann Romney rally in wealthy Winter Park, Florida, and who did not hesitate to repeatedly describe the president of the United States as "evil." Members of Congress repeat lines straight out of the Obama Haters Book Club, talking about Obama's "Gangster Government," "Thugocracy," Muslim Brotherhood infiltration of his administration, his Communist influences and tyrannical ambitions. One Romney campaign ad even spoke of the president's "War on Religion."[57]

This doesn't even qualify as dog-whistle politics—it directly repeats the core drumbeat of the Obama Haters Book Club: that President Obama is un-American and anti-American.

Look over all these disparate threads of Obama Derangement Syndrome—from comparisons to Hitler to Communists to the Antichrist—and you'll see some common themes.

There is a recipe that keeps being repeated—a Wingnut claim that riffs on foundational fears is posted on a fringe website (usual suspects include *WorldNetDaily* or *Free Republic*) and then gets passed around. These dispatches from the outer limits get repeated on talk radio—and then get repeated on Fox News, usually introduced with the infamous "some people are saying" frame. They trickle down to the grassroots and appear on signs at protests. Eventually, some elected official parrots the paranoia, playing to the base while venting his or her spleen. It makes news not only because the statements are outrageous but because they crystallize what's crazy in our politics.

THE BIRTH OF WHITE-MINORITY POLITICS

There's one thing I can't help but notice every time I go to a Tea Party or a town hall, let alone the Republican National Convention: a lot of white people.

The crowds are weirdly monochromatic. Even in the heart of Washington, DC, a city that is 55 percent African American, I didn't see a single black person among the tens of thousands in the crowd at the 9/12 rally on the Washington Mall—it was a columnist's version of *Where's Waldo?*

Some liberals look at the opposition to Obama, and they blame it all on racism. Actress and activist Janeane Garofalo vented her spleen on behalf of many when she said, "This is about hating a black man in the White House. This is racism straight up. That is nothing but a bunch of teabagging rednecks."[1] Reflexively playing the race card may be emotionally satisfying for some on the left, but after covering the Tea Party protests and town halls up close, I still don't believe simple, stupid, ugly segregation-era racism is driving most opposition to President Obama.

Yes, there is the drip-drop of racist e-mails from small-town conservative officials and racially overtoned netroot nicknames for Obama like "Ogabe" (a riff off Zimbabwe's dictator Robert Mugabe). Yes, American voting patterns are still largely split on racial lines, and race has been a fundamental fault line in US politics since the original sin of slavery.

But as Barack Obama once pointed out, he was black before the election. His breakthrough caucus victory occurred in

96-percent-white Iowa. America has come a long way from the brutal bigotry of the Bull Connor era. Something more complex is going on.

We are witnessing the birth of white-minority politics. In some ways, it resembles the identity politics of past groups—for instance, the millions of Irish or Italian immigrants who arrived annually at the turn of the last century—complete with the competing emotions of pride and victimization. There was a focus on preserving ancestral heritage against the onslaught of change in the New World. But this time the economic struggle isn't about climbing the ladder of success; it's about not falling further behind. With an increase of more than 2.2 million white males unemployed in the first year after Obama's election,[2] some white voters felt they were getting squeezed by a changing America—a bad economy combined with a slow-moving demographic tsunami.

These folks feel like a minority because they fear they are going to be a minority. The year 2050 has special resonance—that's the year that the US census estimates whites will no longer be a majority in America.[3] In their eyes, Obama's election represents the rise of a new urban onslaught of educated minorities and immigrants who are pushing the rural whites who used to define what it meant to be an American down the economic food chain.

White-minority politics can be defined as a politics of resistance to social change propelled by resentment. It resonates with people who feel like members of an oppressed minority, under siege by a modern multicultural America that is being imposed on them and that disrespects traditional American values in the process. It is an echo of what Richard Hofstadter described as a core characteristic of the paranoid style a half century ago:

America has been largely taken away from them and their kind, though they are determined to try to repossess it and to prevent the final destructive act of subversion. The old American virtues have already been eaten away by cosmopolitans and intellectuals; the old competitive capitalism has been gradually undermined by socialist and communist schemers; the old security and independence have been destroyed by treasonous plots having as their most powerful agents not merely outsiders and foreigners but major statesmen seated at the very center of the American power.[4]

It's no surprise then that their signature rallying cry is "Take Our Country Back"—a slogan that surfaces at Tea Parties and town halls ("I want my country back, I don't want my flag to change!"). It is used on Wingnut websites, serves as a signature line on talk shows, and provides the title for a conservative conference. (Coincidentally but perhaps not incidentally, the white-supremacist British National Party uses a similar slogan: "We Want Our Country Back.") It accompanies talk about the assault on American values and the undermining of our constitutional republic, of slavery via socialism, tyranny, and totalitarianism. Rush Limbaugh tells his audience, "We're living in occupied territory. . . . We, the people of this country, need to be liberated. We are oppressed now."[5]

This desire to take the country back is combined with an idealized vision of America's past, a more pastoral time of small-town values and small government. It is unspoken that this was a largely white America. It's consistent with the way Confederate flags that occasionally wave in protest crowds are explained away by saying they represent "heritage, not hate." The appeal is so emotional that one sign I saw read simply, "Preserve Mom,

Apple Pie and the American Way." In the eyes of these super-patriots, the ideal of America is under assault.

Right-wing radio show host Michael Savage has been beating the drum of resistance and resentment hard. "In the past people would come over and become Americans. Now they come over and they want you to become them. They want you to speak Spanish, they want you to act Muslim, they want you to give up going to the church and go into a mosque," Savage said on August 20, 2009, as town hall protests were erupting into fistfights.

"We're gonna have a revolution in this country if this keeps up," Savage continued:

> The rage has reached a boil. If they keep pushing us around and if we keep having these schmucks running for office catering to the multicultural people who are destroying the culture of this country, the white male—the one without connections, the one without money—has nothing to lose . . . He is still the majority, no one speaks for him, everyone craps on him, people use him for cannon fodder, and he has no voice whatsoever. You're gonna find out that if you keep pushing this country around, there is an ugly side to the white male that has been suppressed for probably thirty years right now but it really has never gone away.[6]

It's not just the complaint of a few isolated shock jocks strutting their psychoses and doing the latest version of the angry white guy rant.

Conservative pundit and former Reagan communications director Pat Buchanan has been a prophet of white-minority politics for decades, building a successful career on the concept from President Richard Nixon's Southern strategy to his own pitchfork populist campaigns for the presidency. Although he has earned a reputation as a personally genial conservative voice on political talk shows, Pat Buchanan is not just an incidental advocate for these forces. His 2006 book, *State of Emergency,* was subtitled *The Third World Invasion and Conquest of America.* Buchanan has appeared twice on the avowedly white supremacist radio show *Political Cesspool,* most recently in July 2008. The host of *Political Cesspool,* James Edwards, attributes volunteering on Buchanan's 2000 presidential campaign to his political awakening. Since Obama's election, Buchanan has been particularly prolific on the subject, writing about the plight of white voters: "America was once their country. They sense they are losing it. And they are right."[7]

Like Savage, but far more eloquent, Buchanan feels a forced cultural conversion is under way: "Without the assent of her people, America is being converted from a Christian country, nine in 10 of whose people traced their roots to Europe as late as the time of JFK, into a multiracial, multiethnic, multilingual, multicultural Tower of Babel not seen since the late Roman Empire."[8]

And Buchanan laments the new heroes of our evolving multicultural America: "Old heroes like Columbus, Stonewall Jackson, and Robert E. Lee are replaced by Dr. King and Cesar Chavez."[9]

The fact that Pat singled out not one but two members of the Confederate Army—including the now semi-obscure Jackson, whom Southern Civil War historian Shelby Foote once described as having "a curious indifference to suffering"—speaks to the impulses behind this allegedly pro-America traditionalist movement.[10]

But a more popular metaphor than the defeated Confederacy is the founding of the United States, the American political scripture of the War of Independence.

Opposition to health-care reform was presented in online ads as a re-creation of the Continental Army's struggle against British tyranny, recast as a struggle for individual freedom against British-style big-government health care. It's not a policy debate but a life-or-death fight for the soul of America, pitting conservatives against liberals, patriots against tyrants. The president's position is therefore fundamentally un-American.

This call provokes a response. At the 9/12 march, scattered among the crowd were dozens of folks who'd responded to an online call to wear Revolutionary War period garb, so as to make their deeper allegiance clear. The e-mail notice said reams about their hotbox loss of perspective:

> Continental Soldiers Wanted for 9/12 March: Attention all Revolutionary War re-enactors: arise, ye Patriots, to the hallowed cause of liberty! If you have a Revolutionary-era uniform—be it militia, frontiersman, rifleman, musician or regular Continental Army—please bring it with you to the 9-12 march and be part of the Continental fife and drum procession that will be leading the march. What better way to send a message to those who would take away our liberty than to remind them WE have not forgotten those who sacrificed so much to give us our liberty.[11]

Beyond the odd enthusiasm for fife and drum reenactments, the broader point is one of fidelity to the Founding Fathers' America. These marchers see themselves as defending America's heritage against a usurper in the White House who wants to "take away our liberty." In their eyes, Obama doesn't understand the national heritage because he's not part of it—he's an internationalist who grew up in Indonesia with the middle name Hussein. He's not one of "us"—his administration is called a "Thugocracy" or a "Gangster Government." They point to the comment Michelle Obama made during the campaign—"For the first time in my adult life I am proud of my country"—as evidence the president doesn't take pride in our nation's history. He doesn't share our heritage. He's not a real American.

Think back to the rapturous response Sarah Palin got when she toured what she called "real America." She debuted the divisive sound bite at a speech in Greensboro, North Carolina: "We believe that the best of America is in these small towns that we get to visit, and in these wonderful little pockets of what I call the real America, being here with all of you hard working, very patriotic, very pro-America areas of this great nation."[12]

Of course, if "real America" is pro-American, then there is also a false America—by intentional implication, the increasingly diverse and urban areas where most Americans now live—that is anti-American. This is an applause line for people staring into the political abyss.

It's fair to assume that Palin's "real America" riffs were not meant to be about race directly, but they applied almost exclusively to white small-town America.

Candidate Obama validated the fears of the emerging white minority—and the perception of him as an overeducated elitist—when he unwisely and unkindly dismissed the "bitter" working-class Americans of western Pennsylvania: "They cling to guns or religion or antipathy to people who aren't like them or anti-immigrant sentiment or anti-trade sentiment as a way to explain their frustrations."[13]

But unlike previous African American presidential candidates, Obama rarely referred to his race on the campaign trail—he was determined not to run a protest candidacy like Jesse Jackson or Al Sharpton before him. He wasn't running to be the president of black America, he was running to be the president of the United States of America. But there were moments when the curtain came back on the role of race.

In Virginia, Bobbie May, the chairman of the Buchanan County McCain campaign, was forced to resign after he published an article in a local paper describing "the clarified platform of Barack Hussein Obama." It included the Second Amendment applying only to "gang-bangers" and "Islamo-fascist terrorists," "free drugs for Obama's inner city political base," "mandatory Black Liberation Theology courses taught in all churches," and hiring the rapper Ludacris to paint the White House black. The kicker predicted lines we've heard endlessly since: Obama wants to "change liberty and freedom to socialism and communism."[14]

Throughout the campaign there was the occasional racially overtoned vandalism of Obama field offices, and not infrequent outbursts from crowds. In eastern Ohio, news cameras caught flashes of unfiltered racial anxiety at a GOP rally, with one woman saying, "I'm afraid that if he wins the Blacks will take over. He's not a Christian, this is a Christian Nation, what is our country going to end up like?"[15] Another said, "I don't like the fact that he thinks us white people are trash, because we are not."

At a Palin rally in Johnstown, Pennsylvania, amateur camera crews caught crowds yelling out "Osama Obama," "the only difference between Obama and Osama is the BS," "Hussein Mohammed Obama" and "Al Qaeda for Obama"—the confluence of Muslim rumors and terrorist fears—while one heavyset guy sported a Curious George monkey doll with an Obama bumper sticker on its head and paraded it before the camera with a grin and a cackle, saying: "This is little Hussein. Little Hussein wanted to see truth and good Americans."[16]

There's an implicit dare in these defiantly politically incorrect protests—the bully's defense that resentfully says, "Can't you take a joke?"

Another incident was revealing in the response it provoked. Two weeks before the election, McCain volunteer Ashley Todd claimed that she had been attacked at an ATM near Pittsburgh by a six-foot-tall, two-hundred-pound black man who saw her McCain bumper sticker, stole $60, and carved a "B" in her face. She said he told her: "You are going to be a Barack supporter."

Todd quickly became a conservative cause célèbre—evidence of an incipient race war that would no doubt be great for ratings and possibly for election results. Fox News senior vice president for news editorial John Moody fired off a grave op-ed on the online *FoxForum,* titled, ironically, "Moment of Truth."

> It had to happen. Less than two weeks before we vote for a new president, a white woman says a black man attacked her, then scarred her face, and says there was a political motive for it . . . This incident could become a watershed event in the 11 days before the election. If Ms. Todd's allegations are proven accurate, some voters may revisit their support for Senator Obama, not because they are racists (with due respect to Rep. John Murtha), but because they suddenly feel they do not know enough about the Democratic nominee.[17]

Eighteen hours later, Todd admitted she'd fabricated her tale to get attention for herself and the McCain campaign. A cadre of conservative commentators quietly muttered a collective "never mind" but the impulse to climb the barricades of racial conflict was chilling.

On Election Day, the results of these appeals to "real America" came into clearer focus. In a country that is becoming more diverse and urban, McCain and Palin found their strongest support from older white traditionalist voters in towns with populations under 50,000.[18]

Dig a little deeper and a fuller picture emerges. Yes, Obama did better than past Democratic tickets in many areas—for example, winning Indiana and Virginia for the first time since 1964. But in the Deep South, he did far worse than past Democrats, losing the forty-nine counties of Alabama, Arkansas, Georgia, Mississippi, and Louisiana where whites make up 90 percent or more of the population.[19] This is an expression of white-minority politics, the feeling of being under siege.

In the year after the election, the racial gap only grew. An October 2009 *National Journal* poll found job approval for President Obama deeply divided between 43 percent for whites and 74 percent for nonwhites, with two-thirds of whites believing that living standards for "people like me" wouldn't grow as fast as they had for previous generations. "Whites are not only more anxious," wrote *National Journal*'s Ron Brownstein, "but also more alienated."[20]

The most striking gap is between whites and nonwhites when it comes to views of the federal government—whites don't trust it, nonwhites do. It's an old wound that's getting wider.

From the 1860s through the 1960s—from the Civil War to the civil rights era—the federal government was seen as the defender of minorities and an imposition on the white South. During Reconstruction, the federal Freedmen's Bureau was attacked as "an agency to keep the negro in idleness at the expense of the white man," echoing today's "big government" welfare-state critiques.[21] The move to disenfranchise African American voting rights through Jim Crow laws occurred under the cloak of states' rights and a white "counter-revolution" to reestablish local control with the rallying cry "the niggers shall not rule over us!"[22]

Almost a century later, when segregation was confronted by Supreme Court rulings, no less than the *National Review* editorialized, "The central question that emerges . . . is whether the White community in the South is entitled to take such measures as are necessary to prevail, politically and culturally, in areas in which it does not predominate numerically. The sobering answer is yes—the White community is so entitled because, for the time being it is the advanced race."[23]

White-minority politics likes to get dressed up as civic conscience in the face of unconstitutional federal interference: witness how the White Citizens Councils of the segregated South of the 1950s and 1960s were reborn in the 1980s and 1990s as the Councils of Conservative Citizens. But the same ugly base alloys keep bubbling up between the cracks. In one infamous photo, white protesters at Little Rock, Arkansas, in 1959 at the height of the school integration debates carry signs that say "Race-Mixing is Communism" and (perhaps even more telling) "Stop the Race Mixing—March of the Anti-Christ"—while flanked by American flags.

These fights have deep roots, even as they have taken on new urgency with the presence of an African American president. One big question remains: How did the Party of Lincoln get left behind on civil rights?

The Party of Lincoln in Name Only

It's a historic irony that the political party that long defended slavery and racial segregation became the first to nominate an

African American for president, whereas the Party of Lincoln, which fought for union and advanced civil rights from Reconstruction to Little Rock, has been left with a pathetic lack of diversity on its political bench.

This role reversal is reflected in the GOP's political philosophy as well. Lincoln's Republican Party was the centrist progressive party of its day, expanding individual freedom and embracing change to preserve the union. The modern Republican Party, however, finds philosophical structure in federalism and states' rights, conservative concepts that defined Southern Democrats of the John C. Calhoun variety. And perhaps not coincidentally, the party's strongest support now comes from the rebellious states of the former Confederacy.

The legacy of Lincoln and the Civil War has formed the basic fault lines of American politics for the past 150 years.

From 1860 to 1960, the current "red" and "blue" states were reversed, with the former slave-owning South voting solidly Democratic for one hundred years while Republicans generally dominated the North. For all the shifts in party labels since then, Southern conservatives have been consistent. They were conservatives because they believed the rights of individual states had primacy over the interfering federal government. Before the Civil War, they did not want their profitable industry restricted or regulated. They wanted to preserve what they saw as a biblically sanctioned way of life.

In 1860, the election of Illinois's Abraham Lincoln was enough to make South Carolina fire on Fort Sumter and secede—resisting the results of the election as an unconstitutional usurpation of power. The South did not want what it saw as Northern values imposed upon it.

During Reconstruction, African Americans were not only freed but elevated to elected office—including the Congress and governorships—as Republicans. The Knights of the Ku Klux Klan was formed by Confederate veterans such as Nathan Bedford Forrest to resist Reconstruction and to intimidate blacks. This was done in the name of defending the integrity of the white Southern family, but the larger political agenda was clear: "In effect, the Klan was a military force serving the interests of the Democratic party," wrote historian Eric Foner in his book, *Reconstruction*.[24] In time, the federal troops withdrew from the South. Segregation was imposed along with the renewed dominance of the Democratic Party. The few local Republicans left were brave liberal reformers, a minority party in every sense.

Outside the South—throughout the North, Midwest, and West—the smart money remained with the Republicans. From Ulysses S. Grant to William McKinley and Theodore Roosevelt, they were the party of federal power and patronage, the party of industrial expansion and the Gilded Age. All the while, the South stayed stubbornly Democratic. People who lose wars have long memories, and they were not about to vote for the Party of Lincoln.

The pendulum of political power eventually swung back to the Democrats, whose national political dominance reached its peak with FDR's four-term New Deal coalition of liberal reformers, big-city bosses, union leaders, farmers, and Southern conservatives—held together by the benefits of power and the glue of crises. This coalition began to crack with Harry Truman, who desegregated the armed forces by executive order after World War II as Southerners howled.

At the 1948 Democratic National Convention, when the young liberal mayor of Minneapolis, Hubert Humphrey, proposed that the party platform back anti-segregation civil rights legislation, South Carolina governor Strom Thurmond stormed off the convention floor, leading a delegation of social conservative pro-segregation Southern Dixiecrats. He mounted a third-party Dixiecrat campaign for the presidency that year, with the intention of proving the South's power by denying Democrats the White House. Strom won four states in the Deep South—South Carolina, Mississippi, Alabama, and Louisiana, but Truman stayed in the White House.[25]

But it was the expansion of federal power from the Supreme Court of Chief Justice Earl Warren—a Republican former governor of California, appointed to the bench by Eisenhower—that really alienated conservatives and put the Republican Party on the path to renouncing the legacy of Lincoln.

In 1954's *Brown v. Board of Education*, Warren cultivated a unanimous decision outlawing segregation. But some conservatives wanted to stand athwart its history and yell, "Stop!"

"We consider the Supreme Court's decision in the key segregation cases (*Brown v. Board of Education* and *Bolling v. Sharpe*) to be one of the most brazen acts of judicial usurpation in our history," editorialized the *National Review*, "patently counter to the intent of the Constitution, shoddy and illegal in analysis, and invalid in sociology."[26]

The fear of betrayal by the Court has persisted in the intensity with which conservatives fight to keep "liberals" off the bench today and renounce alleged RINO (Republican in Name Only) judges such as Sandra Day O'Connor.

The ground was shifting beneath the political map. It finally flipped one hundred years after the Civil War when Southern

Democratic president Lyndon Johnson proposed civil rights legislation.

Some conservative Republicans smelled electoral opportunity in the Democrats' shift. It came in the form of the missing piece of the post–Civil War political puzzle—the Western libertarian conservative. While North and South were fighting, the West was still being won by pioneers with lots of guns and little government.

Enter Barry Goldwater, born in the Arizona Territory in 1909. Goldwater's libertarian values were clear and consistent. He helped create the modern conservative movement with his absolute belief in individual freedom from government control. But there was one gnawing exception.

Goldwater opposed the Civil Rights Act of 1964. Like Republican icons Ronald Reagan and George H. W. Bush, who also opposed the act, Goldwater was no segregationist—he had desegregated his family's department store and the Arizona Air National Guard. But on advice from Phoenix lawyer and future Supreme Court chief justice William Rehnquist, Goldwater decided that the Civil Rights Act was an unconstitutional infringement upon states' rights.

"It may be just or wise or expedient for Negro children to attend the same school as white children," Goldwater reasoned, "but they do not have a civil right to do so which is protected by the federal Constitution or which is enforceable by the federal government."[27]

At the 1964 GOP convention, Goldwater famously declared, "Extremism in the defense of liberty is no vice. And moderation in the pursuit of justice is no virtue."

Jackie Robinson had been campaigning for Goldwater's primary Republican opponent, New York governor Nelson

Rockefeller—who was shouted down at the convention for proposing a platform condemning extremist groups such as the Ku Klux Klan. "A new breed of Republicans had taken over the GOP," wrote Robinson. "I had a better understanding of how it must have felt to be a Jew in Hitler's Germany."[28]

On Election Day, Goldwater won only six states—his native Arizona and the Deep South, including every state Strom Thurmond carried as a Dixiecrat in 1948. Mississippi cast 87 percent of its votes for Goldwater—the first time the state had voted Republican in its history. In turn, Vermont voted Democratic for the first time in its history.

And so the electoral map began the slide toward the red-blue alignment we know today. When he signed the Civil Rights Act over Southern conservative objections, Lyndon Johnson presciently remarked to his press secretary, Bill Moyers, "I think we delivered the South to the Republican Party for your lifetime and mine."[29]

Former Senate majority leader Trent Lott was among the many conservative Southern Democrats who switched parties in the ensuing decades. In 1984, the Mississippi congressman gave a revealing interview to *Southern Partisan* magazine in which he said, "I think a lot of the fundamental principles that [Confederate President] Jefferson Davis believed in are very important to people across the country, and they apply to the Republican Party."[30] The party labels had changed, but the Southern conservative power structure remained largely the same. In 2008, a young Republican operative from Mississippi apologetically admitted to me, "Let's face it—the base is racist."

The Party of Lincoln may have sold its soul, but the Faustian bargain contributed to four decades of political gain. Between 1968 and 2004, Republicans won seven of ten presidential elections. Before 1968, the opposite was true—Democrats won seven of ten.

But now the bill is coming due. Demographics are destiny, and America is becoming less white and rural—more diverse and urban. Republicans find themselves in danger of becoming a regional party, based in the socially conservative South. In 1999, Republican governors dotted the Northeast in New York, Massachusetts, and New Hampshire. Ten years later, those states were under Democratic control. In New York, there were thirteen Republican congressmen and -women at the time—in 2009, there were two. And after the 2008 election there was not a single GOP member of the House left in all of New England, the historic home of the Republican Party.

To contemporary ears, it almost sounds like an urban legend to hear that the first African American and the first woman freely elected to the Senate were both Republicans: Edward Brooke of Massachusetts and Margaret Chase Smith of Maine. Likewise the first Asian American senator, Hawaii's Hiram Fong, who was first elected in the Eisenhower era. And so too with the first Native American senator, Charles Curtis—who went on to be Herbert Hoover's vice president. The first Hispanic senator, Octaviano Larrazolo, also was a Republican. And here's a stat that puts the cost of the Southern strategy in sharp perspective: of the twenty-three African Americans who served in Congress before 1900, every single one was a Republican. They would not have dreamed of being anything but members of the Party of Lincoln.

"The Republican Party was the party that gave hope and inspiration to minorities—and there was a coalition at first," says Ed Brooke, now ninety-two and living with his wife, Anne, in Miami. "My father was a Republican. My mother was a

Republican. They wouldn't dare be a Democrat. The Democrats were a party opposed to civil rights. The South was all Democratic conservatives. And the African American community considered them the enemy."

But between the civil rights era and the 2008 election, there were only three African American Republicans elected to Congress—Senator Brooke and Representatives Gary Franks (CT) and J. C. Watts (OK)—whereas there have been ninety-three Democrats.

The Party of Lincoln has almost entirely lost the allegiance of the African American community to the point where the reasons for this historical alliance seem dusty and irrelevant. There have been historic appointments of African American Republicans to high office—such as Secretaries of State Colin Powell and Condoleezza Rice—but to date the electoral aspirations of African American Republicans have been basically DOA because the party is not seen as representing their community.

"They can't appeal to African Americans and at the same time oppose everything that's in the interest of African Americans," says Brooke. "When you talk about equality and justice, you can't just preach, you've got to act. That old statement of Abraham Lincoln's—that government should do for people only what they cannot do for themselves—depends on knowing that there are some people who cannot do for themselves. It's got to be a party with a head and a heart."

Young Republicans and Racist E-Mails

"Obama Bin Lauden [sic] is the new terrorist . . . Muslim is on there [sic] side . . . need to take this country back from all of these mad coons . . . and illegals."[31]

So typed a man named Eric S. Piker on a Facebook page operated by Audra Shay—a thirty-eight-year-old army veteran,
mother, and event planner from Louisiana—who was running
to be chairwoman of the Young Republicans.

Shay responded to Piker's post eight minutes later: "You tell
em Eric! lol."[32]

It didn't take long for other posters on Shay's page to do the
math. First, a regular poster, Derek Moss, wrote: "What's dis-
heartening is the use of the word 'coon' in 2009. Wow . . . I'm
usually outnumbered about 500-to-1 on Audra's threads so go
ahead, lemme have it, I deserve it." He clearly expected to be
criticized among this crowd for calling out the racist comment.

Cassie Wallender, a national committeewoman from the
Washington Young Republican Federation, then wrote: "Someone please help a naïve Seattle girl out, is Eric's comment a racial slur?" She answered her own question one minute later:
"Okay, why is this okay? I just looked it up. 'It comes from a
term baracoons (a cage) where they used to place Africans who
were waiting to be sent to America to be slaves.' THIS IS NOT
OKAY. And it's not funny."[33]

This was followed soon after by the African American chairman of the DC Young Republicans, Sean L. Conner, who wrote,
"I'm really saddened that you would support this type of racial
language . . . wow! Thanks Cassie for standing up. . . ."[34]

Word started spreading throughout the Young Republican
circuit, open to GOP members under forty. For hours, Audra
Shay stayed silent.

Finally, she took action. She "unfriended" Wallender and
Conner—in the world of Facebook, that means cutting off rela-
tions—after calling Wallender out. Piker, who made the original "coon" comment, remained her Facebook "friend."

Basically, Shay's immediate concern was damage control. She deleted the controversial exchanges from her page (but not before screenshots were taken) and tried to tamp down the fire internally.

Almost eight hours after Piker's comments, and Shay's ensuing "lol," Shay posted an official-sounding Facebook status update stating that neither she—nor her Young Republican political slate, ironically called Team Renewal—"condones the use of racial slurs on my wall . . . It is not right to nor appropriate to talk that way and will not be accepted!" But soon she was back in jaunty country-girl denial mode ("amazed at all the fuss so here is what you need to know. The 6th song on the new Billy Currington CD is the most awesome song!").

At 10:31 p.m., a friend named Dale Lawson raised the PC flag, writing, "the over reaction to it was a little amusing." Then Eric S. Piker came roaring back: "I agree with dale . . . this is still America . . . freedom of speech and thought is still allowed . . . for now any ways . . . and the last time i checked I was a good ole southern boy . . . and if yur ass is black don't let the sun set on it in a southern town. . . ."

The next morning, the black conservative site HipHop Republican.com posted a story on the exchange.

"There is a culture war going on inside the Republican Party," one of the site's founders, Lenny McAllister, told me. "At some point, we will see one of two things—either a decline that comes from our inability to move away from the image of an older, exclusive, white-males-only party or to a party that befits the Party of Lincoln, one of more diversity that reflects America today."

It probably doesn't help that Audra Shay grew up dancing in the shadow of a Confederate flag. She was a popular cheerleader for the Southside High School Rebels in Fort Smith, Arkansas, Class of 1990. It was a predominantly white school in those days, with the town's African American population attending rival Northside High School. The racial disconnect was symbolized by Southside's mascot, Johnny Reb, a Confederate soldier in the mold of Ole Miss's white-mustachioed mascot. Supporters would wave the Stars and Bars in the stands. Even then, the mascot came under fire for its politically incorrect imagery. "Save Johnny Reb" was a rallying cry for students who sought to save their mascot from what they saw as censorship.

"I'm ashamed to say it, but looking back, we didn't have many black students, and that kind of stopped many of us from appreciating what the big deal was," explained one former classmate. "In our white suburban neighborhood, cultural conservatism was more important than what political party you belonged to."

After graduating from Southside, Audra attended the University of Arkansas for one year and then joined the army, eventually serving in the Second Infantry Division in Korea. After finishing active duty at Fort Benning, she worked in internal affairs of the Muscogee County Police Department and had the first of two children.

She divorced, then married for a second time in 1999 and moved to Louisiana, where she opened a small events-planning business and got involved in local Young Republican politics, eventually serving as field director for pioneering Indian American Bobby Jindal's first, and unsuccessful, gubernatorial campaign. Audra was subsequently hired to be the state grassroots director for the free-market-advocacy organization Americans for Prosperity—which later was instrumental in funding the Tea Parties—and concentrated on climbing the ranks of the national Young Republicans. Her bio proudly states that "she helped to showcase the YRs at the Republican National Committee's Southern Republican Leadership Conference by manning a booth [and] rubbing elbows with Presidential hopefuls."[35]

The Young Republicans have always included a mix of young idealists, aspiring politicos, and ideological warriors, and occasionally that combination has veered from ambition into rank ugliness. During the mid-1960s, the crew-cut militants of the young conservative movement had their own scandals to contend with.

One pungent if forgotten incident involved a group of Young Republicans from the mid-Atlantic states known as the "Rat-Finks," who amused themselves with mimeographed racist songbooks at events like the Young Republicans' national conventions. Here is a sample lyric to one choice anti-Semitic number, which was to be sung to the tune of "Jingle Bells":

> Riding through the Reich, in a Mercedes Benz,
> Shooting all the kikes, making lots of friends.
> Rat tat tat tat tat, mow the bastards down,
> Oh what fun it is to have the Nazis back in town![36]

The Rat-Finks were eventually censured in a close vote of twenty-five to nineteen by the Young Republican Federation in 1967, but Audra and others have reason for comfort that scandals don't preclude a life in politics: one of the Rat-Finks' leaders went on to a successful career as a New Jersey state senator and judge.

In the past, racist incidents could be relegated to a distant stack in the library, but now the Internet provides indelible evidence of every racist aside. Racist jokes that may have passed

in pool halls and country clubs become permanent proof of cal-
lousness and cruelty online.

You'd think the right would have gotten the message when
e-mails provided the initial smoking gun in the notorious Jack
Abramoff scandals. The story gained traction in part because
of the difficult-to-defend sensationalism of e-mails in which
uber-lobbyist Abramoff described his multimillion-dollar Native
American casino clients as idiots, troglodytes, and monkeys—as
in, "I have to meet with the monkeys from the Choctaw tribal
council" and "We need to get some money from those monkeys."[37]

They haven't:

- Election Night 2008, South Carolina GOP operative Jeffrey
  Sewell tweeted: "The agony of defeat, we just elected Curious
  George president." And "Breaking: Obama replaces Secret
  Service with Black Panthers."[38]

- Florida Republican state committeewoman Carol Carter sends
  out the following e-mail a week after the inauguration under the subject line "Amazing!" "How can 2,000,000 blacks
  get into Washington, DC in 1 day in sub zero temps when
  200,000 couldn't get out of New Orleans in 85 degree temps
  with four days notice?"[39]

- Los Alamitos, California, Mayor Dean Grose forwarded an
  e-mail in April showing a watermelon patch lining the White
  House lawn under the title "No Easter egg hunt this year."
  He said that he was unaware of racial stereotypes about African Americans and watermelon. No word, in that case, why
  he thought the e-mail was funny enough to forward.[40]

- Former South Carolina state election director and Richland
  County GOP chairman Rusty DePass "joked" on his Facebook page in June that First Lady Michelle Obama was

descended from a gorilla that had gone missing from a local zoo: "I'm sure it's just one of Michelle's ancestors—probably harmless."[41] DePass initially reached for a defense from the Scopes Monkey Trial era, claiming that Michelle believed in evolution and was therefore descended from apes. He later apologized to the local NAACP.

- Three days later, Tennessee state legislative aide Sherri Go-forth e-mailed out an image labeled "Historical Keepsake"— showing august portraits of all the presidents of the United States, ending with a pair of googly-eyes peering out from a black background to symbolize President Obama.[42] When confronted, the aide to state senator Diane Black said only that she regretted sending the image to the wrong e-mail list and from her government address. She was "reprimanded" by her supervisors but not otherwise punished (a forced furlough at Memphis's National Civil Rights Museum would have been an inspired penalty).

- Florida neurosurgeon, GOP fund-raiser, and founder of Doctors for Patient Freedom David McKalip forwarded an image of President Obama as a New Guinea witch doctor with a bone through his nose to a Tea Party listserv group under the subject header "funny stuff." There was a Soviet-style hammer and sickle through the "c" in "Obama Care."[43]

- The million-dollar relaunch of GOP.com hit a snag in October 2009 when its Facebook fan page featured a rogue posting of a photo showing President Obama eating a chicken wing over the old-school racist slogan, "Miscegenation is a crime against American values: Repeal Loving v. Virginia"—the 1967 Supreme Court decision that outlawed bans on interracial marriage.[44]

- When President Obama's speech announcing 30,000 new troops for an Afghanistan surge preempted a December 2009 airing of a *Charlie Brown Christmas Special,* Arlington, Tennessee, mayor Russell Wiseman took his frustrations out via Facebook, writing about "our Muslim president." "Try to convince me that wasn't done on purpose. Ask the man if he believes that Jesus Christ is the Son of God and he will give you a 10 minute disertation [*sic*] about it . . . when the answer should simply be 'yes' . . . you obama people need to move to a muslim country . . . oh wait, that's America . . . pitiful . . . you know, our forefathers had it written in the original Constitution that ONLY property owners could vote, if that has [*sic*] stayed in there, things would be different."[45]

This is the environment that incubates an incident like the slur on Audra Shay's Facebook page. This time, the uproar grew louder and began to get widespread attention when I wrote about it on *The Daily Beast*. But Shay was not about to let a little racist e-mail scandal stop her Tracy Flick Meets *Strangers with Candy* quest for election as Young Republican chairwoman.

And so an online whisper campaign against Shay's opponent Rachel Hoff began. An anonymously built temporary website targeted Hoff's support for same-sex civil unions as the real scandal, expressed in li'l Lee Atwater tones:

As one of only a very few Young Republicans nationwide in favor of Civil Unions, Rachel Hoff attempted to convince the YRNF in 2007 to adopt a stance IN FAVOR OF CIVIL UNIONS. Although Rachel was not wearing a dress like her female counterparts, but her typical suite [*sic*], her attempt was met with ridicule and frustration. It was overwhelmingly shot down and left the idea in many delegates minds of: Why would Rachel Hoff support Civil Unions?

Got to love the all-caps for her support IN FAVOR OF CIVIL UNIONS, a brave stance entirely consistent with the party's stated belief in individual freedom (and well short of conservative icon Dick Cheney's belated support for gay marriage). Then there's the weird 1920s-era antifeminist dig at her for "not wearing a dress like her female counterparts." And the last sentence, with all the subtlety of a Tom DeLay sledgehammer. It's an exceptionally ugly piece of insinuation and propaganda, casting new light on Shay's campaign claim that "the only way to change something you don't like, is to get in and get your hands dirty."

As the two candidates wound their way to the Young Republican Convention in Indianapolis, it became apparent that this was not an isolated incident.

In October 2008, in the wake of news that an effigy of Sarah Palin was being hung outside an affluent Hollywood home as an offensive Halloween decoration, Shay posted: "What no 'Obama in a noose?' Come on now, its [sic] just freedome [sic] of speech, no one in Atlanta would take that wrong! Lol." She picked up the thread again the next morning with a clubfooted clarification. "Apparently I could not spell last night. I am wondering if the guys with the Palin noose would care if we had a bunch of homosexuals in a noose."

She posted a conspiracy-theory video that attempted to prove that Obama believes he can only "ensure his own salvation" and "fate" if he helps African Americans rise above whites, complete with Barnum-esque captions ("LISTEN AS HE ATTACKS WHITE PEOPLE").

After Obama's overly cautious take on the Honduran "coup" crisis infuriated Shay, she posted: "This is an outrage and I CAN NOT believe this nation has him as our leader! It makes me sick!" She posted a few minutes later: "My disdain for Obama is directly proportionate for his disdain of this country."

A Facebook friend of Shay's weighed in: "Here's what I am getting tired of: If you call Obama a socialist, terrorist, anti-American, whatever, then you're kinda calling me that, too, cause I voted for him and support him (for the most part). Or, you can claim that I didn't really know what I voted for, and in doing so you're kinda saying I'm ignorant and questioning my intelligence."

Three minutes later, Shay replied: "I think that you are ignorant if you believe this man is anything but anti american. He freely rights [sic] about Marxist philosophies. I never called him a terrorist, but if his policies are socialist (which they are) then what would you call him? His actions speak very loudly and his actions are very anti american. You just can not get past it. You might not like it but the truth is what it is."

With all this ugly information on the table, some thought and hoped that Shay's campaign might collapse under the weight of the Facebook scandal. "I saw something that was morally wrong, and as a conservative I took it upon myself as an individual to stand up, and I do not regret it at all," Cassie Wallender, national committeewoman for the Washington State Young Republicans, wrote in a letter to the committee. "I was attacked for wanting better for Young Republicans—in my lifetime of work for the Republican Party I have never been accused of being a 'RINO,' until now, by Audra's supporters."

But Kentucky delegate Katherine Miller reflected the myopia of movement politics when she told the *Indianapolis Star*, "This controversy really is not the decisive factor for the majority of people voting here . . . It really has been played up a little bigger than it really is."[46]

The eventual vote took eight hours, with parliamentary fights to hold a voice vote instead of a secret ballot (it turns out that some conservatives do like card check, if it benefits them). Fistfights nearly broke out between the two camps, and a Hoff supporter from the Oklahoma delegation, who was handing out fliers protesting Shay's Facebook comments, had to be physically removed. "I believe that people were intimidated," said North Carolina delegate John Ross. "Without a secret ballot, many people did not have the opportunity to vote their conscience." In the end, Audra Shay got her prize in a vote of 470 to 415.

"They just took a vote that may have set the party back thirty years," said HipHopRepublican.com's Lenny McAllister, speaking from the floor of the convention hall. "They just voted for a candidate who has a demonstrated tolerance for racial intolerance. She has joked about lynching and then claimed to be a victim. As a black man, I still don't see what's funny about that."

At least Team Renewal had a sense of humor about the oddly named Indianapolis bar where they told supporters to meet after the vote in an irony-free tweet: "Come join the NEW YRNF Administration at Rock Bottom!!"

6

PARTISAN MEDIA: POLARIZING FOR PROFIT

We are self-segregating ourselves into separate political realities. Both Fox News and MSNBC have profited from preaching to a narrow but intense audience—conservative Republicans at Fox and liberal Democrats at MSNBC. Loyal viewers see their favorite opinion-anchors as the only "truth tellers" in town and reject the rest of the media as cowardly or biased. The ideal of objectivity is in danger of being dismissed as a myth. We are devolving back to the era when newspapers were owned and operated by political parties.

Talk radio and Wingnut websites pump up the hate and hyperpartisanship all day, creating a feedback loop of talking points for true believers. They are polarizing for profit. It may be good for ratings, but it's bad for the country.

The result: partisan warfare is on the rise, and trust in media is on the decline. The Pew Research Center for the People and the Press has documented the trend and concluded that "virtually every news organization or program has seen its credibility marks decline" over the past decade.[1]

Even C-Span, which offers unedited coverage of public events without commentary, has experienced a steep—and absurd—decline in believability.[2] In this hyperpartisan environment, people literally don't trust what they see with their own eyes.

The cynicism began with credible accusations of longtime liberal bias inside such institutions as CBS News and the *New York Times*. This in turn ignited conservative talk radio and

Fox News as alternatives, the latter sold under the slogan "fair and balanced." The idea was sinisterly simple: only explicit bias could balance the implicit bias of the establishment press.

The problems accelerated with the institution of the "split scream" on twenty-four-hour cable news more than a decade ago—two amped-up partisans from opposing parties screaming talking points at each other, divided by the thin line on your TV screen. The networks pretended that all the heat generated amounted to light as well.

Things have gotten improbably worse with the innovation of this echo chamber—angry people from the same party inciting each other to extremes on television or online, demonizing a phantom opposition, and engaging in a partisan pile-on. Half the time it's an amen corner and half a hothouse of hate, a reminder of the wisdom behind the old adage that "in a place where everybody thinks alike, nobody thinks very much."

The echo chamber is a route to radicalization. As Cass Sunstein explains in his book *Going to Extremes,* "A good way to create an extremist group, or a cult of any kind, is to separate members from the rest of society. The separation can occur physically or psychologically, by creating a sense of suspicion about non-members. With such separation, the information and views of those outside the group can be discredited, and hence nothing will disturb the process of polarization as group members continue to talk."[3] This dynamic is now a daily occurrence.

It's been said that the secret of the demagogue is to make himself as stupid as his audience, so they believe that they are as clever as he is. Demagogues are heroes in the echo chamber. They're selling special knowledge, combining old fears with new technologies and reaching a wider audience than ever before. Their telltale signs are much the same as detailed by

Richard Hofstadter five decades ago: "The paranoid spokesman sees the fate of this conspiracy in apocalyptic terms . . . He is always manning the barricade of civilization. He constantly lives at the turning point: It is now or never in organizing resistance to conspiracy. Time is forever just running out."[4]

This apocalyptic urgency is familiar to listeners to talk radio and viewers of opinion-news today. But maybe Wingnut hosts are also nervous because they fear their time is running out. What's got them anxious isn't just politics, it's their pocketbook.

Because people have more choices about where to receive their news and opinion, broadcasters are left fighting for a smaller and smaller slice of the pie. "The key to success in modern media is narrow market segmentation," author and columnist David Frum explained to me. "It's much better to own *Ski Magazine* than it is to own *Life Magazine*. And it's better to own *Cross Country Ski Magazine* than *Ski Magazine*. The more precise your marketing the more it delivers eyeballs to advertisers. But in politics, you have to put people together, not slice them apart. So the imperative thing for a successful cable network is very different from a successful national political coalition."[5] This dynamic is driving pundits to the political extremes, providing a financial incentive to incite the Wingnuts.

It's a particular problem in talk radio. According to the radio ratings service Arbitron, nearly two-thirds of talk radio's listeners are over age fifty, and almost 90 percent are white: talk radio is preaching to a declining demographic.[6] It's not surprising that according to some industry experts, talk radio has lost 30 to 40 percent of its ad revenues over the past two years alone.[7] Its slice of revenue is shrinking.

Radio host Michael Medved explained it this way to journalist Tim Mak: "In this [economic] environment, you have something of a push to be outrageous, to be on the fringe, because what you're desperately competing for is P-1 listeners [those who tune in most frequently]. And the percentage of people on the fringe who are P-1s is quite high."[8]

As a result, broadcasters who used to present themselves as independent—for example, MSNBC's Ed Schultz—now dial the partisan anger up to eleven every night. These political per-formers become prisoners of their own shtick—they cannot evolve or they will be called traitors by the tribe they have cul-tivated. They can only move in one direction: further out into the extremes.

This dynamic also inspires the peddling of paranoia to pump up ratings. "What Glenn Beck does is spend three shows specu-lating about whether the Earth is flat," contends Mark Potok of the Southern Poverty Law Center, "and then on the fourth show announces with great fanfare that he, Glenn Beck, has discov-ered the Earth is round."[9]

Political entertainers pretend to sell ideology and integrity, but what they are literally selling is advertising—and the pur-suit of coin can also lead to some compromising positions.* For example, given the conservatives' criticism of Obama's over-spending and invocations of Weimar Republic–like inflation (leading, of course, to the rise of a new Hitler), companies selling gold have been buying up the advertising slots on their shows. Again, Glenn Beck's pitch is typical, blurring the paid adver-tisement with his personal opinion: "If you've been watching for any length of time, and you still haven't looked into buying gold, what's wrong with you? . . . When the system eventually

---

* In 2014, records revealed that Beck had been paid $6 million by the non-profit FreedomWorks to promote its message on air (Ken Vogel and Mackenzie Weigner, "The Tea Party Radio Network," *Politico*, April 17, 2014).

collapses, and the government comes with guns and confiscates, you know, everything in your home and all your possessions, and then you fight off the raving mad cannibalistic crowds that Ted Turner talked about, don't come crying to me. I told you: get gold."[10]

It's a heated appeal and apparently effective; fear is a powerful motivator. But conflicts of interest were alleged when one advertiser, Peter Epstein of Merit Financial Services, admitted to Politico's Kenneth P. Vogel that gold retailers expect favorable coverage from their commentators. "You pay anybody on any network and they say what you pay them to say," said Epstein. "They're bought and sold."[11]

Loyal audiences are perhaps less understanding of the arrangement. In a complaint filed by Mary Sisak of New Castle, Pennsylvania, she stated that she'd bought gold after she saw a television ad featuring Beck, and online endorsements from radio hosts Fred Thompson and Mark Levin. After spending $5,000, Mary said she learned she could have purchased the same coins for $1,600 less. "How could I be misled by Glenn Beck, Fred Thompson and Marvin [sic] Levin?" she asked. Once you've invested your trust in partisan "truth tellers," heartbreak is sure to follow.

The cycle is self-reinforcing, providing fodder to a larger partisan enterprise. It's a dynamic that David Frum calls the Talk-Fox Complex: "Fox News Broadcasting and the major talk radio shows are staffed by many of the same personalities—like Sean Hannity and Glenn Beck—and they really work together. Talk radio creates a buzz that the news side of Fox then reports on as if it were straight news."[12]

One favorite rhetorical bridge is the "some say" formulation, as in, "Some say Barack Obama may not be eligible to be president."

This is one of the mechanisms by which Wingnuts have been able to hijack our media and, by extension, our politics.

There is a recipe for mainstreaming hyperpartisanship: A rumor is posted on a blog site like *Free Republic* and becomes the subject of heated speculation. A site like *WorldNetDaily* publishes fearmongering as fact or opinion. Now it's got a thin veneer of respectability and a shot at becoming part of the talk-radio conversation, often in the form of "just askin'" speculation (as in, "Is Obama our first Muslim Marxist president?"). When a Beck or a Rush Limbaugh picks it up, it's hit the big time. It's heading to a protest poster and then a TV screen near you.

The seamless success of this model in creating issues and crafting narratives has made the out-of-power Republican Party effectively subservient to the conservative media crowd. The tail is wagging the dog; partisan media is driving the GOP's message and not the other way around. So Glenn Beck declares, "Our country might not survive Barack Obama," and a few months later, the Republican National Congressional Committee fires off a fund-raising letter saying, "America cannot survive on this new course."[13] The danger is that the narrow niche-building strategy of partisan news and views is the opposite of the coalition building that political parties use to win elections. Case in point: Glenn Beck.

Beckology

The most influential Wingnut leader in the first year of the Obama administration wasn't an elected official. He isn't even a Republican, but an independent conservative—a former Top Forty radio DJ, self-described "borderline schizophrenic,"[14] and recovering drug addict turned Mormon convert with a taste for confrontation and confession. He presents a manic mix of politics and religion, loftily billed as "the fusion of entertainment and enlightenment."[15]

In the course of a few years, Glenn Beck transformed himself from a talk-radio curiosity into a multimedia cottage industry, with a nationally syndicated radio show, 5:00 p.m. Fox News program, a magazine, and five books—both fiction and nonfiction—on the best-seller lists.[16] He's hosted massive rallies on the Washington Mall—and since leaving Fox News in 2011, Beck has turned his fans into an online annuity, charging them each month to access his own network, known as The Blaze.

Behind Beck's tearful Mad Hatter act, the man is crazy like a fox—a talented and intelligent radio artist, an entrepreneur of anxiety and redemption. His loyal customers constitute a standing army, and he has already proven they can be deployed at will to the tune of tens of thousands.

"We ♥ Glenn Beck" read a sign at the 9/12 Tea Party rally on the Washington Mall. Each letter was spelled out stadium-style on an individual placard with an American flag filling out the heart. The group holding the placards was clustered under a parchment-colored banner that read: "Rainy Day Patriots: We the People Fighting to Restore our Constitutional Republic." Other evidence of his influence dotted the crowd in the form of signs and hand-painted T-shirts: "Answer Glenn Beck's Questions," "God Bless Glenn Beck," and "Glenn Beck is my Hero."

This was something of a hometown crowd for Beck. He had first proposed the rally on air months before, telling his listeners they were "the only thing standing between slavery and freedom," and more than 50,000 citizens came from across the country.[17] No member of Congress could have inspired the same attendance.

Over Thanksgiving week 2009, Beck came up with a new cause to coincide with the launch of an upcoming book—*The Plan*—in August 2010. With his ambition hitting new heights, Beck announced the creation of a new political movement, part *Meet John Doe* and part Father Coughlin, complete with public-education seminars. "Today, I have stopped looking for a leader to show us the way out," Beck declared, "because I have come to realize that the only one who can truly save our country . . . is us."[18]

Echoes of Obama's "We are the change we have been waiting for" aside, self-empowerment is the theme that runs throughout Beckology. Like a classic evangelical preacher who connects with his audience by detailing his days of sin and depravity, Beck uses humor and self-deprecation to sell his own story of salvation through a return to personal responsibility. Beck comes armed with the dry drunk's distrust of the middle ground in life and politics, where everything is good versus evil, conservatives versus "the cancer of progressivism," George Washington versus Barack Obama. But in the duel of opposites, nothing compares to the struggle between Good Beck and Bad Beck.

The Good Beck genuinely cares about people and this country. It's one of the things that makes him so emotional on air.

The Bad Beck is such a talented broadcaster that he knows how to manipulate an audience's emotions. He uses fear, anger, and resentment to keep their attention day after day, buying his books, attending his rallies.

The two coexist uneasily under the justification that the Bad Beck promotes the Good Beck. He is advancing himself in order to advance a greater cause.

To understand Beck's political appeal, you need a window into his personal life, a story of small-town values remembered from broadcast studios in the skyscrapers of Manhattan and Dallas. He grew up in Mount Vernon, Washington, a hamlet perhaps best known as the tulip-bulb capital of America. His dad, William, ran a bakery called the Sweet Tooth and the family attended the Immaculate Conception Catholic Church. The town provided a vision of small-town "real America" that Beck would riff off for decades to come and that would provide the title for his first book.

But bucolic visions always obscure a more complicated reality. In addition to tulips, Mount Vernon was earning a reputation as the leading pot producer in the Pacific Northwest. Nor were things as they seemed on the surface in Beck's family. His mom, Mary, wrestled with addiction and depression, leading to a marital split and her death by drowning, which police called an accident but Beck believes was a suicide.[19]

Before she died, Mary gave Glenn a present that would illuminate his life's path: a record collection of classic radio broadcasts called *The Golden Age of Radio*. "I was mesmerized by the magic radio was," Beck remembered, "how it could create pictures in my head."[20] He became a student of the art form, idolizing pioneers like Orson Welles and practicing his radio voice into a tape recorder in his bedroom.

By the time he was a junior in high school, Beck was commuting to Seattle by bus every weekend to broadcast on a local FM rock station. He was also on the road to smoking pot every day for the next fifteen years (by his own estimation) and spinning records by the late-1970s white-bread rock troika of Cheap Trick, Supertramp, and Electric Light Orchestra.

Rock 'n' roll radio would be Glenn Beck's university. By 1983, at the age of nineteen, Beck was the youngest morning-radio show host in the nation, broadcasting from the coastal military

enclave of Corpus Christi, Texas. He was a one-man morning zoo, with on-air skits and imaginary guests like a clueless
Muppet-voiced foil Beck named "Clydie Clyde," which still surfaces in his act.

Beck's mentor and manager at the station was a former marine and surfing Mormon named Jim Sumpter. "I never had a
doubt that Glenn was headed for huge things," Sumpter told
me on the phone from his radio-show studio in Florida, "but I
didn't see any indication of an interest in politics. I never for a
moment dreamed that Glenn was, based on his lifestyle choices,
a political conservative. If you asked me if Glenn would have
ever been on the cover of *Time* magazine, I would have asked
you what you were smoking."

Beck was busy channeling the decade of excess, doing cocaine, driving a DeLorean, and cultivating a collection of thin
ties. He played the fool but did not suffer fools gladly. "When
we were in Texas, Glenn hated Texans, hated 'em," Sumpter
said. "Now he talks about how he just loves the people in Texas.
He used to make fun of them—their belt buckles, the chunky
jewelry, I mean the whole deal. And he just hated Mormons."

It wasn't just Mormons. Beck's self-described mantra at the
time was "I hate people." Despite occasionally sharing the mic
with a chimp named Zippy, despair was seeping in through
the cracks and Beck's mood swings were alienating colleagues;
one remembered him as "a sadist, the kind of guy who rips the
wings off flies." His competitive edge could certainly contain a
cruel streak. When he faced off against a former friend in the
Phoenix market, Beck called up the man's wife on air after she
had a miscarriage and mocked his friend-turned-rival, saying it
was evidence that he couldn't do anything right—he couldn't
even have a baby.[21]

Beck's own personal life was suffering. His first marriage was crumbling, and a daughter was born with cerebral palsy. Amid drug use and manic behavior, Beck wrestled with suicidal fantasies, writing later, "There was a bridge abutment in Louisville, Kentucky, that had my name on it . . . Every day I prayed for the strength to be able to drive my car at 70 mph into that bridge abutment. I'm only alive today because (a) I'm too cowardly to kill myself . . . and (b) I'm too stupid."[22]

By his late twenties, the onetime radio wunderkind had burned most professional bridges and found himself working at a radio station in New Haven, Connecticut—a comparative Siberia from previous postings. Divorced and with drug use and alcoholism spiraling out of control, Beck hit bottom. He went to his first Alcoholics Anonymous meeting in 1994 and began a skeptic's search for faith, starting with a self-taught Great Books seminar that included tomes from Hitler, Carl Sagan, and Pope John Paul II and culminating with his baptism into the Mormon Church.

Personal rebirth was followed by professional rebirth. Clean, sober, and remarried, Beck was tiring of the bubble-gum Top Forty morning-zoo format. Talk-radio icons like Rush Limbaugh and WABC's race-baiting Bob Grant were his on-air idols now. Beck began peppering his banter with political references and pushing executives for a talk show to call his own. In January 2000, the *Glenn Beck* show debuted in Tampa Bay, Florida. "I don't really consider myself a conservative. I know I don't consider myself a liberal," he said. "I have a brain and I like to use it sometimes."[23]

In 2006, CNN's *Headline News* brought him to cable television to host a political talk show from an independent perspective. But Beck chafed against the billing and enjoyed only middling ratings. He was liberated by an offer from Fox News and the election of Barack Obama.

The *Glenn Beck Program* debuted on Fox News the night before Obama's inauguration, and he came out swinging. Sarah Palin was among the first night's guests and within weeks Beck was pumping up "the Road to Communism" and offering "Comrade Updates," declaring "the destruction of the West is happening"[24] and that "the president is a Marxist . . . who is setting up a class system."[25]

Sometimes Beck pivoted his imagery to the right, saying, "The government is a heroin pusher using smiley-faced fascism to grow the nanny state,"[26] and claiming that "the federal government is slowly drifting into fascism." Other times he indulged both sides of the spectrum, as on April 2, when he asked, "Is this where we're headed?" and showed images of Hitler, Lenin, and Stalin.[27]

Beck's opposition to the health-care bill in the summer of 2009 hit all the bases. First there was fascism, as in the "[healthcare] system is going to come out the other side dictatorial—it's going to come out a fascist state."[28] Then there was health care as "good old socialism . . . raping the pocketbooks of the rich to give to the poor."[29] And finally, race: "The health care bill is reparations. It's the beginning of reparations."[30]

Beck's ratings soared, and his credibility was bolstered by on-air investigations into Obama personnel, for example, "Green Jobs czar" Van Jones, who had once described himself as a Communist and signed a 9/11 Truther petition calling for an investigation into whether President Bush had known in advance about the attacks of September 11. Beck hammered home the story while other news outlets resisted it. Jones ultimately resigned. Beck had both a scoop and a scalp.

Beck's newfound firebrand politics and effectiveness in driving the news cycle had some old friends scratching their heads. "I never got the impression that Glenn is as naturally curious as he appears to be, to be bringing the information forward that he is," said Jim Sumpter. "I don't know if Glenn's being fed or if Glenn's really the driving force. I have no idea. If he's the driving force, that's a Glenn Beck I never saw. If he's being fed, then the showmanship that goes into all of this is classic Beck. Now if Glenn is the showman and the driving force behind bringing the information to the forefront, then, then I think we're probably looking at near genius in terms of what he's doing . . . [but] I don't think this is Glenn. The catalyst in this thing is not Glenn. Glenn's the vehicle, not the catalyst."

Catalyst or not, Beck was hitting all the Wingnut themes with perfect pitch. When Iowa's supreme court legalized gay marriage, Beck declared, "I believe this case is actually about going into churches, and going in and attacking churches and saying, 'You can't teach anything else.'"[31] To nervous gun-rights advocates, he asserted that Obama "will slowly but surely take away your gun or take away your ability to shoot a gun, carry a gun."[32] He brought avowed secessionists on his show and gave them an interested hearing. Beck drew the widest denunciations when he called President Obama "a racist" with a "deep-seated hatred for white people."[33] An advertiser boycott began, but the zealotry of his advocates more than compensated as yet another Beck book went up the charts in 2009. First there was Glenn Beck's *Common Sense: The Case Against an Out-of-Control Government* and then *Arguing with Idiots: How to Stop Small Minds and Big Government,* featuring Beck leering on the cover in a Soviet-style commissar's uniform.

In the books, as on air, it's always a wrestling match between the Good Beck—humorous, self-effacing, and calling on a higher power for a sense of purpose—and the Bad Beck, peddling political apocalypse, the opinion equivalent of a horror film: "We are a country that is headed towards socialism, totalitarianism, beyond your wildest imagination"[34] and "There is a coup going on. There is a stealing of America . . . done through the guise of an election."[35]

Beck's message resonates beyond Main Street and the Tea Party protests. Down in the white supremacy cesspool of *Stormfront,* some contributors thought they recognized a fellow traveler. "Glen [*sic*] Beck can be useful," wrote SS_marching. "When Glen beck said 'Obama Has A Deep-Seated Hatred For White People' he is able to reach a much wider audience than we can. They will [be] predisposed to the idea and the next time Obama pushes an anti-white policy they will see it as such."[36] Frequent *Stormfront* poster Thor357 sees Beck as a recruiting tool: "I have talked to 6 people in two days because Glenn Beck woke them up, it's amazing how angry they are. They are pissing fire over Obama, this is a good thing. Now I educate them."[37]

America hit peak Beck in August 2010, when the man with a "100-year Plan for America" held what was essentially a revival meeting on the Washington Mall, offered up forty-seven years to the day on the same space where Martin Luther King Jr. gave his historic "I Have a Dream" speech—a coincidence Beck modestly chalked up to "divine providence." Instead of being flanked by civil rights leaders, Beck chose to surround himself with the likes of Sarah Palin and special guests such as Ted Nugent at the Rally to Restore Honor. Supporters were asked to keep their signs—and their firearms—at home.

The presence of Nugent—a 1970s hard-rocker known as the Motor City Madman—now inclined toward displays of paranoid hate undercut the protest's promise. In an interview just days before the rally, Nugent denounced Obama's "Islamic, Muslim, Marxist, communist and socialist agenda." And when asked if he believed the president is a Muslim, Ted Nugent replied, "You're damn right I do! He says he's a Christian so he can continue with his jihad of America-destroying policies." So much for Restoring Honor.

But Nugent's view is entirely consistent with the self-righteous conservative populism that Beck and Palin have pumped up and profited from, the old formula of the flag and the cross, predicated on a fundamental vision of division—"real Americans" versus subversive secular socialists; true patriots versus the president.

Then, in April 2011, Fox News abruptly announced that the nightly nervous breakdown would no longer be televised. Glenn Beck would be going off the air—a remarkable reversal of fortune for a man who just one year earlier was banking $32 million annually, teaching Americans how to fearmonger for fun and profit. But with his ratings down nearly 50 percent and advertisers abandoning the show, the apocalyptic shtick had been getting rancid fast. Beck was the boy who cried wolf, constantly ratcheting up the rhetoric to get attention, and ultimately becoming a parody of himself. Nonetheless, *The Glenn Beck Show* was the closest the John Birch Society has ever come to having its own national program, reaching millions and poisoning political debate in the process.

On Beck's last show on Fox News, he compared himself to Paul Revere and predicted the end of the world. His chalkboards prominently listed the Muslim Brotherhood, Bill Clinton, Michael Moore, Mahmoud Ahmadinejad, Bill Ayers, Frances Fox Piven, and Hugo Chávez, as Beck counseled the audience on the connections between them all just below the surface. Another board offered side-by-side comparisons of "Islamic Unrest" and "Unions, Socialists and Anarchists." After a twenty-minute monologue, he took his first commercial break. It was, inevitably, someone selling gold, followed by a pitch for survival seeds to those who want to "declare food independence."

The most successful of modern conspiracy entrepreneurs, Beck left Fox to concentrate on his own media empire, The Blaze—a subscription cable TV outfit and companion website. Feeling the winds shifting, he tried different poses to remain relevant from his Dallas bunker. When he announced that he was now a born-again libertarian—and promised that "we're not going to play in that crazy space as a network"—irony died. Maybe Glenn Beck has belatedly discovered that his own brand of bile is the problem in our political discourse—or maybe he's just realized that unhinged hate doesn't sell as well as it used to. Either way, his aspiration to be an independent, sane, and substantive voice doesn't even begin to pass the laugh test. Instead, it's just the latest reminder of what Eric Hoffer once said: "Every great cause begins as a movement, becomes a business, and eventually degenerates into a racket."

Olbermania

In the beginning there was Phil Donahue. The soft and snowy-haired advocate of liberal causes, a caring, not confrontational 1970s-style talk-show host—he wanted to feel your pain.

Then there was Keith Olbermann—he wanted you to feel his pain.

Liberals' new assertiveness accompanied the rise and fall of this unlikely on-air advocate, a sportscaster turned straight news anchor turned partisan pit bull.

Smart, funny, and acerbic, Olbermann also has a reputation for being prickly and paranoid. But his instinct to pick fights provided important utility: at a time when conservative-opinion anchors were ruling the cable news world, Keith Olbermann decided to return fire.

Here's a measure of his success. When Olbermann started his 8:00 p.m. show, *Countdown,* on MSNBC in 2003, there were no overtly liberal prime-time anchors in all of cable news. When he left the network eight years later, MSNBC was established as the liberal corollary to Fox, featuring a full lineup of liberals in the orbit of his 8:00 p.m. slot.

Aiming to echo the moral authority of Edward R. Murrow down to his lifting of the sign-off "Good Night and Good Luck," Olbermann trades in self-righteous indignation. His signature shtick is the special commentary, five minutes of Keith staring right into the camera delivering a diatribe that he has written himself. It's a radio sermon made for TV, delivered in a born broadcaster's baritone. His targets are anyone—or anything— to his political right.

It's tempting to describe his commentary style as full-contact, to reach for an available sports metaphor for combat, but it wouldn't be accurate—because Olbermann doesn't have guests on his show who disagree with him. It is an amen corner, an echo chamber presented as a truth-telling moment for America. Keith Olbermann isn't interested in any opinion but his own.

Like his alter ego Glenn Beck, Olbermann had his roots in radio, as a precocious if isolated teenager running a half-watt station at his high school in Westchester, New York, and then graduating to the Cornell University radio station. His love of radio is evident in his pauses and diction, delivering a point with dramatic effect. He doesn't talk so much as deliver.

However, it wasn't politics but sports that drove him, and after bouncing around local sportscaster gigs in regional markets, he landed at ESPN in 1992, selected to co-host *SportsCenter* at 11:00 p.m. with Dan Patrick. Their repartee redefined the model: with amped-up humor and sly asides ("If you're scoring at home, or even if you're alone . . . "), they mocked the formalities of the format and made the show an event, a return to the frat house for exhausted adults. Most of all, they made the news fun to watch, a lesson that would last.

But Olbermann did not last at ESPN. In 1997, at the height of his public popularity as a sportscaster, he left. One colleague recalled, "He didn't burn bridges, he napalmed them."[38]

Olbermann's reputation as a malcontent would dog him as he hosted shows on Fox and MSNBC. Sometimes contracts were not renewed, sometimes he was fired. After an ESPN exposé portrayed Keith as a sour, insular man who made co-host Suzy Kolber cry after shows, Olbermann felt compelled to write a public mea culpa in *Salon*. More than a face-saving PR stunt, the 2002 essay was a reflective walk through Olbermann's psyche, full of competing insecurities and perfectionism: "I have lived much of my life assuming much of the responsibility around me and developing a dread of being blamed for things going wrong," he wrote. "If anything would have cut through my neuroses, it would've been a colleague's tears. If I had known, I think I could've jumped over the fence I'd built around myself and said what the inner guy always knew: No TV show is worth crying over. Suzy: I'm sorry."[39]

In 2003, Olbermann got a rare second chance to host a prime-time show on a network he'd left on strained terms, MSNBC. *Countdown* was a late March replacement for Phil Donahue's brief return to television, a ratings failure that was seen as the end of experimenting with liberal views in prime time. "MSNBC takes sharp right turn" was one typical reading of the tea leaves. Ironically, the night of Olbermann's debut, he announced, "Our charge for the immediate future is to stay out of the way of the news . . . News is news. We will not be screwing around with it."

He played it straight down the middle and enjoyed middling ratings. He cultivated a feud with Fox News's Bill O'Reilly, naming him one of "the worst persons in the world" more than fifty times in four years.[40] He reenacted news stories with puppets (another thing he shares with Glenn Beck). Humor was his calling card as a news broadcaster. His personal political beliefs were unknown even to people close to him, and Olbermann has said he doesn't vote.[41]

But that profile changed dramatically in August 2006. Then–general manager Dan Abrams had written a memo encouraging hosts to offer opinions on air. Waiting for a flight at Los Angeles Airport, Olbermann happened upon a speech given by Bush secretary of defense Donald Rumsfeld in which he compared opponents of the administration's war and counterterror strategy to Nazi appeasers, saying that America was fighting "a new type of fascism." Fired up and fueled by a few Screwdrivers, Olbermann wrote his first special comment.

"The man who sees absolutes where all other men see nuances and shades of meaning is either a prophet or a quack," he began.

"Donald H. Rumsfeld is not a prophet." Olbermann accused the secretary of impugning "the morality or intelligence—indeed, the loyalty—of the majority of Americans who oppose the transient occupants of the highest offices in the land . . . This is a Democracy. Still. Sometimes just barely. And as such, all voices count—not just his."[42]

It was a forceful but odd addition to prime time, a counterspeech with an inner history-nerd erupting from within: Churchill, Neville Chamberlain, Hitler, Nixon, Joe McCarthy, General Curtis LeMay, and Ed Murrow all mentioned within five minutes. The audiences loved it. The special commentaries continued, and ratings spiked along with the rhetoric.

Olbermann offered thirteen more special commentaries in 2006, dialing up the outrage, casting himself as the liberal avenger against the Bush administration. "Bush: Pathological Liar or Idiot-in-Chief?" he asked. He accused Bush of "panoramic and murderous deceit," having an "addled brain," and "laying waste to Iraq to achieve your political objectives," and he told the president to "Shut the hell up!"—all in one broadcast. He argued that "the leading terrorist group in this country right now is the Republican Party,"[43] called on Bush to resign, hinted at impeachable offenses, and—in an apocalyptic riff worthy of Glenn Beck—said his policies could bring about "the beginning of the end of America."[44] All this led *New York Magazine* to pay him the ultimate bittersweet compliment, calling Olbermann "the Limbaugh of Lefties."

When Secretary of State Condoleezza Rice compared Saddam Hussein to Hitler, Olbermann's wrath was again predictably vast. "Invoking the German dictator who subjugated Europe; who tried to exterminate the Jews; who sought to overtake the world is not just in the poorest of taste, but in its hyperbole, it insults not merely the victims of the Third Reich, but those in this country who fought it and defeated it."[45]

True. But Olbermann himself couldn't help but wade into the hyperbole and equivalency game at times, calling Bush a "fascist" and acting "dictatorial." One of his favorite routines was offering a Nazi "Sieg Heil" salute while holding a picture of Bill O'Reilly across his face, prompting the Anti-Defamation League to write a strained letter of complaint. "Your repeated use of the Nazi salute has resulted in many complaints from our constituents, including Holocaust survivors and their families . . . In light of these concerns, we hope that you will reconsider your use of the Nazi salute in the future."[46]

The subject of rival Fox News drove Olbermann even deeper into a frenzy of moral equivalency. "Al-Qaeda really hurt us but not as much as Rupert Murdoch has hurt us, particularly in the case of Fox News. Fox News is worse than al-Qaeda—worse for our society. It's as dangerous an organization as the Ku Klux Klan ever was. Fox News will say anything about anybody and accepts no criticism. Half the people there ought to be in an insane asylum."[47] Pot, meet kettle.

With Bush out of office, some wondered how Olbermann would fare without nightly opposition. They shouldn't have worried. After Obama backed an extension of the Bush administration policy on warrantless wiretapping, Olbermann declared: "Welcome to change you cannot believe in."[48] As a series of pragmatic compromises on health care began to enrage the party's left wing, the Olbermann of the Bush years came boiling back to the surface. With the public option effectively out of the picture, Olbermann started making demands of the president. "It is, above all else, immoral and a betrayal of the people who elected you, Sir. You must now announce that you will veto any bill lacking an option or buy-in, but containing a mandate."[49] He named centrist Democratic senator Ben Nelson "the worst person in the world" for comparing him to Limbaugh and Beck, while suggesting that Independent-Democrat senator Joe Lieberman drive off a bridge in suicidal penance for his centrist voting record.[50]

But his truly primo venom was reserved for Republicans. During a live broadcast covering the special election to fill Ted Kennedy's Senate seat, Olbermann unloaded on the Republican nominee who was on his way to a surprise victory: "In Scott Brown we have an irresponsible, homophobic, racist, reactionary, ex-nude model, teabagging supporter of violence against women and against politicians with whom he disagrees."[51]

He went after conservative commentator Michelle Malkin by saying that without her "totally mindless, morally bankrupt, knee-jerk, fascistic hatred," she "would just be a big mashed up bag of meat with lipstick on it."[52]

The vitriol recalls something a wise man once said: "The man who sees absolutes where all other men see nuances and shades of meaning is either a prophet or a quack."

Olbermann's moral outrage had not yet faded, even as his ratings did at the start of 2011. He was open about dealing with his father's death and began an admirably quixotic practice of reading James Thurber stories to his audience on Friday nights. Then in late January, he abruptly announced he was leaving the network. Months of behind-the-scenes conflicts with executives—including a brief suspension for donating to Democrats without disclosure—spurred the midcontract divorce. He soon reemerged at Al Gore's Current TV, but personality conflicts prematurely ended his tenure there as well. As of 2014, Olbermann was back on the air, but out of politics, instead calling the balls and strikes of ball games at ESPN.

Wingnuts on the Web: *WND*

Harry Truman used to say that "the only thing new in the world is the history you don't know." Harry Truman never met the Internet.

The Internet is a force multiplier for Wingnuts, empowering them to reach far broader audiences faster than ever before. It is the best breeding ground for every imaginable conspiracy theory. It provides a national megaphone for what in earlier years might have been just a whisper campaign. It enables like-minded individuals to ignore their isolation and come together as an opinion army.

While the right was dominating talk radio, the left rallied its partisans through the Internet. Within a few years, groups like MoveOn.org and blogs like *Daily Kos* went from being outside agitators to inside players. Their fund-raising powers and ability to fire up activists were too impressive for the Democratic establishment not to forgive and forget their outbursts of radicalism: MoveOn's infamous "General Petraeus or General Betray Us?"[53] ad and the comments of *Daily Kos* founder Markos Moulitsas after the killing of four military contractors in Iraq. ("I feel nothing over the death of mercenaries . . . They are there to wage war for profit. Screw them.")[54]

The GOP was slower to adapt from the AM dial. There were popular and influential conservative news aggregators like the *Drudge Report* that filtered the news through a subjective lens, but there was initially very little in terms of effective online activist organizing. During the 2008 campaign, I'd been told by a conservative strategist that "our voters don't use the Internet"—while he was surfing the Web. The McCain-Palin campaign seemed to take that advice to heart (no doubt under the influence of the direct-mail mandarins who'd made their fortunes while building the conservative movement). Republicans even sent out a fund-raising letter designed to look like an emergency telegram—the instant message of the horse-and-buggy era—two years after the last real telegram was sent by Western Union. They looked like the Party of the Telegraph.

The technology gap could be seen in the GOP's 2008 online outreach. Obama had 3.1 million Facebook supporters, compared to 600,000 for McCain. Obama had 113 million YouTube views, compared to 25 million for McCain. And when it came to Meetup.com—a site famously used by Howard Dean supporters in 2004—McCain got outhustled not only by Obama but also by Libertarian candidate Bob Barr. McCain ran a twentieth-century Get Out the Vote campaign in which phone calls and mailings to supporters were the key metric. The McCain campaign spent $18 million in postage and shipping costs, and $3 million on the Internet, according to opensecrets.org. By comparison, Obama spent $15 million in postage and shipping costs and $14 million on the Internet.

But after the election, grassroots conservatives woke up to social media and the Internet. They were energized by being in the opposition—supplementing their talk-radio diet with Twitter, the social networking service that pushes text messages of 140 characters or less. Ironically, McCain—whose campaign hadn't collected cell phone numbers for text messaging during the campaign—created his own Twitter account three days after the election, and ten months later had 1 million followers.[55] By mid-2009, there were twice as many conservative congressmen on Twitter as Democrats, and Sarah Palin was using her Facebook page as her primary means of communicating with supporters. The Tea Parties and town hall protests were organized online, and with an assist from Fox News's pre-game promotion, they started to feel like populist uprisings.

This conservative netroots revolution is an evolutionary leap—a higher degree of specialization—beyond the niche partisan network approach innovated by Roger Ailes at Fox News. Now what conservatives dismiss as "mainstream media"—because it does not reflect movement politics—can be completely bypassed. You can have news tailored to fit your beliefs and chat with like-minded activists. The logical conclusion is already upon us: conservatives trying to create their own online encyclopedia, an alternative to Wikipedia known as Conservapedia.[56] It's the actual expression of what Stephen Colbert only joked about when he denounced reference books as "elitist—constantly telling us what is or isn't true or what did or didn't happen."[57]

In the isolation of the echo chamber, the influence of fringe news sites is increased, and the tallest midget in that corner of the Wingnut world is *WorldNetDaily*. It was the brainchild of Joseph Farah, a mustachioed longtime newspaperman from Paterson, New Jersey, turned outer-limits conservative activist. Farah was a generation older than most Internet entrepreneurs, but as editor of the *Sacramento Union* in California, he'd gotten to know the Silicon Valley crowd and saw the news potential of the evolving medium. Farah convinced his friend Rush Limbaugh to pen front-page columns for the *Sacramento Union*. But it was too late for the *Union;* circulation continued to decline and the paper soon shut its doors. Subsequently, Farah embarked on a career as a Clinton critic from the perch of the Western Journalism Center, funded by Richard Mellon Scaife (and including the then-conservative Arianna Huffington on its board of advisers).

At the time, right-wing opposition to Bill Clinton was still essentially an analog event, pumped out over radio, magazines, direct mail, and videotapes that purported to offer evidence of rape, murder, and drug deals perpetrated by the forty-second president. While repeatedly "investigating" a conspiracy theory that longtime Clinton aide Vince Foster had not committed suicide but had been murdered with the White House's knowledge—a theory determined to be false by three official reports—Farah began aggregating anti-Clinton articles on a site called eTruth.com. He upped the ante in 1997 with the launch of *WorldNetDaily* with his wife and quickly claimed to have 10,000 visitors a day.

Twelve years and two presidents later, *WorldNetDaily* established itself as a clearinghouse of right-Wingnut information and paraphernalia with twenty-five employees. Visitors spiked in the wake of Obama's election.[58] Farah claims an impressive 6 to 8 million unique visitors a month, and millions in annual sales from its superstore, peddling books like *Muslim Mafia* and $80 jars of earth from Jerusalem's Temple Mount, while offering special departments for Tea Party paraphernalia. There are gimmicks to trade on voter anger, like a "pink slip" you can send to every member of Congress for the discounted price of $29.95, and a lawn sign that says, "America was founded by Right-Wing Extremists."

The gear may be profitable, but it's the stories that keep people coming. With its blurring of news and opinion, *WorldNetDaily* draws a devoted audience, claiming credit for breaking the Obama–Bill Ayers connection,[59] Hamas's alleged endorsement of Obama,[60] and investigations into Obama's Chicago church.[61] Some of its stories are picked up by other conservative outlets quietly and not a little shamefacedly because of

the sub-tabloid reputation of the outfit. ("Glenn Beck was reading *WorldNetDaily* copy without attribution, and that's how he
ended up claiming the scalp of Van Jones," Farah told me.)

But aspirations to credibility are diminished with stories
about H1N1 microchip implants[62] and Federal Emergency Man-
agement Agency (FEMA) concentration camps,[63] leading to
nicknames like WorldNutDaily. And for all the biblical beliefs
professed on the site (such as Creationist-inspired stories that
try to debunk ideas that fossil fuels came from fossils) and strict
stands against pornography, there is preoccupation with proving Democratic opponents are secretly gay.

The site repeatedly published a thoroughly discredited drift-
er's claim that "he took cocaine in 1999 with the then Illinois
legislator [Obama] and participated in homosexual acts" with
him[64] and regurgitated bilge about Hillary Clinton's "well-
known bisexuality and her lesbian affair with her beautiful
assistant."[65]

All in all, it offers a relentlessly grim prognosis for America
short of the Second Coming (predicted for 2015),[66] full of plans
for Obama to bring back "inquisitions"[67] and "destroy capitalism."[68] No wonder its primary advertiser appears to be a mar-
keter of "survival seeds" for your very own "crisis garden" and
a "crisis cooker" to "prepare hot meals when the power is off."[69]
They are profiting off the paranoia they intentionally inflame in
their readers.

But the real growth industry for *WorldNetDaily* in 2009
was the enthusiastic advocacy of Birther claims that Obama
was not born in the United States and is therefore ineligible
to be president. Farah rented twenty roadside billboards that
read, "Where's the Birth Certificate?" at a cost of $300,000
and collected online donations to help fund the effort. A

WND-produced DVD, *A Question of Eligibility,* documents the claims of Birther proponents, including Alan Keyes and Orly Taitz, but darkly states that credits for the movie are being withheld by the filmmakers because "they fear reprisals from their government."

Farah sees himself as an old-school newspaper editor rather than a partisan advocate. He claims to take a disinterested view of the op-eds on his home page. "You ought to see some of the wacky stuff that they write. Doesn't mean I agree with it," he told me. "I don't even look at the columns before they get published in *WorldNetDaily*. We have a commentary editor who does that . . . I don't even read most of the commentary in *WorldNetDaily* after it's published 'cause I'm not a commentary kind of a guy, to be honest with you."

His own commentaries, however, are a different matter, and they do not pretend to be the work of a journalist aiming for objectivity. Instead, the political and the religious are often entwined with a relentlessly hostile view of Democrats in general and President Obama in particular. On Inauguration Day, for example, Farah offered readers a specially written prayer for the president's failure: "I do not hesitate today in calling on godly Americans to pray that Barack Hussein Obama fail in his efforts to change our country from one anchored on self-governance and constitutional republicanism to one based on the raw and unlimited power of the central state. It would be folly to pray for his success in such an evil campaign. I want Obama to fail because his agenda is 100 percent at odds with God's. Pretending it is not simply makes a mockery of God's straightforward Commandments."[70]

At the end of Obama's first year, did Farah agree with the calls to impeach Obama that are advertised on his site?

Oh, hell yeah, I think there are grounds for impeaching Obama. I think there were grounds for impeaching Bush. I think there were grounds for impeaching Clinton . . . There's nothing in the Constitution that would even remotely justify a national take-over of health care. [Before the election] I predicted that Americans would wake up from this slumber that they've been [in] for so long and start marching in the streets again to reclaim their liberties and that's exactly what I see happening today. Obama could end up being, [in the] long term, a blessing in disguise.

I ask whether he worries that *WND*'s stories could provoke an ugly response from an unstable reader. His response:

I think the media establishment should ask themselves that question. When they see hundreds of thousands of Americans rallying in Washington and call it tens of thousands and ignore grassroots protest movements around the country, they are doing a disservice to a vibrant debate in a free republic. They are promoting other methods for grievances to be addressed. There are only a few other possibilities—peaceful civil disobedience is one, and violent force is another. I believe reporting events accurately is the best protection of a vibrant debate in a free republic. Covering up events and silencing voices is much more irresponsible and dangerous.

Farah doesn't deny that *WND*'s stories add to the heat on the Wingnut street but says, "I don't think anger is necessarily an all bad thing. We should be angry at Hitler. We should be angry at Charles Manson." But what about when people start comparing President Obama to Hitler? I ask. "Well, if the analogy fits, it would be irresponsible not to make it," he replies. "Obviously, you can't compare him to Hitler's genocidal Holocaust policies, right? He hasn't done anything remotely resembling that. But I think it's fair to point out that Hitler nationalized health care and that Stalin did that and Hugo Chávez did that and Fidel Castro did that."

For *WorldNetDaily* and others on the Wingnut Web, extremism in defense of liberty is no vice.

Escaping the Echo Chamber

The pioneering television journalist Edward R. Murrow once said, "To be persuasive, we must be believable; to be believable we must be credible; to be credible we must be truthful."[71]

Truth doesn't come tailor-made for any one ideology or political party. But hyperpartisanship has become an industry unto itself, and it is thriving at a time when the old news industry seems to be fading. The fragmentation and self-segregation we are experiencing with television, radio, and the Internet exacerbate our political differences while they decrease the confidence we had in the honesty and integrity of journalism altogether.

Today, with newspapers fighting for survival, faith in the accuracy and fairness of the press is at twenty-five-year lows.[72] You can't blame people for being cynical. The clearest path to profit seems to come from abandoning the ideal of objectivity and nakedly playing to the base. But even at a time when pundits sound like paid shills for political parties, it was shocking to learn that black conservative columnist Armstrong Williams had accepted $250,000 in taxpayer money from the Bush administration to promote its No Child Left Behind education policy in print and on air.[73]

Ironically, Williams had previously complained about the partisan straitjacket he felt imposed upon him by the split-scream formatting of cable news, telling Tina Brown on CNBC's *Topic A:* "One of the things that I struggle with when I go on television, like, let's say, a *Crossfire,* [or] Wolf Blitzer, I'm expected to take a certain side. I'm expected to defend the president [Bush]. Now there are some areas I don't want to defend the president in because I don't necessarily believe that, but you're put in that position. And I think sometimes you're in a predicament that the public is not really getting what you think is their best interests served. So I think sometimes we get caught up in these labels and these stereotypes . . . [and] we do the public a disservice."[74]

The spin cycle is baked into the booking of guests where predictable partisanship is encouraged. Conflict sells and balanced analysis is considered bad for ratings—it takes too long to get to the truth.

Politicians have an interest in encouraging an increasingly partisan media. By drumming home the message of media bias, they try to diminish the credibility of their critics while developing contacts more likely to present their side of the story. This self-serving mission requires loss of perspective. Texas Republican congressman Lamar Smith, for instance, told students in the summer of 2009 what he believed to be "the greatest threat to America." It was not necessarily a recession, he said, or even another terrorist attack. "The greatest threat to America is a liberal media bias."[75]

Washington is the only city in the nation where the most important thing about you is what political party you belong to. Partisan media reinforces the rampant "team-ism." If you walk into a congressman's office and see Fox News on the TV and a

Washington Times on the table, you'll immediately know what party he or she belongs to, just as you would if MSNBC was blaring or the *Washington Post* was the paper of choice. It's no surprise that Republicans and Democrats are so divided. They are consuming different versions of the truth, interpreting the same events in fundamentally different ways.

Likewise, the echo chamber isolates and intensifies grassroots politics, breeding groupthink in tiny platoons that can have disproportionate influence on political debates. When it extends to a national level, it can create a Tower of Babel, condemning us to mutual incomprehensibility. It's easier to demonize people who disagree with you if you don't know them. In the constant partisan spin cycle, everyone has lost sight of the fact that only 15 percent of Americans call themselves conservative Republicans and only 11 percent describe themselves as liberal Democrats.[76] Slicing and dicing that demographic is going to produce diminishing returns, while leaving the other 74 percent of Americans in the center available and unaccounted for.

There are already signs of a demand for something different. "Nationwide, I think we are seeing a trend of some weakness in the hard right and the hard left on both sides," explains Jack Swanson, the program director at San Francisco's KGO-AM. "I do believe we're at a tipping point in talk radio, though . . . It's not just a Left or a Right or a Republican or Democrat thing. It's a million points of light out there on the Internet in terms of the discussion of ideas and ideals. And one size doesn't fit all anymore."

"There are a lot of program directors whose radio 'spider-sense' is tingling," concurred Randall Bloomquist, a longtime radio executive and president of Talk Frontier Media. "They're thinking this conservative thing is kind of running its course. We're saying the same things from morning 'til night and yes, we've got a very loyal core audience—but if we ever want to grow, if we want to expand, we've got to be doing more than 18 hours a day of 'Obama is a socialist.'"

One reflection of this trend came in the form of a *Time* magazine online poll that found *The Daily Show*'s Jon Stewart was the most trusted man in news.[77] When self-professed "fake news" surpasses real news in terms of credibility, it can be counted as a protest vote against the status quo. Media manipulation by professional partisans on both sides has become so predictable and pervasive that satire has emerged as the last best way to cut through the spin cycle. Viewers' intelligence is respected even as they are entertained, and between laughs the civic backbone begins to straighten a bit because someone is calling bullshit. If humor can help rebalance politics by pointing out the absurdities of what passes for debate, it is definitely preferable to the split scream or the echo chamber.

In a high-water mark of this demand for something different—and in direct response to Glenn Beck's Rally to Restore Honor—Jon Stewart announced a "Rally to Restore Sanity" on the Washington Mall the weekend before the 2010 election.

"We live in troubled times, with real people who have real problems," Stewart said at the announcement on *The Daily Show*. "Problems that have real but imperfect solutions, that I believe 70 to 80 percent of our population could agree to try, and ultimately live with. Unfortunately, the conversation and the process is controlled by the other 15 to 20 percent. You may know them as the people who believe that Obama is a secret Muslim planning a socialist takeover of America . . . or that

George Bush let 9/11 happen to help pad Dick Cheney's Halli-
burton stock portfolio. You've seen their signs: 'Obama Is Hitler'; 'Bush Is Hitler' . . . But why don't we hear from the 70 to 80
percenters? Well, most likely because you have shit to do."

Stewart then suggested a few signs for the rally: "I disagree
with you, but I'm pretty sure you're not Hitler" and "9/11 was
an outside job."

On October 30, the crowds came—more than 200,000 strong
—in far larger numbers than had attended partisan rallies on
the mall in past years. And though for his own rally, Beck had
asked his supporters not to bring signs (presumably for fear of
the media distraction they might create), and signs at the Ed
Shultz–emceed liberal "One Nation Working Together" rally
were mostly prefab jobs printed up by unions and activist
groups, the signs at the Restore Sanity rally were clearly homemade. Inspired by hosts Jon Stewart and Stephen Colbert, the
sign makers at the Rally to Restore Sanity used satire to comment on the Wingnuttery that surrounds us. Among the signs I
saw on the mall that day:

- Restrain the Craziness
- Civil War was an Inside Job
- Texans for Staying in the Union
- Obama: At Least He Isn't James Buchanan
- Hitler was Hitler
- Want Less Government? Move to Somalia (not that there's
  anything wrong with that . . .)
- Real Patriots Can Handle a Difference of Opinion
- Real Americans Don't Use the Term "Real Americans"
- I read the Constitution for the Articles
- Moderate to the Extreme

The content from the stage was essentially a comedy show mixed with musical guests, and the message was communicated mostly in "show, don't tell" sketches. In one, Yusuf Islam, the artist formerly known as Cat Stevens, came out to play the hippie anthem "Peace Train," interrupted by Ozzy Osbourne playing "Crazy Train," culminating with the O'Jays performing "Love Train"—a train we can all get onboard.

But the crowd was making a fairly consistent, if irreverent, political statement—from the couple who drove up from Florida with a sign that quoted from a 1970s pop song: "Clowns to the left of me, Jokers to the right, here I am—stuck in the middle with you," to a sign that read, "What do we want? Moderation! When do we want it? In a reasonable time frame!"

College students from Massachusetts made their point for the media: "Can we get some airtime, please?—The Moderates."

"I think there's too much polarization going on—and of course the squeaky wheel gets the grease," said Reba Winstead of Virginia, who was holding a sign that read, "One of the Moderate Majority." "And so the extremists on both ends are the ones screaming the loudest and so the rest of us are in the middle thinking that we're not being heard."

Another woman held a sign that quoted Edward R. Murrow: "We will not be driven by fear into an age of unreason."

Some partisan journalists tried to spin the rally as just a liberal event, but they missed the point by reinforcing the idea that has helped get us into this mess: that if you're not with us, you're against us; that if you're not a card-carrying conservative, you're liberal.

In comparing rallies, size matters—and the Restore Sanity rally was much larger than the grim partisan marches that preceded it. This is fitting, because there are more Americans in

the center than those who are on the right or left. And there are
certainly more Americans who prefer the leavening effects of
laughter to ideological fearmongering.

But for all the humor and affirmation, the Restore Sanity rally
ultimately had a serious if commonsense point—namely, that
we have to work together to solve problems, but our polarized
politics and the partisan media are stopping our ability to reason together as Americans. As Stewart said in his instant classic
of a closing speech: "Why would you work with Marxists actively subverting our Constitution or racists and homophobes
who see no one's humanity but their own? We hear every damn
day about how fragile our country is—on the brink of catastro-
phe—torn by polarizing hate, and how it's a shame that we
can't work together to get things done. But the truth is we do.
We work together to get things done every damn day. The only
place we don't is here [in Washington] or on cable TV."

So this celebration of sanity and humor came with a challenge to hyperpartisans in politics and media—stop playing
to the lowest common denominator. The American people are
smart, and as Stewart said, "Most Americans don't live their
lives solely as Democrats or Republicans or conservatives or
liberals."

The Rally to Restore Sanity's size and enthusiasm was evidence of a growing demand for something different—an alternative to predictable talking points and the partisan spin cycle,
a desire for humor and honesty, independence and integrity—
both an opportunity and an obligation.

7

SARAH PALIN
AND THE LIMBAUGH BRIGADES

The morning after the 2008 election, David Kelly hung the American flag upside down outside his Colorado Springs home.

"I felt our nation was in distress, going in the wrong direction," he explained. "I was exercising my God-given, unalienable right as a citizen of this great nation to express myself. That flag in distress was telling me and my whole neighborhood that our nation is in distress and we must stand tall and turn the tide."

A week later, Kelly filed papers to form the Draft Sarah 2012 Committee.

"Sarah Palin represents the silent majority of this nation, which I think scares the left and the liberal media," the self-described Scots-Irish American told me. "She's everybody's mom or sister or the girl next door. They can imagine themselves running into her at the supermarket and having casual conversation . . . She just invokes and embodies what conservative America's all about: God and Country."

Rarely has anyone gone from obscurity to obsession in America's psyche faster than Sarah Palin.

Her supporters feel a personal connection to the woman they see as a salt-of-the-earth supermom, a straight-talking, pro-life, pro-gun icon—the face of conservative populism. Her detractors call her the Queen of the Wingnuts.

Geraldine Ferraro, she ain't. She proved able to parlay a historic but losing vice presidential bid into the kind of devotion that led supporters to sleep in parking lots to meet her, buy a million copies of her memoir in less than a month, and at least briefly push her into the top ranks of the consideration set for the 2012 GOP presidential nomination.

Not bad for someone who was a small-town Alaska mayor at the start of the decade and spent just thirty-two months governing America's forty-ninth most populous state before abruptly quitting. But there's a slight wrinkle in this conservative Cinderella story: even at the height of her popularity, 63 percent of Americans said they would "never" consider voting for her for president.[1]

This stark enthusiasm gap reflects the deep disconnect between conservative populist true believers and the rest of the country. It is reinforced by the Wingnut media and their followers, who overflow small venues, turning them into amen corners. In this environment, there are no enemies on the right and no such thing as too extreme—the more outrageous a statement, the more it will be applauded. Narrow but intense support may be good for ratings. It may even be enough to take over a political party. But if such a political posture is defiantly uninterested in reaching out, can it lead to national victory?

When John McCain announced her as the surprise pick for vice president in late August 2008, Sarah Palin's profile was very different. Instead of the most polarizing figure in American politics, she was the most popular governor in America, boasting an approval rating that had been as high as 93 percent in a state where independents outnumber Republicans or Democrats. She had earned a reputation as a courageous reformer, taking on the corrupt Alaska Republican political machine. Her most pronounced policy expertise was in the broadly popular area of energy independence, and she sounded themes designed to appeal to independent voters: "This is a moment when principles and political independence matter a lot more than just the party line." She checked all the basic boxes when it came to the social conservative litmus tests, but they did not seem to define her. And no one was going to confuse her with Dick Cheney.

Questions about Palin's political ability evaporated after her nomination speech in Minneapolis—an instant classic written by Matthew Scully, a former Bush speechwriter and book-length defender of vegetarianism (an odd pairing with the newly famous moose hunter)—was rapturously received by the conservative crowd. Here was a formidable talent, able to smile while sliding in a rhetorical knife, the newest symbol of small-town values squaring off against the liberal elite—Spiro Agnew in a dress.

But the combination of one of the least nationally known picks in history, paired with the oldest nominee in history, had reporters—and opposition researchers—furiously doing their due diligence on the woman who could have been one chicken bone away from the presidency. The Republican spin room seemed prepared.

"The media doesn't understand getting up at 3:00 a.m. to hunt a moose; they don't understand eating a mooseburger,"[2] attested Florida representative Adam Putnam in an awkward attempt to preempt liberal media bias.

It wasn't the mooseburgers that would cause trouble.

Problems began when some of her more socially conservative policy positions were unearthed—like opposition to abortion even in the cases of rape and incest (a detail that had not been known by the McCain campaign senior policy staff). Then it came to light that her seventeen-year-old daughter, Bristol, was pregnant, unmarried, and keeping the baby.

This news had the unexpected effect of helping Sarah Palin hit the pro-life trifecta, with a special-needs baby (the governor had given birth to a son with Down syndrome four months before), a perfect pro-life record, and an unmarried pregnant daughter carrying her child to term while in high school. If a Democratic nominee had a pregnant teenage daughter, reflexive family values attacks might have been deafening—after all, this was the party that two decades before had Vice President Dan Quayle attack Candice Bergen's television character Murphy Brown for having a fictional child out of wedlock because it set a bad example for the nation.

But now the same social conservative voices who weeks before had been tut-tutting over the teenage pregnancy of tween idol Jamie Lynn Spears found a bracing honesty and integrity in Bristol's situation, evidence of a real American family that folks could relate to. (It should be remembered that the media feeding frenzy was stopped by none other than Barack Obama, who simply stated to reporters one disarming fact: "My mother had me when she was eighteen.")

Palin quickly became a lightning rod for the left. The netroots took their ideological opposition and added tabloid attacks that aimed at her family. Feminist icons like Gloria Steinem attacked her for representing the wrong kind of change. It was reminiscent of the anger directed at Clarence Thomas after the first President Bush tapped him to succeed Thurgood Marshall on the Supreme Court. Not just his qualifications for the office, but the legitimacy of his voice for African Americans was at issue. Palin was the same kind of apostate—in this case, a traitor to her gender.

All of which made her more beloved to conservatives. As long as all the social conservative and fiscal conservative litmus tests are met, they will not hesitate to rush to the defense of a fellow traveler who is under attack from the liberal media. It is both a sport and a pastime. And with Palin, they were defending a lady's honor, which is always worth an extra dose of moral outrage.

But the woman nicknamed "Sarah Barracuda" by her high school basketball team was no shrinking violet. She reveled in the traditional VP nominee attack-dog role, delivering most of the memorable sound bites from the GOP team:

- "Our opponent is someone who sees America as being so imperfect that he's palling around with terrorists who would target their own country . . . This is not a man who sees America as you see America and as I see America."[3]
- "We believe that the best of America is in these small towns that we get to visit, and in these wonderful little pockets of what I call the real America, being here with all of you hard working very patriotic, very pro-America areas of this great nation."[4]
- "Barack Obama calls it 'spreading the wealth,' Joe Biden calls higher taxes patriotic, but Joe the Plumber and Ed the Dairy Man, I believe that they think that it sounds more like socialism . . . Friends, now is no time to experiment with socialism."[5]

She sounded more like a right-wing talk-radio host than someone on a presidential ticket, but that was the key to their resonance. Just as with a talk-radio host hammering home a point, there was no such thing as too extreme: the more outrageous, the more memorable and therefore the more effective. Their accuracy or broader impact was unimportant, an elitist concern. These sound bites not only owned their own news cycle, they ended up metastasizing into the body politic.

The more populist conservatives loved her, the more liberals loathed her. Tina Fey's impersonation of her on *Saturday Night Live* often simply used Palin's own words as a script. When she epically botched her interviews with Katie Couric, her combination of innate confidence with a disinterest in policy details caused critics to hear echoes of George W. Bush. Her fans saw Ronald Reagan.

But some Reagan-era alumni of the conservative movement were starting to have their doubts. David Brooks pronounced her "a fatal cancer to the Republican Party. . . . Reagan had an immense faith in the power of ideas. But there has been a counter, more populist tradition, which is not only to scorn liberal ideas but to scorn ideas entirely. And I'm afraid that Sarah Palin has those prejudices."[6] Kathleen Parker called on her to resign from the VP slot to "save McCain, her party, and the country she loves."[7] They weren't the only ones: McCain staffers were starting to spew out their regrets in the press, accusing her of "playing for her own future" as a party leader and potential presidential candidate. Palin saw herself "as the beginning and end of all wisdom," vented another.[8]

No matter. Out in "real America," Palin was the star on the circuit, drawing crowds that sometimes outnumbered the top of the ticket. She was relatable and relevant, a symbol of comforting change compelling almost spooky devotion. At a rally in Ohio, one teenage supporter offered a contrast between Obama and Palin: "He seems like a sheep, or a wolf in sheep's clothing to be honest with you. And I believe Palin, she is filled with the Holy Spirit and I believe she will bring honesty and integrity to the White House."[9]

Sarah Palin wasn't just polarizing the electorate, she was polarizing the Republican Party, driving a wedge between populists and centrists. Some hard-core conservatives who had long disliked McCain's unpredictable independence—his co-authoring of legislation with Democrats such as his friend and supporter Joe Lieberman—went to the polls because of Palin. "John McCain was not our guy," explained David Kelly. "McCain is Republican in Name Only—too much of the moderate views of leaning towards the middle . . . When I voted I had to hold my nose because had McCain not picked Sarah Palin I would not have voted for the Republican Party candidate personally."

For all her success at energizing the base, there was evidence Palin was losing more votes than she was attracting. By the end of October 2008, 59 percent of American voters believed that Sarah Palin was not ready for the job,[10] and 47 percent of centrists said they were less likely to vote for McCain because of Palin's presence on the ticket.[11] And oddly, though the campaign expected Palin to attract women to the GOP, polls showed that she was less popular with women than men.[12]

Nonetheless, after the election, the Palin star was undimmed among the true believers. She didn't attend the Conservative Political Action Conference (CPAC) in February 2009, but she was well represented. Buttons and bumper stickers saying, "Don't blame me, I voted for Sarah" were pinned and plastered on unlikely surfaces; her face poked out of pamphlets and posters. Competing Draft Palin organizations were in attendance, including Team Sarah, whose website had rolled right over from supporting her in the 2008 campaign to priming for 2012. A look into the comments on that website revealed a combination of adulation ("Most people [like the media] who try to make others believe that Sara is dumb and stupid or inexperienced actually fear her because of her faith and goodness") and Obama

Derangement Syndrome. One post caught my eye because of the fury it directed at someone conjured up as the anti-Palin, First Lady Michelle Obama: "I have never actually HATED anyone in politics before now. . . . She is stupid, mean, power hungry, manipulative, corrupt, essentially ignorant—a poster girl for Institutionalized Black Racism and Agression [sic], a take-no-prisoners warrior for Political Correctnes [sic] aka Socialist Realism and a racially driven Communist fellow traveller. Let her go run an African country. She doesn't fit in here with the American People."[13]

Through the spring of 2009's Tea Parties, Palin was in Alaska, but her absence made the heart grow fonder. For all the attempts of presidential hopefuls like Mike Huckabee and Newt Gingrich to ride that wave, Palin was the most popular by far, rivaling even Reagan for references on signs and T-shirts. She was becoming the conservative answer to Obama—a symbol of hope and change for conservatives.

After abruptly resigning from office to "not retreat but reload," Palin communicated to her masses via Facebook and Twitter ("I don't have to go through the mainstream media . . . spinning my words"), firing off policy dispatches and personal updates while writing her multi-million-dollar memoir.

Without any organized effort or op-eds, her post alleging Obama's "death panels" single-handedly moved the summer's health-care debate and drove the tone of the town halls. It was a compact Wingnut classic, combining self-referential patriotism with apocalyptic big government imagery and a threatened baby, to boot. "The America I know and love is not one in which my parents or my baby with Down syndrome will have to stand in front of Obama's 'death panel' so his bureaucrats can decide, based on a subjective judgment of their 'level of productivity in society,' whether they are worthy of health care. Such a system is downright evil."[14]

Here again the talk-radio model was proving its effectiveness—if you throw a bomb, people notice. And when criticism came, it could be dismissed as just the liberal media knocking her again. Defenders would come rallying to her side. There would be no apologies, and Sarah's army loved it that way.

Palin's support was deep but not broad. With approval ratings north of 80 percent among Republicans, her disapproval ratings were just as high among Democrats. And 58 percent of independents believed she did not understand "complex issues." Given Palin's increasingly public professions of her Christian faith on the political stage—and the news that she believed her nomination for vice president was "God's Plan"—it's perhaps not surprising that her strongest support was coming from white evangelical Protestants, regular churchgoers, and the self-described "very conservative."

But Palin was also hugely popular with the talk-radio crowd, especially fans of Rush Limbaugh. Forty-eight percent of Limbaugh's listeners said that Palin best represented Republican core values out of all likely party leaders in 2012, with 45 percent saying they would vote for her in their state's presidential primary.[15]

As it turns out, the Birthers were also big fans—66 percent of those who believe that Barack Obama may not have been born in the United States chose Sarah Palin as their favorite out of the likely 2012 presidential pack.[16] And when Palin was subsequently asked about Obama's birth certificate on the *Rusty Humphries* radio show, she offered just enough encouragement to keep those home fires burning. "I think the public, rightfully, is still making it an issue. I don't have a problem with

that. I don't know if I would have to bother to make it an issue, because I think enough members of the electorate still want
answers."[17]

Sarah Palin fans were so eager for 2012 that they offered up
vice-presidential candidates on signs at rallies and on websites,
reflecting their vision of a Wingnut dream team. A Palin-Beck
ticket has been imagined, an outside-the-beltway celebrity duo
selling a return to common sense. After Joe Wilson shouted
"You lie!" at Obama during a Joint Session of Congress, Palin-
Wilson 2012 signs popped up days later at the 9/12 rally.

I asked Adam Brickley, the blogger who successfully started
the push to get the McCain campaign to nominate Palin in 2008,
what he made of this rush to pair Palin with some of the more
angry and uncivil voices in the GOP. "Those people who are
hard-core enough to carry a 'You Lie!' sign tend to like bluntness
and straight talk and that's what they get from Sarah Palin."

Bluntness and straight talk—no apologies. That's a mantra fitting a Fox News contributor or a radio talk-show host. And the
big daddy of them all, Rush Limbaugh, had nothing but good
things to say about Sarah Palin: "This woman has far more patriotism and love of country and decency in her than Barack
Obama could hope to have. This woman would be so much better leading this country than what we have now because we are
being led into destruction . . . We are being led by a man who's
got a chip on his shoulder for some reason about this country
and doesn't like it. She loves it."[18]

The Limbaugh Brigades

Rush Limbaugh is the founder of the modern Wingnut feast.
The political entertainer and professional polarizer was slapped

on the cover of *Time* magazine as the voice of conservative populism in the wake of the 1994 Republican Revolution, and he's been going strong ever since. A generation of conservatives had grown up listening to him trash liberals, the Clintons, and "elite, country club Rockefeller Republicans." Social issues, with the exception of abortion, are rarely discussed—he is, after all, a man of appetites. Loyal fans are called "dittoheads," a label that both mocks and encourages their tendency to fall in line with El Rushbo. The son of Cape Girardeau, Missouri, is now the $400-million man, with the most lucrative contract recorded in any medium, reaching 20 million people a week.[19]

But there's a secret beneath those numbers that reflects the Republican Party's broader problem—nearly half of Rush's listeners are over sixty-five.[20] Analysis of industry data shows that in market after market, Rush's ranking has declined decisively over the past five years among advertisers' coveted 25–54 age group. For example, in Charlotte, North Carolina, Rush fell from sixth to twelfth between 2005 and 2010. In Portland, Oregon, he fell from fourth to eighth. Among listeners sixty-five and older, however, Rush remains number one. Limbaugh can sell bedpans and resentment forever, but the demographic trend is not his friend. And though he has favorable ratings from 60 percent of Republicans, only 25 percent of independents and 6 percent of Democrats agree.[21] Unlike Republicans, Rush can afford not to care.

After the 2008 election, Rush dubbed himself "the last man standing." In the lead-up to inauguration, a magazine asked Rush to write four hundred words on his hopes for the Obama administration. "I don't need four hundred words," he told his audience. "I need four: 'I hope he fails.'"[22]

His opposition to Obama was alternately philosophic—seminars about the virtues of conservatism versus the evils of liberalism—and just plain weird. "We are being told that we have to hope he succeeds, that we have to bend over, grab the ankles, bend over forward, backward, whichever, because his father was black, because this is the first black president."[23]

As long as Rush was in the news, it was good for ratings. And the Obama administration initially liked it that way. In a "don't throw me in that brier patch" moment, Chief of Staff Rahm Emanuel said that Limbaugh was "the voice and the intellectual force and energy behind the Republican Party."[24] It was a contrast that worked to their advantage.

When newly elected RNC chair Michael Steele was asked whether Rush was the de facto head of the GOP, he said, "Rush Limbaugh is an entertainer" and described his style as "incendiary" and "ugly." Steele told the truth, but the blowback among the base was so great that he was compelled to engage in an extended grovel of an apology. "I have enormous respect for Rush Limbaugh," Steele told *Politico*. "I went back at that tape and I realized words that I said weren't what I was thinking . . . I wasn't trying to slam him or anything."[25] When he tried to phone in an apology, Rush did not immediately take the call.

Here's the thing: Rush Limbaugh has political power without responsibilities. He does not need to worry about governing or winning elections, only keeping his audience engaged and enraged. He uses conflict, tension, and resentment to increase his ratings. And his influence has inspired a new generation of Wingnut politicians who are choosing to follow the narrow but intense popularity of his model.

These are the Limbaugh Brigades.

In the past, they might have been blocked from office for being too extreme. But the rigged system of redistricting has helped push political power to the margins. The creation of safe seats has resulted in a 96 percent reelection rate,[26] effectively ending competitive general elections. That makes the only real contest a partisan primary—and if only 10 percent of the electorate turns out, 5.1 percent makes a majority. It's a paradise for activists, empowering ideological warriors who do not have to worry about winning voters in the center of the political spectrum. Instead, they can focus on playing to the base.

Their extreme politics makes them popular in their party but deeply polarizing figures to the electorate-at-large—just like Limbaugh.

The more angry and unhinged their claims, the more they are celebrated as courageous by activists in the base—just like Limbaugh.

Michele Bachmann

Minnesota congresswoman Michele Bachmann is a prime example. Elected to Congress in 2006, after she told supporters God called on her to run, Michele first made a national name for herself by declaring that Obama "may have anti-American views"—and calling for an investigation of other Democrats with "anti-American" views in October 2008.[27] The media fallout casting Bachmann as a neo-McCarthy made her, if anything, more beloved by conservatives.

She continued with a string of howlers and incitements in the first year of the Obama administration. On cap-and-trade pollution programs, she urged Minnesotans to be "armed and dangerous on this issue of the energy tax because we need to fight back."[28] She opposed funding for AmeriCorps, saying she foresaw "a very strong chance that we will see that young people will be put into mandatory service" with "re-education camps"[29] (her son later voluntarily enlisted). On health care, she urged an audience: "What we have to do today is make a covenant, to slit our wrists, be blood brothers on this thing. This will not pass . . . Right now, we are looking at reaching down the throat and ripping the guts out of freedom."[30] She's called for an "orderly revolution," saying that "where tyranny is enforced upon the people, as Barack Obama is doing, the people suffer and mourn."[31] She's declared that the Founding Fathers "worked tirelessly to end slavery," that HPV vaccines cause mental retardation, and has blamed hurricanes on God punishing the United States for fiscal irresponsibility. The media covers her because she makes great copy, and conservative populists love her because they think she's talking truth to power. She parlayed her unapologetically unhinged play-to-the-base notoriety into a powerful national fund-raising network before briefly running for president in 2012. Her spectacular flameout and subsequent ethics scandals culminated in her decision not to run for reelection in 2014.

Louie Gohmert

Texas congressman Louie Gohmert was an early adopter of the "Kill Granny" arguments against health-care reform, proclaiming "this socialist health care . . . is going to absolutely kill senior citizens. They'll put them on lists and force them to die early."[32] He took to the House floor to argue against the hate crimes bill, saying if gays and lesbians were covered by the bill, then "if you're oriented toward animals, bestiality, then that's not something that could be held against you . . . which means that you'd have to strike any laws against bestiality. If you're oriented toward corpses, toward children. You know, there are all kinds of perversions, some would say it sounds like fun, but most of us would say were perversions . . . and there have been

laws against them and this bill says that whatever you're oriented toward sexually that cannot be a source of bias against
someone."[33] He is also one of the eleven co-sponsors of the
Birther bill. First elected to his safe seat in 2004, he has been re-
elected on autopilot ever since, despite a steady string of howlers, including telling the Values Voter Summit that John McCain
"supported Al Qaeda."

Steve King

Iowa congressman Steve King earned a rebuke from John Mc-
Cain in 2008 when he said that if Obama "is elected president,
then the radical Islamists, the al-Qaida, the radical Islamists and
their supporters, will be dancing in the streets in greater numbers than they did on September 11 because they will declare
victory in this War on Terror."[34] He raised eyebrows as the only
member of Congress not to vote for a resolution acknowledg-
ing the use of slave labor in the construction of the US Capitol Building. In response to the "day without an immigrant"
protests, King wrote in an op-ed for his local paper, "The lives
of 12 U.S. citizens would be saved who otherwise die a violent
death at the hands of murderous illegal aliens each day . . . Eight
American children would not suffer the horror as a victim of a
sex crime."[35] And when commenting on Representative Joe Wilson, King argued that "the President threw the first punch" and
then called Wilson "an officer and a gentleman and a patriot."
"God bless him," King said. "He said what we were thinking."[36]

King managed to alienate not just immigrants but GOP leadership when he lashed out at the children of undocumented
immigrants, known as the "Dreamers." "For everyone who's
a valedictorian, there's another 100 out there who weigh 130
pounds—and they've got calves the size of cantaloupes because

they're hauling 75 pounds of marijuana across the desert," King told *Newsmax*. In response, Speaker of the House John Boehner offered this clarification to a group of congresspeople about King: "What an asshole," the Speaker said.

Paul Broun

Georgia congressman Paul Broun proudly takes credit for being the first member of the House of Representatives to compare President Obama to Hitler and call him a Marxist—just days after the 2008 election. What's more significant is that the congressman refused to apologize, seeing political benefit in the unhinged outburst. In fact, Broun went on to brag about the attack in fund-raising letters, writing, "I was the first Member of Congress to call him a socialist who embraces Marxist-Leninist policies like government control of health care and redistribution of wealth."[37] A veteran and doctor whose father served in the Georgia statehouse, Broun is perhaps best known for a 2012 speech in which the member of the House Science Committee declared evolution and the big bang theory "lies straight from the pit of hell," because "the Earth is but about 9,000 years old." The hunter and taxidermy enthusiast is also a vocal gun-rights advocate, telling MSNBC that "our Founding Fathers knew an armed citizenry was the best means of protecting this country from having our government totally destroy our freedom and liberty." He also opposes immigration reform, telling the Tea Party Express, "If John Boehner were to press on with comprehensive immigration reform, it will be disastrous for Republicans . . . and it would be disastrous for anybody who is freedom-loving."[38] Broun also has a fondness for "domestic enemy" language in domestic politics, as when he declared in 2009, "I was sworn into the Marine Corps, I was sworn to

uphold the Constitution against every enemy, foreign and domestic. We've got a lot of domestic enemies of the Constitution
and one of those sits in the speaker's chair of the United States
Congress, Nancy Pelosi."[39] In 2014, Broun ran for the US Senate
from Georgia and was trounced in the primary.

Alan Grayson

It is not only happening on the right. In 2009, freshman Florida
Democratic representative Alan Grayson went on a search for
hyperpartisan accolades as he tried to label himself "the congressman with guts." In a speech on the House floor, he said,
"The Republican health care plan is this: 'Don't get sick, and
if you do get sick, die quickly.'" Days later, he attacked Republicans as "foot-dragging, knuckle-dragging Neanderthals who
think they can dictate policy to America by being stubborn."
That was mild compared to what came next: calling Republicans
"the enemy of America" and "certainly the enemy of peace."[40]
He rounded out the diatribes by calling an aide to Federal Reserve chair Ben Bernanke a "K-Street whore" on 9/11 Truther
Alex Jones's radio show. Here's what was most impressive:
Grayson made all these comments in the space of one month.[41]
Even more impressive was the tough-talking congressman's sen-
sitivity to criticism. When a Florida resident from a neighboring district created a website titled mycongressmanisnuts.com,
Grayson wrote a letter to US attorney general Eric Holder accusing the site of lying and being "utterly tasteless" as well as "ju-
venile." He concluded by asking that his critic be put in jail for
five years.[42] Seriously. Grayson lost reelection in a swing district
during the 2010 midterms after calling his opponent "Taliban
Dan" in an ad. He was reelected from another district during
the 2012 presidential election.

This culture of unhinged commentary from the conservative Limbaugh Brigades may have been crystallized when Joe Wilson shouted, "You Lie!" But Wilson's outburst was soon outdone by Arizona congressman Trent Franks's remark that President Obama "has no place in any station of government and we need to realize that he is an enemy of humanity."[43]

"An enemy of humanity"—let that roll off your tongue for a while. It's hard to find a more global condemnation than that—and yet the comment was brushed aside as overheated and unremarkable, just one more conservative getting carried away by playing to the base.

Congressman Franks offered his impassioned rant in front of the How to Take Back America Conference, hosted in St. Louis by Wingnut matriarch Phyllis Schlafly ("Feminism is the most destructive force in the world") and *WorldNetDaily* columnist Janet Folger Porter.

To get a taste of the Take Back America crowd, take a look at some of the workshops offered to attendees: "How to Counter the Homosexual Extremist Movement," "How to Defeat UN Attacks on Sovereignty," "How to Stop Feminist and Gay Attacks on the Military," and, inevitably, "How to Recognize Living Under Nazis and Communists." A companion DVD featuring a shadowy Hitler-like figure plotting a takeover of the USA was for sale under the title "Freedom to Dictatorship in 5 Years."

Given this lunatic fringe festival, you might imagine that few elected officials would attend for fear of guilt by association. But as you might have guessed by now, you'd be wrong.

Once and future presidential candidate Mike Huckabee (the "Huckster") had taken time from his Fox News TV and radio show to give the keynote speech, railing against the UN: "It's time to get a jackhammer and to simply chip off that part of New York City and let it float into the East River, never to be seen again!"[44] After he spoke, a PowerPoint offered these parting wishes: "Where would America be today if Gov. Huckabee were President Huckabee? We sure wouldn't be celebrating Rama-dan . . . Huckabee 2012."[45]

Michele Bachmann brought the crowd to its feet by decrying the "gangster government" that was now running the White House, an alliterative riff off the "thug-ocracy" conservatives had predicted.[46] She spoke of the dangers of a "one-world currency" and advocated defense of "American sovereignty, even if President Obama's czars want to give it away."[47] And she promised that if Republicans took back Congress in 2010, "defunding the left is going to be so easy and it's going to solve so many of our problems."[48]

Steve King was on hand to present Joe the Plumber with the coveted Golden Wrench Award ("for throwing a wrench in the works") and a Golden Plunger ("to help flush out Washington"). King told the crowd, "I ran for public office because of what the government was doing to us, not because of what I wanted the government to do for us" and warned that in the effort to stop liberals, "every conversation matters; every prayer matters; every Tea Party matters."[49]

Conservative blogger and convention speaker Brian Camenker of MassResistance pronounced it "the best conference of its kind in memory. It was God and country—and unflinching, refreshing non-politically-correct sanity."[50]

The How to Take Back America Conference may have been extreme, but it was not an exception. It is part of a circuit tour. The Conservative Political Action Conference provides an annual echo of these themes for the party faithful. Often derided as "the Star Wars bar scene of the conservative movement," the shindig features an uneasy balance between presidential aspirants and an activist fringe festival, including panels with titles like "Saving Freedom from the Enemies of Our Values" (hosted by Phyllis Schlafly), "Friend or Foe? Abraham Lincoln on Liberty" (the jury is apparently still out for some at CPAC), and "When All Else Fails: Nullification and State Resistance to Federal Tyranny."

The speaker at "Friend or Foe? Abraham Lincoln on Liberty," Thomas DiLorenzo, made his intentions clear when he said, "I consider Abraham Lincoln an enemy of the Constitution" to a round of applause. He's offered book-length attacks on America's first Republican president, now characterized as the original progressive despot because of his violations of the Tenth Amendment, and explications of how Confederate president Jefferson Davis "championed states' rights in defense of liberty"—not slavery.

The CPAC seminar "When All Else Fails: Nullification and State Resistance to Federal Tyranny" was, if anything, less subtle. It echoed the language of Civil War–era secession and civil-rights era defense of segregation, which Martin Luther King, in his "I Have a Dream" speech, alluded to when he spoke of "vicious racists," like Alabama governor George Wallace, with "his lips dripping with the words of 'interposition' and 'nullification.'" That seminar's speaker, Dr. Thomas Woods, author of *The Politically Incorrect Guide to History*, has written about "the conservatives' traditional sympathy for the American South and its people and heritage" and participated in the founding of the neo-Confederate organization League of the South, which advocates "independence of the Southern people" from "the American Empire."

Populist conservative appeals, anti–federal government impulses, and threats of secession are nothing new, but they take on special resonance with a black president in a bad economy.

The next stop on the conservative cattle-call summit was the Values Voter Summit, held amid the Art Deco halls of Washington's Omni Shoreham Hotel. The usual suspects all appeared—including Huckabee and Bachmann—but they were joined by presidential hopefuls Mitt Romney, Newt Gingrich, and Minnesota governor Tim Pawlenty. There were religious figures, ranging from the Family Research Council's Tony Perkins to born-again B-movie actor Stephen Baldwin. And rounding things out was former Miss California-turned-conservative-sex-symbol Carrie Prejean, a martyr to the liberal media for support of what she called "opposite marriage" as opposed to same-sex marriage.

The How to Take Back America themes were in full force, with breakout sessions titled "Thugocracy: Fighting the Vast Left-Wing Conspiracy" and "ObamaCare: Rationing Your Life Away." Minority Whip Eric Cantor got in touch with his inner Glenn Beck by saying, "Right now, millions of Americans are waking up realizing that they don't recognize their country anymore." During Mitt Romney's address, an audience member channeled Joe Wilson and shouted, "He lies!" to which Mitt quipped, "I approve of that comment."[51]

But it was the Huckster who walked away the event's big winner with a speech rejecting calls to modernize or moderate the party. "I'm not sure the center makes a whole lot of sense when it's coming from people who certainly don't have our interest, or our country's interest, at heart."[52] This was a new assault—saying that centrist Republicans were not just trying to subvert the GOP, but that they "certainly" did not have America's best interest at heart. It was the kind of attack that had previously been directed at liberals, but now the enemy's list was growing to include all but the true believers. These appeals helped the ordained minister and former Arkansas governor win the Values Voter straw poll easily, apparently answering the question the title of one book for sale in the hall asked: *Who Would Jesus Vote For?*

Beneath the heartfelt talk of God and Country, there is a strangeness seeping into our politics, not just incivility but outright hostility. It is a sign of the increasing influence of the extremes, embracing the slash-and-burn techniques of talk-radio entertainers instead of the coalition-building skills of political leaders.

The would-be leaders of the conservative populist movement hail from the right wing of the Republican Party. In the wake of the 2008 election, Sarah Palin's popularity was astronomical among Republicans and conservatives, but she was decidedly unpopular with independents and centrists. Likewise, Rush Limbaugh is hugely popular with conservatives and Republicans, but his brand of harsh partisanship is kryptonite to independents and centrists. The source of this disconnect is not a mystery.

A 2008 survey by TargetPoint Consulting found that 96 percent of centrist voters consider themselves conservative to moderate on fiscal issues, whereas 86 percent of centrists see themselves as liberal to moderate on social issues. To put it another way, only 4 percent of centrists describe themselves as fiscal liberals and just 14 percent describe themselves as social conservatives. The rise of independent voters has been in reaction to the increased polarization of the two parties, though conservative populists believe that the parties are not polarized enough. For all the libertarian talk, the only independence their leaders advocate is moving further to the right on social as well as fiscal issues. Conservative populists' threats to bolt from the Republican Party may not be a bluff, but they are an attempt to hold the GOP hostage to its most fundamentalist elements. You cannot unite a country by first trying to divide it.

Time cools passions and adds perspective. This seems especially true for the tumultuous Republican love affair with Sarah Palin. It was intense, it was irrational—and then it was over. The initial fever of speculation surrounding a possible 2012 presidential run fueled obsessive media coverage of her every sound bite, but the decision to abandon elected office in Alaska in favor of giving high-priced speeches and starring in a reality TV show about her home state did not help her cause of being taken seriously.

In the course of 24/7 coverage, it was in some ways a slow-motion implosion. One year after the 2008 election, 63 percent of Americans said they "would not seriously consider her for president." By the spring of 2010, at the height of Tea Party enthusiasm, even 47 percent of Tea Party supporters were saying that Palin would not "have the ability to be an effective president."[53] By the fall of the following year, a McClatchy-Marist poll found that "by 72 percent to 24 percent, Republicans and Republican-leaning independents do not want Palin to run for president in 2012. Even among Tea Party supporters—a group that likes Palin—68 percent do not want her to run." It was a judgment call by the people who knew her best.

But perhaps the unkindest cut came from David Kelly, the Colorado Springs supporter who rushed out to register the Draft Sarah 2012 Committee the day after Obama was elected and subsequently served as the committee's treasurer.

"You may be shocked to hear that I am no longer a Palin supporter," he told me over the phone in the summer of 2012. "I
think what attracted me to her in the first place was the fact
that she'd say things that you'd hear at the Thanksgiving table
when your relatives are there and go, 'There's my crazy aunt,
but she nails it every time.'"

But now? "I realize that she's another Republican talking
head," says Kelly, who converted to count himself a strong Ron
Paul supporter. "I don't think she has the caliber to make a
great leader for this nation in these times . . . She's off my radar.
It's a sad statement."

8

RINOs AND DINOs: HUNTING FOR HERETICS

Hunting for heretics is an expensive hobby. The most competitive Senate race in 2008 was in Minnesota between Al Franken—the longtime *Saturday Night Live* comic, liberal Air America host, and author of such bestsellers as *Rush Limbaugh Is a Big Fat Idiot*—and the incumbent Republican senator Norm Coleman, a onetime Woodstock–attendee–turned prosecutor and the former mayor of St. Paul. Although Obama won the state by 10 percent, Coleman's broad center-right profile helped him gain enough crossover votes to make the race too close to call, with a gap of 0.01 percent—or 225 votes out of the 2.9 million cast.

But the morning after the election, some Wingnuts on the right were calling for Coleman's defeat. Here's the logic of young conservative radio host Ben Ferguson: "I think a lot of people last night think this was a cleansing for the party. We got rid of some dead weight, we got rid of some RINOS—Republicans in Name Only. There are Republicans today, like myself, that are rooting against Norm Coleman, hoping Al Franken wins, just so we can at least have a real Republican next time around. I mean, for me I'm like 'Let's kick 'em all out,' you know. The ones that act like they're real conservatives that weren't, hey, go on home."[1]

Ferguson eventually got his wish. Eight months later, the Minnesota Supreme Court rejected Coleman's appeal and the Senate Democratic caucus got precisely the sixty votes it needed to beat back a filibuster, the tactic Republicans had counted on to check Obama's agenda.

Six years later, Al Franken was cruising toward reelection, crushing conservative opponents in the polls—and Democrats controlled all the statewide elected offices in Minnesota.

The convictions that led some Wingnut conservatives to find a paradoxical satisfaction in defeat were neatly expressed by a sign I saw paraded at the Tea Partiers' 9/12 march on Washington: "All progressive or liberal democrats or republicans are communists."

These folks are not interested in rebuilding the Republican Party if it means forming coalitions with anyone who is not a strict social conservative as well as a fiscal conservative. They want to see the party purged, Stalinist-style, before it rebuilds—even if it means being defeated by Democrats. It's an inquisition based on ideological purity. Conformity is courage. Dissent is disloyal.

Centrist Republicans are targeted by conservative groups like the Club for Growth, which runs right-wing candidates in closed primaries who win and then often promptly lose the general election to Democrats. In 2006 and 2008, such self-inflicted losses included Representatives Heather Wilson and Wayne Gilchrest. "They don't make any bones about losing elections so long as they purify the party," said Senator Arlen Specter, who abandoned the GOP ship after twenty-four years in the face of a tough primary challenge from Club for Growth president Pat Toomey. "I don't understand it . . . There ought to be an outcry."[2]

Another example came in a 2009 special election for an upstate New York congressional seat that had been held by Republicans since 1872. It was won by a Democrat because the Wingnuts split the right. New York state Conservative Party candidate Doug Hoffman challenged local Republican elected

official Dede Scozzafava, drawing national support from Sarah
Palin and conservative pundits who characterized the GOP
nominee as a "radical leftist" because she was pro-choice and
pro–gay marriage. Brian Brown, executive director of the National Organization for Marriage, made his intentions clear:
"The Republican Party cannot take someone as liberal as Dede
Scozzafava and thrust her out on the voters and expect the voters just to accept it."

"You can have a very, very intense movement of 20 percent.
You can't govern," Newt Gingrich cautioned a week before the
election, explaining his support for the party nominee. "To govern, you got to get 50 percent plus one."[3] And for that bit of
pragmatic math, the leader of the 1994 Republican Revolution
was dubbed "King of the RINOS" by the Wingnut netroots.[4]

Soon after this election debacle, a ten-point party-purity petition was advanced by members of the Republican National
Committee, proposing that any candidate who broke with conservatives on three or more of these issues—in any votes, public statements, or on a questionnaire—would be denied party
funds or the party endorsement.[5]

There is a struggle going on between the fifty staters and the
51 percenters—those who want a broad, diverse, and national
Republican Party against those who are content to only play to
the base in pursuit of narrow victories. Right now, the 51 percenters seem to be winning. The hunt for heretics has helped
make congressional Republicans extinct in an entire region.

In 1997, the Club for Growth's Stephen Moore published an
article in the *American Spectator* titled "Is the Northeast Necessary?" in which he suggested Republicans should "[write] off
this dying region once and for all."[6] Twelve years later, Moore
had gotten his wish. After the 2008 election, there wasn't a

single Republican representative left in all of New England. This is what success looks like in the all-or-nothing world of the RINO hunters.

There is a special fury inside the conservative movement directed at Republicans who don't walk in lockstep with both social and fiscal conservatives. The goal of the RINO hunters is spelled out on the website of conservative activist Bob MacGuffie at Right Principles: "The RINO is a destructive animal that tramples on many people's hard work. It has no useful objective in an American sense because it feeds on destruction of our individual liberties and freedoms. It is a parasite that needs to be driven into political extinction!"[7]

Abraham Lincoln and Teddy Roosevelt are dubbed RINOs (because they were "progressive plutocrats"), and the site goes on to offer a RINO hit list, including Senators John McCain, Richard Lugar, Lindsey Graham, Kit Bond, Lamar Alexander, Mel Martinez, Judd Gregg, Susan Collins, and Olympia Snowe. Among the House members mentioned are Representatives Mark Kirk, Jeff Flake, Mike Castle, Mary Bono Mack, David Reichert, John McHugh, Chris Smith, and John Sullivan.

The RINO hunters enjoyed high-profile advocates in the US Senate—most notably South Carolina senator Jim DeMint, who took it upon himself to break ranks and endorse (and fund-raise for) what he called "constitutional conservative" candidates against incumbent Republicans. "I'd rather have thirty Republicans in the Senate who believe in the principles of freedom than sixty who don't believe in anything," DeMint thundered. This was a textbook example of the appeals that Cass Sunstein detailed in his book *Conspiracy Theories and Other Dangerous Ideas:* "The overall size of the group may shrink; but the group may also pick up new believers who are even more committed. By self-selection, the remaining members will display more fanaticism."

Such party purification rituals led DeMint to spend more than $5 million through his leadership PAC, the Senate Conservatives Fund, winning only eight of twenty-seven races. But embracing the lost-cause rhetoric of the old South, DeMint explained away such losses by telling ABC News, "I'd rather lose fighting for the right cause than win fighting for the wrong cause." Regardless of his record, DeMint was beloved by social conservative activists and the talk-radio crowd.

The RINO hunters could claim some high-profile scalps: Richard Lugar was defeated in a Tea Party primary by Tea-Vangelist candidate Richard Mourdock, who flamed out in the general election after pronouncing a pregnancy that resulted from rape as God's will. Senator Olympia Snowe declined to run for reelection in disgust and was replaced by an independent candidate from Maine, Angus King. Other targets rose despite the RINO hunting: Jeff Flake of Arizona and Mark Kirk of Illinois were elevated to the US Senate.

But perhaps the most telling target remains John McCain—a pro-life, fiscal conservative war hero—who has been a target of RINO hunters over the years because of his political independence and willingness to criticize both conservative and liberal excesses. After the election, when McCain's daughter Meghan began advocating on *The Daily Beast* and television that the party should modernize itself on issues like gay rights, she became a target of Wingnut familial suspicions. When Arlen Specter defected, Rush Limbaugh invited the GOP's recent nominee to do the same: "Take McCain and his daughter with you."

We've seen the hunt for heretics before.

During the Southern conservative "massive resistance" to de-segregation, moderate critics were derided as traitors, double-crossers, sugar-coated integrationists, and cowards.[8]

During the anti-Communist heyday of Joe McCarthy and the John Birch Society, a new umbrella term was introduced, "com-symp"—for "Communist sympathizer"—that allowed any skeptics to be stigmatized without the difficulty of actually proving they were Communist. At the time, Republican senator Milton R. Young of North Dakota reflected on the Birchers' obsession with what would become known as RINO hunting: "Strangely enough, most of the criticism is leveled not against liberal public officials but against more middle of the road, and even conservative Republicans."[9]

And though Nixon VP Spiro Agnew invented the use of the word "squish" to refer to radical liberals in the late 1960s and early 1970s, by the Reagan revolution it was used by conservatives to denigrate centrist members of their own party, notably Reagan chief of staff (and future secretary of state) James Baker and then–vice president George H. W. Bush.[10]

But the hyperpartisan hunt for heretics really got main-streamed during the administration of the second Bush. At the outset, conservative activist Grover Norquist gleefully told Pat Robertson's 700 Club that "there isn't an 'us and them' with this administration. They is us. We is them."[11]

Poisonous partisanship got a new name in the later part of the Bush administration when the actions of Monica Goodling came to light. Goodling was the thirty-four-year-old Justice Department White House liaison—known as "she who must be obeyed" by her staff—who illegally imposed partisan social

conservative litmus tests on prospective Justice Department
civil-service employees.

An investigation found that Goodling—a graduate of Messiah College and Pat Robertson's Regent Law School—asked
about abortion in thirty-four interviews and gay marriage on
at least twenty-one different occasions.[12] She recommended Internet searches be applied to job applicants to gain insight into
their political beliefs, and just before Christmas 2006, Goodling
e-mailed political appointee John Nowacki, urging him to "hire
one more good American"—a phrase he later testified applied
exclusively to conservatives.

Even the pioneering secretary of state and Bush loyalist Condoleezza Rice was considered suspect by second-tier administra-
tration conservatives because of her position on social issues.
When one applicant expressed admiration for Condoleezza Rice,
Goodling frowned and said, "But she is pro-choice."[13]

Over the course of the Bush administration, but especially
during the 2008 election, the excommunications and defections
continued. Individuals who were once considered among the
brightest young minds of the Reagan and Thatcher era have
been caught up in this dragnet—Peggy Noonan, David Frum,
David Brooks, and Andrew Sullivan—all declaring their independence to differing degrees and receiving a hailstorm of right-
wing criticism in return. Some might argue—as Reagan once
did about the Democrats—that they didn't leave the party, the
party had left them. But this was not the time or place for debating differences of opinion.

The son of William F. Buckley Jr. waded into the crossfire by
endorsing Barack Obama for president after the Palin nomination. Christopher Buckley chose *The Daily Beast* as the location

of the announcement instead of *National Review,* which had been founded by his father, because "I don't have the kidney at the moment for 12,000 e-mails saying how good it is he's no longer alive to see his Judas of a son endorse for the presidency a covert Muslim who pals around with the Weather Underground."[14] He got his 12,000 angry e-mails anyway.

Chris Buckley—who describes his politics as that of "a small-government conservative who clings tenaciously and old-fashionedly to the idea that one ought to have balanced budgets. On abortion, gay marriage, et al., I'm libertarian"—found himself no longer welcome in the pages of the magazine his father founded.

When David Frum—another *National Review* alum and a former George W. speechwriter—engaged in a public debate with Rush Limbaugh over the future direction of the GOP, he was barraged with angry e-mails from dittoheads. "Most of these e-mails say some version of the same thing: if you don't agree with Rush, quit calling yourself a conservative and get out of the Republican Party. There's the perfect culmination of the outlook Rush Limbaugh has taught his fans and followers: We want to transform the party of Lincoln, Eisenhower and Reagan into a party of unanimous dittoheads—and we don't care how much the party has to shrink to do it. That's not the language of politics. It's the language of a cult."[15]

The cult-like impulse to hunt for heretics has only escalated. The founder of the acclaimed blog *Little Green Footballs,* Charles Johnson, got his first big boost by railing against Islamist radicalism after the attacks of 9/11. But in the Bush administration's second term, he started to criticize excesses from the far right as well—taking aim at creationism and the increased influence of the religious right.

"I've been pretty much labeled as a heretic now by all the people who used to be what I would consider friends and allies," Johnson told me. "I'm getting more hate mail nowadays than I got even at the height of my popularity as an anti-Jihadist, which was very surprising to me, because I used to get some pretty nasty hate mail from radical Islamists. But the stuff I'm getting right now from right-wingers is an order of magnitude worse."[16]

When it comes to seeing an order of magnitude worse up close, you're not going to outdo what you're about to see from the inbox of nationally syndicated columnist Kathleen Parker.

In late September 2008, Parker had the temerity to criticize Sarah Palin in the pages of *National Review,* concluding after a month of watching that the Alaskan VP nominee was "out of her league." "No one hates saying that more than I do," she wrote. "Like so many women, I've been pulling for Palin, wishing her the best, hoping she will perform brilliantly. I've also noticed that I watch her interviews with the held breath of an anxious parent, my finger poised over the mute button in case it gets too painful. Unfortunately, it often does. My cringe reflex is exhausted."[17]

Within a week, she'd gotten 11,000 e-mails. By week three, the total passed 20,000. She estimates that about 70 percent were negative, with the general theme being that she was a traitor.

"I didn't realize that I worked for the GOP," says Kathleen, "or that my job as a 'conservative' columnist meant I had to defend all things Republican."[18]

Here are some choice cuts from her e-mail bag at the time:

- "You're not one of us, you're one of THEM, the liberal lovers, the flag burners, country haters, the ones who want to kill god and put Stalin in his place and see this nation destroyed by a sea of brown people and gays. Do you secretly date black men, Parker? You make me sick you sickening sick witch!!!"

- "So the republican party is supposed to surrender their traditional values in order to expand the base. Have you always been a dumb, trashy cunt or did sucking Obama's schlong fill your head with such bull-shit that you can't even think straight."

- "You're a fucking, shit-faced whore and you are the reason for the decline of the republican party. Yes. You and every pansy shit-headed fucking liberal republican who caters to the leftist agenda."

- "You like getting cucumbers up your ass, whore? Huh? Stop writing your stupid articles. Conservative Christians don't like you and your ilk, we don't need you or your fucking ideas. We will do fine without republicans, democrats, or anyone else who tries to disregard our values."

- "Kathleen Parker is a lesbian, anti-christian whore and anti-American terrorist who must be eradicated. She is an Adolph [sic] Hitler of this century."

There is something breathtakingly stupid about seeing such bile written down instead of just hearing it screamed. For some unhinged hyperpartisans, a hint of dissent provokes unreasonable rage. When thoughtful criticism is responded to with an avalanche of hate, its absurdity is the only saving grace.

You don't want to indulge in close readings of deranged right-wing dispatches like a high school class reading *Hamlet*, but in those five e-mails you get the whole gamut of paranoid associations—Hitler, Stalin, people who "want to kill God," "Us versus Them," and fear of the nation being "destroyed by a sea of brown people and gays"—a twofer of racism and homophobia. What's especially weird is the abrupt segues between high-minded conservative arguments and then the slide into the psychotic sewer.

Hunting for heretics pretends to be a principled fight for ideological purity, but behind that mask is an uglier impulse, an attempt to intimidate and insist on conformity. Imperiousness and inflexibility in politics are signs of insecurity. It's a reminder of what the Czech dissident-turned-president Vaclav Havel once wrote: "Ideology offers human beings the illusion of dignity and morals while making it easier to part with them."

Burning Down the Big Tent

"I've spent my entire life time separating the Right from the kooks,"[19] reflected William F. Buckley Jr. His friend Ronald Reagan won the White House for conservatives by preaching a "big tent" philosophy—noting as far back as 1967, "The Republican Party, both in [California] and nationally, is a broad party. There is room in our tent for many views; indeed, the divergence of views is one of our strengths"[20]—and reminding activists that an 80 percent friend is not a 20 percent enemy.[21] These axioms echoed Reagan's genial personality, but they were also shrewd politics. In 1984, the tent was big enough to hold 59 percent of the electorate and carry forty-nine states.

But now Wingnuts are trying to burn the big tent down. They have forgotten that the essence of evangelism is winning converts. Reagan's oft-quoted Eleventh Commandment—"Thou shalt not speak ill of another Republican"—is dismissed if the Republican is not considered adequately conservative. Even the term "big tent" itself is regarded as code for liberal subversion.

The tone has come from the top as well as from the grassroots activists. When former vice president Dick Cheney was asked whether the party should follow the lead of Rush Limbaugh or Colin Powell, he chose the professional polarizer instead of the centrist former secretary of state. "Well, if I had to choose in terms of being a Republican, I'd go with Rush Limbaugh," he said with gravelly dismissiveness while sticking in the partisan shiv. "My take on it was Colin had already left the party. I didn't know he was still a Republican."[22]

Here's the irony of today's ideological purists: conservatives' greatest patron saints, Barry Goldwater and Ronald Reagan, would never have met the "You're either with us or against us" litmus tests of today's right wing. Not even close.

Goldwater was a small-government libertarian who believed in getting government out of both the boardroom and the bedroom. On the issue of abortion, Goldwater was frustrated that "a lot of so-called conservatives think I've turned liberal because I believe a woman has a right to an abortion. That's a decision that's up to a pregnant woman, not up to the pope or some do-gooders or the religious right."[23] It wasn't a newfound view— his wife co-founded Arizona Planned Parenthood in the 1930s.

On gay rights, Goldwater took a live-and-let-live attitude at odds with the social conservative playbook, saying: "The rights that we have under the Constitution cover anything we want to do, as long as it's not harmful. I can't see any way in the world that being a gay can cause damage to somebody else."[24] Of gays in the military, he famously said, "You don't have to be straight in order to shoot straight."[25]

Goldwater was also wary of the growing influence of the religious right on the Republican Party, taking to the floor of the Senate in 1981 to decry "the religious factions that . . . are trying to force government leaders into following their position 100 percent. . . . I'm frankly sick and tired of the political preachers across this country telling me as a citizen that if I want to be a moral person, I must believe in 'A,' 'B,' 'C,' and 'D.' . . . I will fight them every step of the way if they try to dictate their moral convictions to all Americans in the name of 'conservatism.'"[26]

Goldwater's libertarian instincts would color him a liberal in the eyes of current social-conservative power brokers. This paradox, in turn, raises questions about the role and influence of libertarians in the party that so many consider their natural home, especially by contrast to the big-spending Democrats. Nick Gillespie, the editor in chief of the libertarian magazine *Reason,* has stated that the split is too obvious to ignore. "The Republicans used to talk about cutting taxes, cutting spending, and cutting regulation," Gillespie told me in the lead-up to the 2006 elections after half a decade of conservative control of Washington. "Now, they only talk about cutting taxes and regulating people's personal lives."[27]

Even the sainted Reagan would come under fire from most in the current Republican Party if his policies were judged absent the hagiography. As governor of California, he signed the nation's most liberal abortion bill into law (an action he later said he regretted). In the 1970s, he opposed California's Proposition 6, the conservative bill backed by Anita Bryant, which would have made it legal to fire gays and lesbians from teaching positions in public schools. He raised taxes by $1 billion to close a budget gap and presided over an increase in the number of state employees by 50,000.[28] Any of these actions could get him disqualified as an untrustworthy conservative or even a dangerous liberal, if he tried to step out on the road to the White House today.

As president, Reagan gave amnesty to illegal aliens in a comprehensive immigration reform. He closed tax loopholes that today would be attacked as raising taxes. He negotiated with the

Soviet "evil empire" and withdrew troops from Beirut after a terrorist attack. He worked amiably with Democrats in Congress and constantly courted their constituents, creating the Reagan Democrat. In fact, as early as 1981, coalition conservative activists were complaining about Reagan, with the director of the Conservative Caucus saying, "He sounds like Winston Churchill and acts like Neville Chamberlain,"[29] and the editor of the *Conservative Digest* reached absurdity by writing, "Sometimes I wonder how much of a Reaganite Reagan really is."[30]

Today, Rush Limbaugh and Glenn Beck are among the chief critics of the big-tent philosophy. Beck attacked South Carolina senator Lindsey Graham for saying the GOP can't be the party of "angry white guys" by sarcastically asking, "Who's left?"[31] How about the 85 percent of Americans who don't identify themselves as "conservative Republicans" or the vast majority of nonwhite citizens who feel unwelcome in what used to be the Party of Lincoln?

Mike Huckabee appears to be building a future campaign around attacking the very idea of a big tent: "One of the things that concerns me is that in the United States there is real talk of maybe we need to have this big tent and accommodate every view . . . That will kill the conservative movement."[32]

He's playing to grassroots groups such as Connecticut's Right Principles that sum up hostility to the big tent: "How long will they accept the fiction of a party that is a 'Big Tent'? . . . How long will it tolerate being politically debilitated by a disease caused by an internal enemy consisting of a disloyal collection of ideological subversives who are, for all intents and purposes, looking to either mutate its host body beyond all recognition or to kill it outright?"[33]

When RNC chair Michael Steele advocated a more inclusive approach to pro-choice Republicans and increased tolerance for gays and lesbians, the Family Research Council's Tony Perkins countered by saying that if Steele was trying to create a big tent for the GOP, the Republican Party would find that it's nothing but an "empty big tent."[34]

There is a core contradiction at the heart of modern conservatism. The party's proudly stated belief in expanding individual freedom is at odds with the agenda of the religious right. A collectivist streak runs through much of social conservatism—a desire to have the government make decisions for individuals, especially on questions of reproductive and sexual freedom.

There's also a secret hiding in plain sight: the far right is far more loud than powerful. The few big-tent Republicans who are left are among the party's most powerful vote getters, even as they are attacked as politically impotent. John McCain won reelection to the Senate in 2004 with 76 percent of the vote. And in 2006, a Democratic year, Republican Olympia Snowe won in liberal Maine with 74 percent of the vote and Republican Dick Lugar won with 87 percent in Indiana, whereas social-conservative senator Rick Santorum lost in Pennsylvania with 41 percent. In 2008, Lamar Alexander won reelection with 65 percent in Tennessee and conservative Senate minority leader Mitch McConnell squeaked by with 53 percent in neighboring Kentucky. And when talk radio advocated a new conservative coalition based on anti-immigrant fervor, two of the border-state candidates backing that approach, Arizona's J. D. Hayworth and Randy Graf, lost their 2006 congressional campaigns.

Joe Scarborough, former GOP congressman and host of *Morning Joe* on MSNBC, provides a conservative's view on the hunt for heretics.

I hear these freaks screaming and yelling about how they're the true believers, they're the true conservatives. They're the ones that are going to root out the heretics . . . It's madness. These are the same people that took a $155 billion surplus when I left Washington in 2001 and turned it into a $1.5 trillion deficit. These are the same so-called conservatives that took the national debt from $5.7 trillion to $11.5 trillion. So when I hear people say the Republican Party's become too conservative, you know what my answer is: They haven't become too conservative. They've become too radical. They stopped being conservative when it came to spending our money. They stopped being conservative when it came to foreign policy. They stopped being conservative in their rhetoric. They have been radicalized by people who don't know what it means to be a small-government conservative.[35]

National Review editor Rich Lowry looks to the future and tells me, "For decades, the way for the Republican Party to grow was to become more conservative and to draw away conservatives from the Democratic Party. But there are various demographic trends that make the Republicans' job tougher and they've sort of tapped out to a large extent that strategy. So now the growth strategy, I think, has to be something different, not to be less conservative but to ensure conservatism is addressing people's current concerns and anxieties."[36]

For the Republican Party, a return to its historic principles of individual freedom, fiscal responsibility, and national security—with renewed consistency—would not only lead to the

GOP's political resurgence, it could help unite our nation. But it will require that social conservatives embrace the big tent again—and not treat allies with libertarian opinions on social issues as loyalty suspects or second-class citizens.

However, when you hear the far right invoking the big tent these days, it's often because they are being forced to defend the indefensible signs that dot the Tea Party and town hall protests. There is a reluctance to repudiate for fear of dividing or demoralizing their partisan forces. Instead, Joe Wierzbicki, one of the GOP operatives organizing the Tea Party Express, contorted himself to avoid judging the occasionally extremist rhetoric and signs amid his crowds: "People who choose to embrace your message or your movement are not the people that you embrace. They have chosen to embrace you."[37] In other words, the big tent should extend as far to the right as necessary to fire up the base. The real disloyalty is not doing violence to civil society but criticizing a fellow traveler. No one is accountable for inciting the mob. It's a sign that the inmates are running the asylum.

DINO Hunting and Occupy Outrage

While the far right set out to eat its own during Obama's first year in the White House, the far left started to indulge the same impulses. The far right's constant drumbeat held that Obama was a socialist, but the far left attacked him for not being radical enough.

As with the right, the furor started on the fringes even before the inauguration. In early January 2009, the folks at Revolution Books in Manhattan's Chelsea neighborhood weren't even trying to restrain their disgust with liberal excitement over the president-elect. "A lot of people got taken with Obama," the clerk at the checkout counter grumbled, "but it's just the same Bush program rebranded." Instead of the near-ubiquitous Obama buttons adorning overcoats in that area, Revolution had a window display selling bottles of "Obamalade" for a buck each. It was an oddly entrepreneurial way to make the point. Each plastic bottle's wrapper contained a tiny political screed:

INGREDIENTS: Massacres in Gaza, Rick Warren, escalation of the Afghanistan war, Hillary Clinton, bailout of big business, Rahm Emanuel, blaming Black people for problems the system inflicts on them, "coming together" with those who hate gay people, Robert Gates, whitewashing torture by the Bush regime, and the Patriot Act.

SURGEON GENERAL'S WARNING: Obamalade causes massive loss of life in Iraq, Afghanistan, Palestine, Pakistan and many other countries; continued attacks on Black people, women, immigrants, gays & lesbians; political cowardice that is dangerous to the health of humanity. If, after drinking Obamalade, you find yourself accepting the crimes of this system—you should immediately take 2 doses of reality and report to the nearest movement of resistance against these crimes.

Peel off the Obamalade wrapper and you'd have a perfect pocket-sized reminder of the far-left Wingnut worldview: America as the world's prime oppressor.

The professional protesters at a group called The World Can't Wait weren't too thrilled about the Obama agenda, either. The group formed "to repudiate and stop the fascist direction initiated by the Bush Regime." After Inauguration Day 2009, they launched "Obama Watch."

The new president's first sin was the choice of evangelist Rick Warren to give the inauguration invocation: "To say that's a bad start would be a colossal understatement," wrote the organization's director, Debra Sweet, going on to describe "Warren's overall Christian fascist program."[38]

Nor were the group members willing to make adjustments in the oft-cited struggle against the racist imperialism of the United States: "Having a Black man at the head of a white supremacist government doesn't mean that white supremacy is over!"[39] *Hasta la victoria siempre.*

But the biggest criticism was reserved for Obama's continuation of what they call "the War OF Terror." Here the list of grievances is long: US troops still in Iraq, an expansion of the war against the Taliban in Afghanistan, striking at targets in Pakistan, and support for what they call Israel's "occupation" of Gaza. Guantánamo is still open, rendition still practiced, and as for torture, well, they're selling stickers with an Abu Ghraib silhouette over the Obama campaign logo saying, "Yes We Can Cover Up Torture."[40]

As Obama's realpolitik agenda—a surge for Afghanistan, a cautious exit from Guantánamo, pragmatism on health care—began to clash with left-Wingnut ideals, Obamalade fervor began leaking into more mainstream voices.

"Right now, Mr. President, your base thinks you're nothing but a sellout—a corporate sellout at that," bellowed MSNBC's Ed Schultz.[41] "Can you really say this White House is on the side of the American people?" asked Arianna Huffington.[42] Obama, they complained, was too quick to compromise, too eager to horse-trade for a single elusive Republican vote and, most of all, too slow to overturn Bush's foreign policies. The activist website *Democratic Underground* conducted an online poll concluding

that Obama was a Democrat in Name Only, while a photo showing Bush's face morphing into Obama's was circulating among
the netroots. Some were already suggesting that progressive former presidential candidate Howard Dean challenge Obama in
the 2012 primaries.[43] The newly emboldened left was taking on
the embattled center. The era of DINO hunting had begun.

Bipartisanship doesn't sell to Wingnuts, left or right. Obama
had promised to appoint a "Team of Rivals"–style cabinet if
elected, and when he followed through, the Wingnuts weren't
happy. Tapping Hillary Clinton to be secretary of state was on
the outside edge of acceptable, despite her hawkish positions on
the Middle East, but the real news was the selection of former
McCain adviser and marine general Jim Jones to be national security adviser and the reappointment of Bush's secretary of defense, Robert Gates. As the executive director of Moveon.org,
Eli Pariser, told the Associated Press: "If they turn out to be
all disappointments, we'll have a good three years to storm the
gates at the White House."[44] For the far left, the reflexive rhetoric of *Ramparts* always lives on.

With sixty votes in the Senate and a 258-seat majority in
the House, liberal leaders viewed Obama's election as an ideological mandate. Congressman Barney Frank quipped, "When
Obama said he was going to be a post-partisan president, I got
post-partisan depression."[45] Columnist Thomas Franks argued
that "bipartisanship is a silly Beltway obsession," writing that
"promises to get beyond partisanship are the most perfunctory
sort of campaign rhetoric"[46]—trying to absolve Obama of the
obligation to govern as he'd campaigned. It was a classic case
of situational ethics: critics of conservative hyperpartisanship
couldn't wait to get their equal and opposite revenge.

Each centrist policy enraged the far left even more. On Afghanistan, congressional liberals like Dennis Kucinich reflexively deployed Vietnam metaphors while Bush nemeses like Code Pink took to the streets to protest Obama's "imperialist war against Afghanistan." Even Cindy Sheehan—the self-styled "peace mom" who declared W. a "bigger terroris than Osama bin Laden"[47]—came out of semiretirement to prote t President Obama on his summer vacation, just like old times: "The body bags aren't taking a vacation and as the U.S.-led violence surges in Afghanistan and Pakistan, so are the needless deaths of every side."[48] She later led protests in Oslo opposing Obama's Nobel Peace Prize acceptance ceremony.[49] The fact that Obama dedicated his speech to the men and women of the US military—and made a thoughtful case for when war is justified—must have infuriated the protesters even more, if they bothered to listen.

The larger problem for liberals wasn't just Afghanistan but Obama's decision to change the style but not the substance of the Bush administration's War on Terror policies. Obama's expansion of detention for terror suspects spurred nationally syndicated ultraliberal cartoonist and columnist Ted Rall to erupt in a Wingnut call for Obama's resignation, titled "With Democrats Like Him, Who Needs Dictators?" His argument: "Obama is useless. Worse than that, he's dangerous. Which is why, if he has any patriotism left after the thousands of meetings he has sat through with corporate contributors, blood-sucking lobbyists and corrupt politicians, he ought to step down now—before he drags us further into the abyss . . . Obama has revealed himself. He is a monster."[50]

On the domestic front, the Wingnuts turned the health-care debate into a circular firing squad. MoveOn.org started targeting centrist Democrats in the Senate with issue ads in their districts, essentially threatening them if they did not back the "public option."[51] The newly formed Progressive Change Campaign Committee aimed to be a liberal corollary to the Club for Growth, targeting ten conservative Blue Dog congressmen for their "Betrayal of Democrats."[52] Joe Lieberman emerged as an especially ripe target for DINO hunters. Al Gore's 2000 VP nominee had emerged as a hawkish "9/11 Democrat." His support of the War on Terror led Democratic liberals to run antiwar candidate Ned Lamont against him in the 2006 primary, but Lieberman created a new party and won the general election in Connecticut as an independent by 10 percent. Lieberman continued to caucus with the Democrats in the Senate, but he inflamed old wounds by campaigning for John McCain in 2008.

Now with Lieberman a health-care holdout, liberal activists started to play "hunt for the heretic" in exceptionally ugly terms. The thoughtful *Washington Post* policy wonk blogger Ezra Klein briefly reached for mass-murder metaphors, writing, "Lieberman seems primarily motivated by torturing liberals. That is to say, he seems willing to cause the deaths of hundreds of thousands of people in order to settle an old electoral score."[53] Victor Navsky, former editor of the *Nation,* accused Lieberman of "the betrayal of his Jewish heritage."[54] Jesse Jackson also wielded the identity politics machete in an attack on centrist Democratic congressman Artur Davis of Alabama, saying, "You can't vote against health care and call yourself a black man." Ralph Nader went so far as to call President Obama "an Uncle Tom groveling before the demands of the corporations that are running our country" because the health-care bill was not liberal enough.

Ultimately, the health-care bill passed the House and Senate along narrow party lines. This not only failed to fulfill the president's postpartisan campaign promises, it broke with precedent.

Every major entitlement expansion or reform in America's past enjoyed broad bipartisan support. FDR's Social Security Act earned the support of eighty-one House Republicans and sixteen GOP senators.[55] LBJ's Medicare Act in 1965 had the support of seventy House Republicans and thirteen Senate Republicans.[56] Even the Newt Gingrich–led 1996 welfare reform bill enjoyed the support of ninety-eight Democratic votes.[57]

All this Wingnuttery had an impact. Approaching the end of Obama's first year in office, the Democratic-controlled Congress's approval rating was down to 21 percent[58]—and though Obama began his term identified with centrist policies, by year's end most Americans saw his agenda as liberal.[59] In November, Democrats lost the governorships of New Jersey and Virginia, swing states Obama carried in 2008.

But the liberal anger at Obama and the Washington establishment only escalated even as pressure increased on Democratic elected officials, especially in red states and swing states heading into the 2010 midterm elections. Their chief complaint was that Obama and congressional Democrats had not been liberal enough. In some circles, they condemned centrist Democrats like Arkansas senator Blanche Lincoln, as "conserva-dems" and argued for her defeat as part of a long-term party purification exercise. In the case of first-term Washington, DC, mayor Adrian Fenty—a prominent supporter of school choice and education reform working alongside his school chancellor, Michelle Rhee—unions dumped over $1 million into his defeat in a 2010 closed partisan primary and knocked him out of office, despite a majority of citizens saying the city had improved under his watch. And then there were the protests.

"We as one nation must stand together, must fight the forces of evil, the conservatives in this country across the board,"

boomed MSNBC's Ed Schultz, emcee of the One Nation Working Together rally on the Washington Mall on a Saturday in
early October 2010. "The conservative voices of America, they
are holding you down. They don't believe in your freedom. . . .
They talk about the Constitution, but they don't want to live by
it. They don't believe in your freedom. . . . They talk about the
founding fathers, but they want discrimination."

The stated intention of the One Nation rally was to promote
an "antidote" rather than a liberal alternative to the Tea Party
rallies, but it fell short of that noble goal.

A pregame rally south of the Washington Monument featured drum circles and papier-mâché puppets. President Obama
was called an "imperialist president" who was insensitive to the
"African community" and "the 2.5 million people in concentration camps called prisons."

"We recognize that the U.S. government is waging the same
kind of war—a counterinsurgency," warned a woman on the
makeshift stage, "that it is waging against the people of Afghanistan—against the people of the African community right here
inside the U.S."

The curious migration of anti-Semitism to the left was evident in signs that read, "End All U.S. Aid to the Racist State of
Israel" and "Fund Jobs, Not Israel." I cringed as these marchers crowded past a group of World War II vets from Columbus,
Ohio, being wheeled to their war memorial as part of the excellent "Honor Flight" program.

The crowds mostly wore union T-shirts—tie-dyes for members of SEIU/1199—with umbrella union UAW members wearing navy-blue shirts that read "Mobilizing for Justice." Justice
is, of course, supposed to be impartial, but in this crowd the
word had ideological overtones, as protesters marched past

people handing out copies of the *Workers World* and selling *The Communist Manifesto* next to the collected works of Malcolm X.

There were plenty of homemade anti–Tea Party signs, including "The Enemies of America" and "Kissing GOP Ass Gets You Tea-Bagged." There were recycled anti-Bush signs, some of which had been repurposed to read "Stop Obama's Wars" (or "Mr. Obama: End These Fucking Wars Now" as the Vets for Peace would have it). Some signs were strikingly sensible ("Who is America being taken back from?"); others waded into policy ("American Jobs for American Workers: No H-1B Visas"). Still others aimed for theology (asking "When Did Jesus Become Pro-Rich, Pro-War and Only Pro-American"), with one simply asserting "Jesus Christ is the Almighty Liberal."

And then there was Death. The man in the Grim Reaper outfit was holding a sign that read: "Death Thanks the GOP For Its Stance on Healthcare Reform. You Guys Sure Make My Job Easy."

It turns out that Death lives in Maryland. His name is Wayne Castle and he's an electrician. He's carried dozens of posters in the guise of the Reaper since 2004. "I wish there were more people here," Death said glumly.

As the DJ played "Everyday People" and high-school students step-danced on the stage at the foot of the Lincoln Memorial, I saw a red flag waving above the crowd, crowned by a gold hammer and sickle. I tracked down the young man holding it, an eighteen-year-old named Adrian, a self-described Marxist-Leninist from Buffalo. I asked him what reaction he'd been getting to the flag. "People love it—I'm getting a very positive reaction," he said. But was he concerned about offending people, given that Communists murdered more than 60 million people over the course of the twentieth century?

"No, not really," he said. His friend Dez broke in: "I feel more upset about the millions of people murdered by the American system and the claim of democracy," Dez said. "No colored person has ever seen democracy."

"What about President Obama?" I asked.

"With Obama they put a black face on a white problem," replied Adrian.

President Obama is called a Communist by the far right, while the far left believes that he is a corporate sellout. That's an absurd political position that says more about us than about the occupant of the Oval Office. But that perspective was one of the animating ideas behind the leftist protests known as the Occupy Movement that briefly burst into national consciousness in the fall of 2011.

It was, at its core, a reflection of understandable anger at the growing gap between the super-rich and the rest of society, disgust at the way the big banks had caused the Great Recession and were bailed out on the taxpayers' dime while middle-class American families found themselves foreclosed on and small businesses could not get loans.

But under the banner of the 99 percent, the protest itself took on the characteristics of a counterculture collective. An anarcho-hippie commune took root in Zuccotti Park, across the street from where the World Trade Center towers once stood, and spread to satellite protests around the country.

Zuccotti Square—the official name of what had been known locally as Liberty Park—is just 26,000 square feet, or roughly half an acre. During the Occupy protest, the park became home to a food line, a clothes bank, a lending library, and a lot of space taken up by sleeping bags. The numbers of protesters swelled to the thousands during the day, then increased on weekends with circling tourists and journalists, but the square still defined the contours of the protests, housing only a few hundred earnest souls overnight.

Across the street, the same battered Burger King on Church Street that was kept open twenty-four hours a day to feed rescue workers in the weeks after 9/11 was used by Occupiers looking for a bathroom. The Brooks Brothers on the corner of Liberty Street that had been briefly used as a morgue became little more than a framing device for the protest, a symbol of the establishment absent any context. Likewise, opposite the Stock Exchange on the corner of Wall Street and Nassau Street was the site of Federal Hall, where the Bill of Rights was passed.

The protesters' historic amnesia, willful or not, could be jarring—the 9/11 "Truther" signs I repeatedly saw scattered among the slogans, the pamphlet by Professor Ward Churchill, who infamously called the workers at the World Trade Center "little Eichmanns" reprinted en masse among the tracts (one called "Public Anarchism"; an abridged autobiography of Emma Goldman; "Women in the Spanish Revolution"), all in the shadow of Ground Zero itself. The fact that Zuccotti Park had been covered knee-deep in ash and debris went unremarked—it was only a place to be occupied.

Over the two-month occupation of Zuccotti Park, support from some thirty-nine unions and community organizations helped bulk up and organize the Occupy Wall Street crowd, and select MSNBC shows and Current TV seemed to be competing to see who could outpromote these protests as Fox News had done previously with the Tea Party.

The Occupy protesters were anarchists with Apple computers—earnest and eager to play for the cameras with slogans that captured emotions but were too often unrelated to solutions.

Social Democrats stereotypically offer an endless supply of pro-
grammatic solutions, but these protests seem to be occurring
in a policy-free zone. For example, one frequent battle cry is
"Replace capitalism with democracy"—which sounds great but
makes not a lot of sense. After all, one is an economic system
and the other a political system. And although signs like "Shit is
Fucked Up and Bullshit" have a certain all-encompassing appeal
on bad days, the thought is not really all that useful as a political statement designed to highlight a problem, let alone offer a
solution.

Likewise, take a look at a list of goals/demands I saw on a
sign the first night Occupy protesters began their weeks-long
encampment at Zuccotti Park. The list of demands was helpfully
addressed "to every man, woman, and child":

1. We want an end to the glamorization of negativity in the
   media.
2. We want an end to status symbols dictating our worth as
   individuals.
3. We want a meaningful universal education system.
4. We want substance in the place of popularity.
5. We won't compromise.
6. We want invisible walls that separate by wealth and race
   and class to be torn down.
7. We want to think our own thoughts.
8. We will be responsible for our environment.
9. We want clarity/truth from our elected officials or they
   should step aside.
10. We want an end to all wars.
11. We want an end to the processed culture of exploitation &
    over-consumption.

Got it. This is heartfelt and ambitious but offers little in the way of action items. It is a stoned wish list and it is part of a piece—among the signs I saw across the street from Ground Zero are: "How Long Can the Corporate-Military Occupation of Earth Go On?" "Corporatism is Fascism," "We are Tunisia, Egypt, Greece, Palestine, Spain, Yemen, Bahrain, Syria, Bolivia and Libya"—this last litany a reference to the Arab Spring protests and their echoes across the Atlantic.

Reality check: populist rallies gain intensity by encouraging a loss of perspective, fueling anger with apocalyptic urgency. In the case of the Tea Party, conservative activists seemed to believe that losing the 2008 election was like living under tyranny. And too many in the Occupy Wall Street crowd tossed around comparisons to Arab Spring uprisings, where state police murdered peaceful protesters.

The perspective-free rush to the ramparts threatens to obscure the very real reasons people should be angry at our screwed-up financial system that led to corruption and collusion and economic malpractice. We should have a fact-based debate about growing gaps between the super-rich and the middle class in America, reinstating Glass-Steagall, or whether a millionaire's tax is the best way to pay for a Jobs Bill while beginning to pay down the debt. Against this backdrop, it's not insensitive to say that comparing the USA to dictatorships while banging away in a drum circle isn't the best way to get taken seriously.

As Occupy Wall Street spread into satellite protests, there was an understandable media impulse to impose an established narrative, asking whether this was the mirror image of the Tea Party protests. Most of the protesters I spoke to dismissed the comparisons abruptly. "The Tea Party is the opposite of Occupy Wall Street. The only thing we have in common is our homemade signs," Eric Seligson of Brooklyn told me, as he folded anarchist pamphlets by the light of a headlamp in Zuccotti Square on Friday night. "The Tea Party is phony, a fake grassroots. They're supported by the Koch brothers and Fox News. They're not representative of workers. They're mostly disenfranchised white people," Seligson said, gesturing to the young and comparatively diverse crowd. "Maybe some of them are losing their jobs but their anger is misdirected, because they're being taught to side with those who crashed the economy," added Sara Quinter, from Queens in New York City. "Instead of identifying with their fellow 99 percent, they're thinking they should identify with the 1 percent."

But at least one man in the crowd, wearing an "End the Fed" T-shirt and a tricorner hat, argued for common cause with the Tea Party. "I believe there's lots of overlap between the message of Ron Paul and Occupy Wall Street," said Gabriel Brown of Long Island. "We're against the war. We're against the Federal Reserve. We're against the police state and the Patriot Act. I think there's lots of unity here. They need to start coming down here and start being in the marketplace of free ideas."

The "marketplace of free ideas" is a great phrase that is needed these days. But populist protests quickly polarize into us-against-them, enforced by partisan media. Healthy skepticism, a sense of humor, and independent perspective are essential but endangered by these dynamics.

There was a tense but courteous standoff between the police and the protesters for weeks. After an announcement that the company that owned the privately maintained public space of the park would attempt to clean it—which would require emptying the Occupy commune—the protesters braced for conflict with the cops as television cameras waited to capture the fight.

Unions like SEIU/1199 dispatched members to bolster the crowd along with the Working Families Party, while the American Civil Liberties Union (ACLU) sent official observers, adding to the atmosphere of impending oppression.

In the tense hours up to the deadline, protesters set about cleaning the park themselves, using soap and water and scrub brushes, trying to prove that they did not need to be displaced. Homemade signs such as "Today we clean up our park; Tomorrow we clean up Wall Street" dotted the perimeter, along with prefab printed jobs like "Stop the War on Workers" and "NYPD Protects and Serves the Rich." Overall, it was a sincere show of self-reliance with characteristically lighthearted touches, like the guy dressed as Santa Claus in the early morning hours, wielding a blue broom, who flashed a peace sign as I took his picture.

Then the announcement came that the park would not be cleared or cleaned—at least not that night. "This is our victory," shouted an exuberant, fat, bearded man with red suspenders from the speaker's wall on the north side of the park, while his words were echoed in waves across the crowd. A rowdy brass band led a dance line through the square as the kitchen area offered scrambled eggs, salad, bagels, and blueberry muffins. "We even got some fucking scones here!" exclaimed one dude in delight.

But the sense of celebration born of reprieve did not last long. In the twilight afterglow, talk of a new march on Wall Street swept the crowd. There was no point in wasting all the media attention already assembled this morning. And so a few hundred protesters began a march down Broadway as the green-and-black-clad brass band played a buoyant version of "We're Not Gonna Take It" by Twisted Sister behind a large cardboard sign saying "Keep the Peace." It would prove disingenuous. I overheard one protester tell a cameraman: "The intersection will be at Exchange Place—that's where we're going to get arrested."

And so it was. One block south of Trinity Church, in sight of Alexander Hamilton's grave, the marchers crossed into the middle of Broadway, blocking the morning traffic. They got less than one block before a dozen cops on scooters rushed up to meet them. Cameras flashed as the sounds of whistles pierced the air.

The sense of relief that had greeted the wise decision to delay the forced cleaning of the square had been replaced with a determination to orchestrate a conflict in front of cameras.

Professional protesters crave the visuals of oppression to help build public sympathy for their movement. Like all extremes, they will ultimately be their own worst enemy, alienating more people than they attract. That morning, they only succeeded in turning a sympathetic story of celebration into a story about manufacturing dissent.

In one cosmic irony, the right condemned the Occupy protests in almost precisely the same terms as the left condemned the Tea Party movement, while the left angrily argued that media bias was behind anything less than uncritical coverage.

For example, here's Republican majority leader Eric Cantor: "I'm increasingly concerned about the growing mobs occupying Wall Street and other cities around the country . . . Believe it or not, some in this town [Washington, DC] have actually condoned the pitting of Americans against other Americans."

And here's Eric Cantor rallying the crowd at 2009's Values Voter Summit: "Right now, millions of Americans are waking up, realizing that they don't recognize their country anymore." Down the hall, his conservative compatriots were hosting seminars with unifying titles like "Thugocracy: Fighting the Vast

Left-Wing Conspiracy" and "ObamaCare: Rationing Your Life Away." Double standards and situational ethics are the way the hyperpartisan game is played.

But it is a two-way street. Liberals loved the telling snapshots of the more unhinged signs at Tea Party rallies. But now they claimed that similar snapshots of the messages penned at the Occupy Wall Street protests were taken out of context and designed to discredit them.

Unlike the Tea Party protests, the Occupy Movement failed to translate its passion into coordinated political action, let alone a takeover of Congress. Instead, many of the protesters I spoke to identified electoral politics as part of the problem. Of course, no alternative vision was given, but this apathetic impulse—driven by the ugliness of our domestic politics—is dangerous for our democracy.

What gets lost in the pendulum swing of populist protests is a sense of citizen responsibility and desire to actually solve problems in a democratic republic—defining the common ground that exists and then building on it. In the current polarized political environment, that just might be the most revolutionary idea of all.

9.

THE BIG LIE: BIRTHERS AND TRUTHERS

Somewhere beyond the far right and far left lies the fright wing of American politics: a murky ground where diabolical plots are hatched by opponents in power and only true patriots with special knowledge of these conspiracies have the courage to ask the tough questions.

The Big Lie can be seductive. It masquerades as reason, but always leads down a path confirming your worst fears about your worst enemy.

In the first decade of the twenty-first century, two Big Lies have preoccupied the fright wingers—the ideas that Barack Obama was not born in America (the Birthers) and that 9/11 was an inside job (the Truthers). On the surface they seem like opposite sides of the same coin—an anti-Obama conspiracy theory for Wingnuts on the right and an anti-Bush conspiracy theory for Wingnuts on the left. But nothing is that simple among the fright wing. As I dug around this dark, dank basement, I discovered that the Birther claims were first circulated by Obama's opponents on the far left during the 2008 primary campaign. And Truther myths are now aggressively promoted by anti-government activists on the far right.

Both conspiracy theories aim at the foundation of the respective president's claim to history—Obama's importance as the first African American president and Bush's leadership after 9/11. Both claims try to undermine the presidents' essential legitimacy by writing an alternate history, one that would reveal them to be monstrous frauds with dictatorial ambitions. Proponents of the Big Lie cast themselves as populist truth tellers taking on powerful interests, but their ultimate goal is to bring down their political opponents while proving that the American people are easily duped, making their own efforts seem both misunderstood and heroic.

Whereas some Wingnut claims take place in the realm of political theory, like casting Obama as a Communist, the Big Lie often poses as scientific inquiry. Those searching for truth behind the Big Lie have wasted countless hours poring through data, learning alternate histories, and ignoring the obvious. The obsessions of the more extreme Wingnuts are impermeable to reason. Those on the periphery have always peddled the Big Lie. What's different now? As the fringe blurs with the base, and the Internet provides an effective platform, more people in American politics are beginning to buy into it.

The Birthers

"I don't want this flag to change! I want my country back!" screams the lady in red at Republican congressman Mike Castle's Delaware town hall.

With brown hair pulled back and wearing an oversized red T-shirt, she's waving her birth certificate and a tiny American flag in her left hand while holding a microphone in her right. "I want to go back to January 20. Why are you people ignoring his birth certificate? He is not an American citizen!" Her voice rises an octave and cracks with anger. "He is a citizen of Kenya!"[1]

The crowd goes nuts with screams of support. The woman known to locals as "Crazy Eileen" has brought a small army, and they have the place packed.

Mike Castle seems taken aback. After a bit of circuitous stammering, he says, "If you're referring to the president, he is a citizen of the United States." He is shouted down in tones that recall the crowd in *Monty Python and the Holy Grail* yelling, "Burn the witch!" Castle continues, "You can boo, but he is a citizen of the United States." Crazy Eileen then led the crowd in a rowdy rendition of the Pledge of Allegiance.

A video of the confrontation soon went viral and America was introduced to the "Birthers"—conspiracy theorists committed to undoing the 2008 presidential election by trying to prove that Barack Obama was not born in the United States.

To them, this president is not just anti-American but constitutionally ineligible for office. It's the ultimate fright-wing paranoid fantasy—we have a Muslim illegal alien in the White House.

It's all part of a carefully constructed plot: "The Muslims have said they plan on destroying the U.S. from the inside out. What better way to start than at the highest level, through the President of the United States, one of their own!"[2] Or so said an e-mail chain during the 2008 campaign. At the same time, Internet rumors were making the case that Obama was born not in the United States but in Kenya, his Muslim father's home country. The ideas got linked: a poll in Tennessee found that one-third of respondents thought that Obama was either "definitely" or "probably" a Muslim or born outside the United States.[3]

But these Manchurian candidate myths seemed too ridiculous to mention in mainstream media until the Birther town hall video clip revolt crystallized a subterranean effort to raise the issue, reaching talk radio, cable news, the armed services, and even the halls of Congress.

The rumor has its roots in the original Obama Haters, the group called Party Unity My Ass, or PUMA. It was a splinter group of hard-core Hillary Clinton supporters who did not want to give up the ghost after the bitter fifty-state Bataan Death March to the Democratic nomination.

In the early summer of 2008, message boards on sites like PUMAParty.com began indulging in the ultimate reversal-of-fortune fantasy—that the party nomination could be overturned on constitutional grounds. "Obama May Be Illegal To Be Elected President!" read one e-mail: "This came from a USNA [US Naval Academy] alumnus. It'll be interesting to see how the media handle this. . . . WRITE TO YOUR LOCAL newspaper editors etc. Keep this out there everyday possible. Also write to the DNC [Democratic National Committee] too!"[4]

In June, the Obama campaign released his birth certificate on its website as part of its "fight the smears" effort. Professionals at Factcheck.org and other organizations examined the document in person and declared it genuine: "Our conclusion: Obama was born in the U.S.A. just as he has always said."[5] But posters at the PUMA sites were unimpressed: "Nobody believes it's for real, except the Kool-Aid drinkers themselves."[6]

A Hillary supporter from Texas, Linda Starr, was particularly fired up by what she called "the daily misogynistic hate speech against Hillary" during the primaries. As a Democratic precinct captain in Medina County, Texas, she had volunteered for the Clinton campaign during the hotly contested June Lone Star State primary and was a Hillary delegate at the state convention. But Linda's real talent was as an amateur opposition researcher—she'd dug up information against Republican congressional leaders such as Dan Burton and Bob Livingston during the Clinton impeachment hearings of the late 1990s and was cited as a key source for CBS's discredited 2004 investigation into George W. Bush's National Guard records that led to

Dan Rather's replacement after twenty-four years as the evening news anchor.[7] After Hillary's concession, Linda Starr turned her attention to Barack Obama. "I determined that I was going to start digging up every bit of dirt that I could find on him," she told me. "Hopefully that I would find something against him that would convince the Democratic Party to dump him and make Hillary the nominee."[8]

In the first week of August, as the Democrats were getting ready for their convention in Denver, Philadelphia attorney Philip Berg got a call from Linda offering a challenge. "She called me up and said, 'Have you heard about Obama not being national born?' I said, 'Yes.' She said, 'Well, now it's for real, and you're the only attorney in the country with brass balls enough to sue Obama.'"[9]

Berg is a Democrat and he'd also been a Hillary supporter. But he was best known as a former deputy attorney general of Pennsylvania and a serial unsuccessful campaigner for state-wide office with a reputation as an enthusiastic litigant. In 2004, he filed a 9/11 Truther lawsuit against President Bush, alleging that the government allowed 9/11 to happen and that the World Trade Center was destroyed from within.[10] Now he had a new conspiracy to push.

On August 21, Berg filed the first Birther lawsuit, asking for an injunction to stop the convention from going forward, al-leging that Obama was born in Kenya, not Hawaii. He faxed notices to the Democratic National Committee (DNC) and Obama campaign headquarters. He launched the website *Obamacrimes .com* the next day, with Linda's assistance. The lawsuit went nowhere. Berg told me: "[DNC chair] Howard Dean at that point should have called Obama and said 'What's the story, are you natural born or not?' . . . Obviously there was collusion there and I think when it's all said and done they should all be tried and put in jail." The media ignored it as well. "I wish I could sue them," says Berg, of the media. "If the American public knew what was going on here Obama would be out of office or we never would have had him in office."

In July 2009, soon after Crazy Eileen's shout-down of Mike Castle went viral, a US Army major, Stefan Frederick Cook, brought the Birther story its first national headlines when he refused deployment to Afghanistan on the grounds that President Barack Obama might not be a natural-born citizen and therefore would be constitutionally ineligible to give orders as commander in chief. Major Cook, a distinguished combat veteran, appears to have been a willing pawn in the Birthers' efforts to bring attention to their cause. He had volunteered for Afghan deployment in May, with the intention of carrying out the political performance-art litigation.

The military shrugged and said since he volunteered to go to AfPak he was within his rights to change his mind. No lawsuit was needed. An e-mail or a phone call would have been fine. But they issued a statement, just to be clear: "This in no way validates any of the outlandish claims made by Major Cook," and a judge threw out the case. Unfazed, the Birthers celebrated it as a smoking-gun victory.

WorldNetDaily trumpeted the news as "Bombshell: Orders Revoked for Soldier Challenging Prez." Cook's lawyer, Orly Taitz, an Orange County, California, dentist with an online legal degree, subsequently announced there were 170 more soldiers willing to file similar protests against the president. The blonde middle-aged mother of three was on a mission.

Taitz first stumbled across the controversy while surfing the Internet. As a native of the former Soviet Republic of Moldova, she sniffed a Communist conspiracy. Or maybe it was Nazi.

"I realized that Obama was another Stalin," she said. "It's a cross between Stalinist USSR and Nazi Germany."[11] On October 25, 2008, two weeks before the election, she e-mailed the California secretary of state's office, asking about the "eligibility of Barack Hussein Obama." When filling out the slot inquiring how she became aware of this problem, Taitz typed "native intelligence."

She may be crazy, but she's not stupid. Taitz became the face of the Birther lawsuits in the media, making twenty-nine trips across the United States in 2009, filing more lawsuits and doing more than one hundred interviews. *WorldNetDaily* profiled her generously: "Meet Fierce Blonde Behind Obama Eligibility Lawsuits."[12] And she's got the snappy name-calling sound bite down: "Obama should be in the Big House, not the White House!"[13]

On her blog, the tone gets a wee bit more unhinged, repeatedly calling the Obama administration the "Gestapo-SS establishment," extending the metaphor with a call for investigation and execution: "They all should and would be tried in Nurenberg [*sic*] style trials for harassing, intimidating, blackmailing and terrorizing fellow citizens, for defrauding the whole country."[14]

Fox News's Sean Hannity picked up the torch, and so did another mainstream heavyweight, Lou Dobbs, who had her on his radio show and segued into a CNN segment on the Cook case by saying, "New questions are being raised about Obama's eligibility to serve as president."[15] Dobbs, whom Taitz refers to as a "supporter," subsequently resigned from the network, contemplated a political career, and then joined the cast of *Fox Business*.

With her fifteen minutes of fame ticking away, Taitz appeared on CNN alongside co-litigant Alan Keyes to debate the issue. I was tapped to take them on alongside my friend Errol Louis, a columnist for the *New York Daily News*. Taitz and Keyes were beaming in remotely via satellite, but I got to watch their pre-game rituals: Keyes had his eyes closed as if in prayer; Taitz was jumpy and pie-eyed.

Anchor Kitty Pilgrim went through a semi-exasperated three-and-a-half-minute dismantling of the Birther arguments, including the long-ago issuance of Obama's August 1961 certificate of live birth; its validation by Hawaii's Republican governor, Linda Lingle; and two birth announcements published in Honolulu papers.

Asked what more he needed to be convinced, Keyes's response was an instant classic in the clueless overconfidence of conspiracy theorists: "Some evidence."

My on-air summation was also four syllables: "You guys are nuts."

The eleven Republican members of Congress who co-sponsored the so-called Birther bill apparently disagree. In response to the hysteria, H.R. 1503 would require presidential campaigns to provide "a copy of the candidate's birth certificate." When asked whether Obama "is a U.S. citizen," bill co-sponsor Randy Neugebauer (R–TX) gave a Texas two-step reply: "I don't know. I've never seen him produce documents that would say one way or another."[16]

But in a refreshing break from the "no enemies on the right" straitjacket, some conservatives knew that things were getting indefensibly overheated. Talk-radio show host Michael Medved memorably denounced the Birthers as "crazy, nutburger, demagogue, money-hungry, exploitative, irresponsible, filthy conservative imposters" who are "the worst enemy of the conservative movement" and "make us look sick, troubled and not suitable for civilized company."[17]

With the Birther controversy ingrained in the Wingnut history of the first year of Obama, I flew to California to reacquaint myself with Birther queen Orly Taitz, this time face-to-face.

Nestled in the hills of Rancho Santa Margarita, Taitz's joint law and dentist offices stand in a Spanish Mission–style office park. In their cluttered corridors, she balances the demands of a small private practice with an effort to prove that the president of the United States is constitutionally ineligible for office.

Taitz greets me at the door wearing a bright purple-and-orange dress. She seems engaging and friendly to her employees, concerned about her clients, and highly organized. Details of the full conspiracy are copied and filed inside black binders with colored tabs.

On the walls of her office are pictures of her three sons wearing their Tae Kwon Do uniforms from years past. When asked to describe herself, she says, "I am a proud mother of three sons and a wife and a professional woman who's been working all her life." In any other context, she would be a classic American immigrant success story, but over the span of one year she has placed herself at the forefront of a massive conspiracy theory.

"I'm just concerned that our constitutional freedoms are being taken away," she explains. She's established the Defense of Freedom foundation and blogs on her website.[18] She talks about the hundreds of e-mails she gets from supporters who want to help with her work, and the death threats that are coming in daily. To show her depth of secret support, she says Sarah Palin has friended her on Facebook, along with Newt Gingrich, RNC chairman Michael Steele, House Minority Whip Eric Cantor, and Israeli prime minister Benjamin Netanyahu. Then it's time to get down to business.

The conspiracy goes deep, and so does the paperwork. She hands me a fifty-page packet that she says is a copy of what she has sent to Attorney General Eric Holder. It is a hodgepodge of letters and legal documents, website home pages, and data lists.

Taitz shows me Obama's official certificate of live birth and contrasts it with the long-form certificate. She presents an oft-touted piece of Hawaiian legislation, Act 182, which makes it possible for children born out of state to receive birth certificates, but the bill itself indicates that it didn't take effect until 1983.

She's got two copies of Obama's alleged Kenyan birth certificate, which she says were sent to her anonymously. "So I had both the registrar copy and a hospital copy from Kenya but yet there wasn't one proper birth certificate from the United States."

Then she hands over the mother lode, her newest project: "I have put together a database showing he used thirty-nine different Social Security numbers . . . This is a felony. For those kind of criminal activities, for those kind of felonies, people spend years and years in prison. And when you multiply this by thirty-nine, we're talking a life sentence." She shows me a new affidavit from an Ohio private investigator swearing that Barack Obama's Social Security number—which she gives me digit for digit—was issued in the state of Connecticut in the mid-1970s but actually belonged to a man born in 1890.

"This is mind-boggling that we have the president and commander in chief of all US military who is using a stolen Social Security number. I did investigation to find out where he got it and what I found out was that his grandmother, Madeline, volunteered in Oahu Circuit Court in Probate Department. Now, Probate Department is the department where you get the Social Security numbers." That's right—according to Orly, Obama's grandma stole him a Social Security number back in the 1970s.

When you've got that many different ways to say that someone is an evil psychotic fraud, it's possible there is some projection going on.

And then there's her legal record to date—a perfect .000 batting average. Phil Berg had warned me about Taitz in paranoid hall-of-mirror terms, saying, "I really think she's a plant. I think she's been put there to disrupt everything to make us look like fools." But could an otherwise intelligent, sincere, and accomplished woman be so single-issue insane, like the political equivalent of a functioning alcoholic?

When I got to the Long Beach airport, I began paging through the full fifty-page packet full of documents and screen shots that she gave me. I started to read her open letter to Attorney General Holder, which was cc'd to fifty state governors and the entire US Senate. It demanded "investigation and immediate action" into fourteen counts of "criminal activity/crimes," among them cyberspace crimes, impersonation of a military officer, libel, defamation of character, intimidation, harassment, interference with judicial proceedings, breaking into the computer system of the Supreme Court, voter fraud, and forgery.

It is a long, rambling letter, and life is short, but early on she sets out her demands and identifies the consequences: "Verify the above facts brought forward by me and demand Obama/Soetoro's immediate resignation or removal from office due to fraud and Constitutional inability. National security and national survival depends on your expedient actions as Obama/Soetoro releases violent terrorists from Gitmo, allocates $900 million to

Gaza ruled by radical Hamas terrorists, signs an executive order that would provide expedient U.S. citizenship and bring hundreds of thousands of Hamas terrorists to this country."

Then she details an alleged pattern of harassment: "When around the same time one gets her case erased from the docket of the Supreme Court and Wikipedia, a tire blows out on her in a car, and a link with a sign in Arabic about somebody's hanging appears, one begins to feel threatened. I believe all the occurrences had to do with my investigation, not only in the area of Obama/Soetoro's ineligibility for the presidency, but also in the financial dealings of Barack and Michelle Obama."

And finally, she offers a bargain to the feds: "As a private citizen I cannot complete this investigation. However, you, as Attorney General, together with the FBI, IRS, Secret Service and local law enforcement can and have an obligation to complete it. I would be willing to complete this investigation if you're willing to grant me a status of relater–special prosecutor. Sincerely, Dr. Orly Taitz, Esquire."

As I finished, I was reminded of US District Court judge Clay D. Land's comments to Taitz when he dismissed one of her Birther complaints: "Unlike in *Alice in Wonderland,* simply saying something is so does not make it so."[19]

But by then the Birther case had been heard about by millions of Americans—and a July 2009 poll found that 58 percent of Republicans either thought Barack Obama wasn't born in the United States or weren't sure.[20]

The 9/11 Truthers

Somewhere in the world of Wingnut conspiracy theories, left and right overlap. And when you can rally around both Texas libertarian Ron Paul and Georgia leftist Cynthia McKinney as presidential nominees, you've hit a very special place of transpartisan paranoia.

Welcome to the world of the 9/11 Truthers.

The attacks of September 11, 2001, were the most digitally documented loss of human life in history, exploding on our television screens in real time. And yet, an Internet-driven conspiracy theory soon set in—fueled by Bush Derangement Syndrome—arguing that the US government, and not al Qaeda, was behind the attack. To quote from one online screed, "The actual forces behind the conception, planning, and execution of this seminal event came not from bearded Islamic extremists living in a cave in Afghanistan, but from within high-level rogue elements of our own government."

This could be dismissed as somewhere between offensive and absurd, if it weren't for the fact that in the years since the attacks, the conspiracy theory's credibility has been on the rise.

Five years after the attack, a Scripps poll found that 36 percent of Americans believed the federal government "either assisted in the 9/11 attacks or took no action" because the administration "wanted to go to war in the Middle East." Sixteen percent thought the World Trade Center might have collapsed because of secret explosives, while 12 percent said a US cruise missile—and not a hijacked airplane—hit the Pentagon.[21]

In the Bush era, liberal congressmen and celebrities were eager to get on the bandwagon.

Cynthia McKinney, a congresswoman at the time, reflexively reached for Watergate rhetoric, asking, "What did this administration know and when did it know it, about the events of September 11?"[22] Congressman Dennis Kucinich rallied the crowd at a Code Pink protest by saying, "We have a plan, Mr.

President, and our plan is to tell the truth about 9/11."[23] Michael Moore told a group of 9/11 Truthers he had questions about the plane that hit the Pentagon. "Why don't they want us to see that plane coming into the building? . . . I don't think the official investigations have told us the complete truth. They haven't even told us half the truth."[24] Celebrity actress and talk-show host Rosie O'Donnell weighed in by saying, "It is impossible for a building to fall the way it fell without explosives being involved." And signatories of the 9/11 Truth petition included Ralph Nader, Janeane Garofalo, Howard Zinn, Edward Asner, and President Obama's onetime Green Jobs czar Van Jones.

Sadly and stupidly, they were not alone. Type "9/11 Conspiracy" into Google and you'll get millions of page matches—8,730,000 as of November 29, 2009. The website *911truth.org* includes a subsection, Lawyers for 9/11 Truth, which presents a score of endorsements by "legal scholars, judges and attorneys" for the statement "We are demanding an end to the 9/11 cover-up, and a full investigation by unbiased people with subpoena power . . . and the courage to demand that the Constitution and rule of law are followed, and all guilty persons held accountable for their actions."

Purple bumper stickers reading "9/11 was an Inside Job" became as annoyingly common in the 2000s as "Andre the Giant Has a Posse" stickers were in the 1990s. And in the summer of 2008, New Yorkers were stopped on street corners by petitioners seeking signatures for the creation of "a new, independent investigation of the attacks" that will "follow the evidence wherever it might lead."

Like many New Yorkers, I lived through the attacks and their aftermath. I saw the first plane scream past my window, and I was covered in ash after the collapse. Afterward, I spent three

months writing eulogies for the fallen firefighters and police officers as a speechwriter for Mayor Rudy Giuliani. So when I see
people in Lower Manhattan indulging the Blame America First
impulse, I lose my sense of humor real quick.

In search of some perspective, I called Professor Patrick J.
Leman, a conspiracy theory specialist at the University of London, to ask a decidedly unacademic question: What the hell is
going on?

"There is an underlying psychological phenomenon called
'major-event/major-cause' thinking," explained Dr. Leman. "If
there's a big event, we like to find a similarly big cause to explain what happened. It provides us with a sense that the world
is a relatively predictable place. Because the alternative—imag-
ining that something big, like the death of a president, can be
caused by something minor like a lone gunman—presents us
with a view of the world that's unpredictable and scary and dif-
ficult to control."

The greatest check against government conspiracy is the up-
close chaos of any human organization. People are simply too
disorganized and indiscreet to pull off a secret worldwide plot.
But it turns out that the Orwellian-named 9/11 Truthers need a
Big Brother for their story to hold.

"Conspiracy theorists need a competent and malevolent con-
spirator," said Dr. Leman. "And if you have a lot of Keystone
Kops messing around, that's not going to work very well. So
there is a kind of contradiction here: 'They're up to no good, but
they're very good at it.'"

This requires that 9/11 Truthers effectively reverse-engineer
a well-documented al Qaeda plot to bring down the Twin Towers. They would rather believe that their own government is

all-powerful and evil than imperfect and well-intentioned. Faced with a real conspiracy, they must invent their own.

Investigating the 9/11 conspiracy websites is a thankless business—as the old saying goes, "When you argue with a fool, you've got two fools."

They drape their paranoia in the American flag and earnest prose. The catalogue of accusations is dizzying—a Top Forty list is available on 911truth.org—but the usual suspects include explosives to bring down the Twin Towers, missiles to hit the Pentagon, Dick Cheney complicit, the military and the Federal Aviation Administration gone MIA. The documentary *Loose Change*—an X-Files–tempoed account of the conspiracy by upstate New York twenty-somethings—has been viewed on YouTube more than 3 million times.

Alternately, you can just take Osama bin Laden's word for it. He repeatedly took credit for the attacks, including on a videotape where he recounts the planning process and his wish for maximum damage: "We calculated in advance the number of casualties from the enemy, who would be killed based on the position of the tower. We calculated that the floors that would be hit would be three or four floors. I was the most optimistic of them all . . . Due to my experience in this field, I was thinking that the fire from the gas in the plane would melt the iron structure of the building and collapse the area where the plane hit and all the floors above it only. This is all that we hoped for."[25]

But this tape is dismissed by the Truthers: "The man shown in the video, though bearded, Arabic, and of darkish complexion, is much heavier than bin Laden. The man in the video is seen writing something down with his right hand. Bin Laden is well-known to be left-handed." Similarly dismissed are the voluminous 9/11 Commission Report and the thorough special report by *Popular Mechanics,* "Debunking the 9/11 Myths." As Dr. Leman says, "A conspiracy theorist is always going to see a conspiracy—whatever evidence you give to them."

The conspiracy theories continued to be pumped up even after the Bush administration ended, promoted by fright-wing anti-government radio hosts like Alex Jones and, disturbingly, mainstream celebrity dupes like Charlie Sheen, who demanded and was denied a request to brief President Obama on the matter.[26]

The dogged search for truth is admirable and essential to a free society. But when that concept becomes twisted by a moral relativism that masquerades as open inquiry, the idea of truth starts to lose its meaning. Ignoring the obvious does not lead to insight. And by entertaining conspiracy theories after being attacked, we run the risk of amusing ourselves to death.

Just because an evil ideology expresses its murderous intentions with cartoonish clarity doesn't mean that its adherents are not deadly serious. We have the body count to prove otherwise. So let's call the 9/11 Truthers what they are—al Qaeda apologists.

10

THE HATRIOTS: ARMED AND DANGEROUS

The plot to assassinate the president was called Operation Patriot. Marine lance corporal Kody Brittingham plotted from his barracks at Camp Lejeune, North Carolina. With maps of the Capitol Building and a dossier on Barack Obama, he penned a letter explaining his reasons for wanting to join the ranks of John Wilkes Booth and Lee Harvey Oswald:

> I Kody Brittingham, write this as a letter of intent. I am in full mental health and clear judgment, having consciously made a decision, and in turn do so choose to carry out the actions entailed. I have sworn to defend my country, my constitution, and the values and virtues of the aforementioned. My vow was to protect against all enemies, both foreign and domestic. I have found, through much research, evidence to support my current state of mind. Having found said domestic enemy, it is my duty and honor to carry out by all means necessary to protect my nation and her people from this threat.[1]

Kody Brittingham was arrested before his plot had a chance to be enacted. President Obama spoke at Camp Lejeune in February 2009 without incident, announcing his plan to draw down US forces from Iraq. But Brittingham's clear, cold-blooded rationalization for assassination—a patriot defending the Constitution against the president by any means necessary—reflected the rhetoric of the emerging Hatriot movement.

The Hatriots are self-styled patriots, armed and ready for a new American Revolution. They talk of martial law, a seizure of guns, and imposition of global government, complete with forced internment camps and mass executions. When love of country is mixed with fear of the government and hate for the president, that's when you become a Hatriot.

"You need to be alert and aware of how close we are to having our constitutional republic destroyed!"

So thundered Stewart Rhodes to a wave of applause on Lexington Green in Massachusetts, on April 19, 2009. The crowd assembled included military veterans and reservists, cops and firefighters, and no small number of Revolutionary War re-enactors. It was the first public meeting of the Oath Keepers. The location and date of the gathering had been chosen carefully. It was the anniversary of the first battle of the American Revolution on that very spot. The Oath Keeper website featured a quote from George Washington to set the tone: "The time is now near at hand which must probably determine, whether Americans are to be, Freemen, or Slaves; whether they are to have any property they can call their own." The Oath Keepers then added their own dark warning: "Such a time is near at hand again."[2]

But April 19 has deeper significance for members of the militia movement and their inheritors throughout the United States. It is the date that federal officers attacked the Branch Davidian compound in Waco, Texas. And it's the day that Timothy McVeigh blew up the Murrah Federal Building in Oklahoma City, killing 168 people and injuring five hundred more. McVeigh was wearing a T-shirt that day with a favorite Hatriot message handed down from Thomas Jefferson: "The Tree of Liberty must be refreshed from time to time with the blood of patriots and tyrants."

Within nine months of their first meeting, Oath Keeper dues-paying membership rose to 3,000—including active-duty military, current and retired police officers and sheriffs—and the organization claims that 15,000 people have signed up to participate on their online forum. The Oath Keepers have established themselves as a nonprofit organization, complete with a board of directors. Describing themselves as "The Guardians of the Republic," they distribute business cards with orders they will not obey—it's a step-by-step tour through the Hatriot vision of America. Among them:

- We will NOT obey any order to disarm the American people.
- We will NOT obey orders to invade and subjugate any state that asserts its sovereignty and declares the national government to be in violation of the compact by which that state entered the Union.
- We will NOT obey any order to blockade American cities, thus turning them into giant concentration camps.
- We will NOT obey any order to force American citizens into any form of detention camps under any pretext.
- We will NOT obey orders to assist or support the use of any foreign troops on U.S. soil against the American people to "keep the peace" or to "maintain control" during any emergency, or under any other pretext. We will consider such use of foreign troops against our people to be an invasion and an act of war.

It's a world of government-sponsored concentration camps, forced disarmament, and international invasion—scary stuff. But where many see fearmongering, the Oath Keepers see themselves as freedom's last defender. Stewart Rhodes is an engaging and intelligent, if angry, guy—he's taken the stage on MSNBC's *Hardball* and won a constitutional prize at Yale Law. He is careful to distance his group from outright advocates of antigovernment violence, writing that "those of you who are in militia have a vital mission which we support and agree with fully. But it is a different mission. We don't mind at all if people belong to both, but keep the two activities separate." He also knows the way to disarm critics: to those who see the rise of the Oath Keepers as a response to Obama, he is quick to condemn George W. Bush—he was just too busy during the Bush years to mobilize his ideas into action. And to those who question the repeated concentration-camp riff, he pulls the ultimate liberal guilt trip: If internment camps happened to Japanese Americans during World War II in this country, why should we think it couldn't happen today? It raises the image of Stewart Rhodes, liberal action hero.

But not all Oath Keepers are as smooth as Stewart Rhodes. In a video posted on the Oath Keepers' site, a man who describes himself as a former army paratrooper in Afghanistan and Iraq calls President Obama "an enemy of the state," adding, "I would rather die than be a slave to my government." Oath Keeper and former Arizona sheriff Richard Mack has said, "The greatest threat we face today is not terrorists; it is our federal government."[3] Extremism is no vice in Hatriot circles: you can even buy T-shirts at the Oath Keeper site that read, "I'm a Right Wing Extremist and Damn Proud of It!"

The Hatriot movement has morphed from the militia movements of the mid-1990s. The Southern Poverty Law Center tracks their growth and found that militia groups grew from forty-two in 2008 to 321 in 2012, while the number of associated Patriot groups exploded more than 800 percent over President Obama's first term, from 149 to 1,360.[4]

"One big difference from the militia movement of the 1990s," the SPLC points out, "is that the face of the federal government—the enemy that almost all parts of the extreme right see as the primary threat to freedom—is now black."[5]

The Three Percenters are another new breed of Hatriot, and like the Oath Keepers, they focus on armed resistance and American Revolutionary War imagery. They take their name from the questionable statistic that only 3 percent of the American colonists actively fought for independence. Therefore, the Three Percenters are not only an elite group but also a direct link to the Founding Fathers, making their extremist alienation from mainstream America a badge of honor and secret knowledge. They describe themselves as "promoting the ideals of liberty, freedom and a constitutional government restrained by law."[6] But beneath the benign bumper sticker, members of the loosely affiliated group also profess to "embrace the American Resistance Movement philosophy"—a survivalist militia-incubating network that teaches its followers how to train for the coming fight against tyranny. Their online forums offer a glimpse into a lunatic fringe that is itching to get the fight on: "This government has failed," writes one registered user known as JV67. "At what point do we follow the example of the Founding Fathers and take up arms against these tyrants?"[7]

Three Percenter founder Mike Vanderboegh of Pinson, Alabama, is a self-described "former leftist" and Students for a Democratic Society (SDS) member who had a political epiphany reading Nobel economist Friedrich von Hayek's *The Road to Serfdom* in the mid-1970s. He became a Second Amendment activist and was involved in the militia movement during the 1990s. The father of three now reluctantly believes the escalation is all but inevitable. As he chronicles the first year of the

Obama administration, particularly the attempts to pass health-care legislation, he is bracing for revolution: "You should understand that we are rapidly coming to a point in this country when half of the people are going to become convinced of the illegitimacy of this administration and its designs upon our liberty. Need I remind you that this side is the one with most of the firearms?"[8]

Now Vanderboegh is warning his supporters to be prepared for "The Big Die Off": "When a computer crashes, you simply discard it and obtain another. When political systems, nations or civilizations fail, they collapse in a welter of blood and carnage, usually ending in mountains of bodies, slavery and a long dark night of tyranny. This is referred to by people today who recognize the existential danger by the short-hand acronym of 'TBDO'—'The Big Die Off.' This is not a video game. There are no do-overs. This is as real as it gets. Your system has experienced one or more fatal errors and must shut down at this time. Whether you survive The Big Die Off with anything left that is worth preserving is up to you."[9] As Vanderboegh's home page warns, "All politics in this country now is just dress rehearsal for civil war."

The Far Right Flirts with Secession

After speaking at an Austin Tea Party rally where the crowd repeatedly shouted, "Secede!," Republican governor Rick Perry was asked about renewed talk of Texas secession: "There's a lot of different scenarios," he said. "We've got a great union. There's absolutely no reason to dissolve it. But if Washington continues to thumb their nose at the American people, you know, who knows what might come out of that? Texas is a very unique place . . . when we came to the Union in 1845, one of the issues was that we would be able to leave if we decided to do that."[10]

The folks from Fox News were carrying the Texas Tea Party live and couldn't help but weigh in on Perry's comments.

Greta van Susteren: You know, from here, Glenn, listening to Governor Perry last night and watching your crowd and listening to the things that are coming out of Texas—I don't want to be too dramatic, but it almost seems like Texas is going to secede from the rest of the nation.

Glenn Beck: I mean, I don't know—can we get this back here? [Points to a banner] This is on the jib back over here. This says "Texas independence" . . . And the reason is—correct me if I'm wrong—these people love America. They just think Texas does America best![11]

Suddenly, somehow, the threat of secession is a sign of superpatriotism.

Just days before, Beck had been musing on-air about the same subject: "Does the individual have any rights anymore? Does the state have any rights anymore? And I know, because I've heard it, from all of the conservative historians and scholars, and everything else. But you can't convince me that the founding fathers wouldn't allow you to secede. The Constitution is not a suicide pact. And if a state says, I don't want to go there, because that's suicide, they have a right to back out. They have a right. People have a right to not commit economic suicide. . . . I sign into this Union, and I can never get out, no matter what the government does? I can never get out? Well that leaves only one other option. That doesn't seem like a good option."[12]

You'd think the Civil War had cleared up any questions about the efficacy of the "other option" Beck is talking about—600,000 Americans died. But conservative activists keep circling back to the concept, something that would presumably have offended them if it had been suggested one year before during the presidency of Texan George W. Bush.

Here's Academy Award–winning actor Jon Voight playing his newfound political role as a conservative pundit in an August interview with the *Washington Times:* "There's a real question at stake now. Is President Obama creating a civil war in our own country?"[13]

Focus on the Family's James Dobson offered a similar applause line at the Council for National Policy: "We are in greater danger right now I think than at any time since the Civil War . . . What this country desperately needs in coming elections are . . . men and women who cherish liberty and are willing to give their very lives for it and will oppose the evil of liberalism."[14]

The impulse occasionally gets dressed up as intellectualism, with a summer 2009 column in the *American Thinker* foreseeing "several regional republics" taking the place of the United States after a civil war inspired by the "overbearing, oppressive leviathan" created by Barack Obama.[15]

In anticipation of a civil war, the Oath Keepers include state sovereignty among their list of orders they will not obey: "In response to the obscene growth of federal power and to the absurdly totalitarian claimed powers of the Executive . . . We will NOT obey orders to invade and subjugate any state that asserts its sovereignty and declares the national government to be in violation of the compact by which that state entered the Union."

And a new Idaho militia was established in 2009 by army veteran James Ambrose, who explained his decision along the same lines: "I formed it to defend Idaho if it wants to secede. If Idaho decides it no longer wants to be part of the United States, we back that decision."[16]

So perhaps it wasn't a surprise that when the Senate Health Care Bill was presented in October 2009, the Wingnut netroots posters were quick to pick up the civil-war talk on sites such as Michelle Malkin's *HotAir*:

- "I don't want to suggest violence, but I think this nation is headed towards a civil war if things don't stop. The American people can't take a whole lot more of this."[17]
- "Maybe it is time the non Marxist states considered 'opting out' of the 'union.'"
- "I'd sooner die a patriot, than a slave. And even if every one of us is killed . . . I will have considered it an honor to be dead amongst other like minded heroes. Secession and civil war are alternatives to this, and by god if those are the only options left . . . so be it, the democrats forced our hand."[18]

Overheated echo-chamber chatter about secession and civil war might seem simply creepy if eight states hadn't passed secession resolutions since President Obama's election.

On April Fool's Day 2009, the conservative Georgia state senate passed a resolution by a vote of forty-three to one threatening to secede from the United States. It was a fool's resolution, but it was not a joke.

It was the work of the Tenthers—advocates of reaffirming the Tenth Amendment. Under the innocuous-sounding banner of "Affirming states' rights based on Jeffersonian principles,"[19] the resolution resuscitated Confederate and segregation-era arguments about nullification—the right of states to nullify the

Constitution and disband the United States if the president or federal government assumes powers not explicitly provided for.

The resolution had been co-sponsored by some of the most senior members of the state legislature, including the senate majority leader and president pro-tem. Among the areas enumerated in the Georgia resolution were "Further infringements on the right to keep and bear arms including prohibitions of type or quantity of arms or ammunition"—in other words, a reinstatement of the federal assault weapons ban could trigger Georgia to secede from the union. It also reserved to Georgia the right to judge "how far the licentiousness of speech and of the press may be abridged without lessening their useful freedom." The Taliban might have approved.

The strangeness of the Tenthers was put into context by *Atlanta Journal-Constitution* columnist Jay Bookman: "The resolution they sponsored is part of a radical right-wing national movement . . . And while the Georgia resolution is legally meaningless and was passed without debate or even knowledge of most senators, it has had an impact. It has been hailed by, among others, those fighting the conspiracy to create a single North American country, by the Confederate States Militia, by the John Birch Society, and the League of the South, which still pines for the cause of an 'independent South' and believes that 'Southern society is radically different from the society impressed upon it by an alien occupier.'"[20]

In its commitment to conservative secession, the League of the South not only echoes the usual Wingnut talking points about "national socialism: coming to a town near you" but offers books that connect Lincoln to Marx and Hitler, calling them a "Band of Brothers."[21] It's the same grouping President Obama is often placed alongside at the Tea Party rallies. Other strains of the neo-Confederate movement find themselves at home in the Hatriot movement, advancing the pseudo-constitutionalist idea of "Fourteenth Amendment Citizens"—aka African Americans—who, because their rights were granted by the US government after the Civil War, do not fall under natural law as described by the Declaration of Independence and are therefore lesser citizens than natural-born whites. It's an arcane example of the lengths to which white supremacists will go to defend bigotry as being sanctioned by the Bible or the Founding Fathers. But I digress.

The *Gone with the Wind* state wasn't the only one to sign up for the Tenth Amendment insanity. Similar resolutions passed in Oklahoma, North Dakota, South Dakota, Tennessee, Idaho, Louisiana, and Alaska—all states won by McCain-Palin in 2008. And Sarah Palin, whose husband was a member of the secessionist Alaska Independence Party for ten years, was one of the few governors to put her signature on the bill, before resigning in the summer of 2009.

Populist conservative appeals, anti-federal-government impulses, and threats of secession are nothing new, but they took on special resonance with a black president in a bad economy.

Hatriot History, Media, and Murder

America has seen militarized right-wing radical groups in the past, playing off the same fears: a tyrannical federal government, a surrender of sovereignty, and seizure of all guns.

Survivalist groups such as the Minutemen began developing a "patriotic resistance" movement patterned after colonial militias in the early 1960s, doing wilderness military drills, hoarding weapons and ammunition to prepare for a Soviet invasion in advance of what they said was a plan to "confiscate all private fire-arms by the end of 1965."[22] Its founder, Robert Bolivar DePugh, briefly tried to form a political party, dubbed the Patriot Party, but his plans for political influence were undone when he was arrested for a plot to blow up the Redmond, Washington, city hall and surrounding power plants, before robbing local banks.[23] Arrests of affiliated Minutemen groups found half-baked plans for a cyanide attack on the United Nations[24] and extensive weapons caches, including bombs, mortars, machine guns, and more than 1 million rounds of ammunition.[25]

Major General Edwin Walker became a hero to mid-twentieth-century right-wing militants when he resigned from the military after coming under criticism for distributing John Birch Society literature to troops. The decorated World War II and Korean War combat veteran then led protests against James Meredith's integration of the University of Mississippi. His rallying cry presaged Wingnut and Hatriot claims today, calling for "a national protest against the conspiracy from within. Rally to the cause of freedom in righteous indignation, violent vocal protest, and bitter silence under the flag of Mississippi at the use of Federal troops . . . This is the conspiracy of the crucifixion by anti-Christ conspirators of the Supreme Court in their denial of prayer and their betrayal of a nation."[26] Two people were killed and six federal marshals were shot in the fifteen hours of riots that followed. (Perhaps inevitably, Walker would later be arrested twice for public lewdness in Dallas park men's rooms.)[27]

The rash of right-wing extremist groups from the explicitly military to overheated anti-Communist compelled former president Eisenhower to speak out on the subject in the early 1960s: "I don't think the United States needs super-patriots," Ike gently scolded. "We need patriotism, honestly practiced by all of us, and we don't need these people [who pretend to be] more patriotic than you or anybody else."[28]

President Kennedy also weighed in, warning of "armed bands of civilian guerrillas that are more likely to supply local vigilantes than national vigilance."[29]

In the ensuing two decades, anti-government left-wing extremist groups dominated headlines, but there were outbursts of far-right violence such as the 1979 massacre in Greensboro, North Carolina, in which KKK and American Nazi Party members shot and killed five leftist protesters, including members of the Communist Workers Party.

The recession of the late 1970s and early 1980s saw the rise of the Posse Comitatus groups, which claimed that the highest government authority lay with county officials like sheriffs and that there had been a "subtle subversion" of the US Constitution that reflected a "criminal conspiracy to obstruct justice, disfranchise citizens and liquidate the Constitutional Republic of these United States."[30]

Posse Comitatus—whose name means "Power of the Country" in Latin—was one of the early radical anti-tax, antigovernment groups that began emerging in the 1970s. Its adherents did not accept any obligation to pay taxes, supported the notion that US dollars were "fiat" currency because they were not backed by gold or silver, and believed that international bankers were conspiring to impose a one-world government. They also gave rise to the sovereign citizen movement, which divides society into "Fourteenth Amendment Citizens"—African Americans who were given their constitutional rights by the government after the Civil War—and so-called sovereign citizens who were not obligated to follow "statutory law," such as paying taxes or carrying a driver's license. The members of the group purchased compounds, such as a 1,400-acre parcel in remote rural Wisconsin, which they considered sovereign territory with its own government.

In 1983, a leader of the Posse Comitatus movement, a World War II veteran named Gordon Kahl, shot and killed two federal marshals in North Dakota when they tried to arrest him on charges of violating probation in a tax-evasion case. He fled to rural Arkansas, where he murdered a sheriff's deputy and was himself killed in a firefight that ignited thousands of rounds of ammunition and explosives. Increased subsequent scrutiny of Posse Comitatus led to the convictions of five members of the group in 1987 on charges of threatening to murder IRS agents and a Nevada state judge.[31]

Loosely affiliated anti-government groups combined tax protests with armed survivalist drills, feeding members a diet of anti-communism and extremist "Christian Identity" theology. By the 1990s, America experienced the rise of the antigovernment patriot militia movement, paramilitary groups featuring a mix of white pride and Christian identity politics, fueled by anger at the Bill Clinton–led federal government after deaths at Ruby Ridge and the Branch Davidian compound in Waco, Texas. The destruction of the Murrah Federal Building in Oklahoma City was the culmination of years of escalation, and subsequent scrutiny reduced the militia's momentum.

But even in the wake of that attack, late-stage militia-related plots were discovered to blow up IRS offices in Austin, Texas; Reno, Nevada; and Portage, Michigan. In 1997, the IRS office in Colorado Springs was set on fire, causing $2.5 million in damages and sending James Cleaver, national director of an antigovernment Sons of Liberty group, to prison for thirty-three years.[32]

In total, the Southern Poverty Law Center has tracked seventy-five plots, attacks, and murders from far-right militia types in the years since Oklahoma City.[33] There were 845 acts of domestic terrorism from far-right and affiliated white-supremacist groups between 1954 and 2004, including shootings, bombings, and arson.[34] The historic record shows this is not a benign movement of patriots, but a dangerous strain of extremism with both a rap sheet and a body count.

Today's Hatriots are potentially even more dangerous because of their ability to recruit and radicalize more people via the Internet. Their job is made easier by Wingnut media heroes and even members of Congress who condone their conspiracy theories.

Alex Jones's syndicated radio show and his websites Prison Planet and Info Wars are a clearinghouse of conspiracy theories from 9/11 to the New World Order—and a home to unhinged Hatriots eager for "information" they can't get elsewhere. A self-described paleo-conservative and "aggressive constitutionalist," Jones is so far right he's left, unsteadily establishing himself at the vanguard of fright-wing politics.

"The answer to 1984 is 1776!" is a typical battle cry that endears Jones to the Hatriots. During the presidency of George W. Bush, Jones eagerly advanced the idea that the Bush administration and bankers were behind the destruction of the World Trade Center (with companion DVDs for sale). Now that Obama is in office, a whole new cottage industry of hate has opened up: he's selling semi-slick productions with such titles as *The Fall of the Republic* and *The Obama Deception*, which are passed on like Grateful Dead bootlegs among the Hatriot underground. The pitch is always apocalypse, telling viewers, "The last vestiges of our free republic are being swept away . . . the destiny of humanity is in our hands." The common ground is opposition to the federal storm troopers Jones sees as trying to impose one-world government on the few remaining patriots left. When Pittsburgh police engaged in modest riot control measures at a 2009 G-20 Summit, Jones was ready to climb the ramparts, referring to the police as "complete enemies of America. . . . Our military's been taken over. . . . This is the end of our country . . . They'd love to kill 10,000 Americans . . . The republic is falling right now."[35]

Given his full-throated embrace of the crazy (always presented as a search for the truth), what's really troubling is that members of Congress go on Jones's radio show. Ron Paul is a frequent guest. Texas Republican Louie Gohmert chose the venue to say: "This socialist health care . . . is going to absolutely kill senior citizens. They'll put them on lists and force them to die early."[36] Florida Democrat Alan Grayson used the opportunity to call a female Federal Reserve aide a "K-Street whore." Going on Jones's radio show isn't just a serious lapse of judgment, it seems to inspire serious lapses in judgment as well.

There is a trickle-down effect to hardworking people who identify with the message of anger and anxiety. The Oath Keeper–affiliated Nevada deli owner Billy Glassberg describes Alex Jones as his "hero": "He stands for the Constitution, for America and sovereignty. Regardless of whether you want to know something or not, you've got to investigate the truth. There's no more right and there's no more left. It's all about Americans and Globalists. That's it. And it was Globalists behind 9/11."[37]

His diner, Brooklyn Billy's, stands less than a mile from the Las Vegas Strip in sight of the Mandalay Bay Casino in the corner of an office park. Next to the sign in the window that boasts "the best pastrami west of New York," another reads, "free speech zone." On the walls are posters of Robert De Niro as Travis Bickle in *Taxi Driver* and Al Pacino in *Scarface,* bearing the slogan "Who I trust? I trust me." Framed on the opposite wall is a yellowing *New York Daily News* cover dated November 23, 1963. The headline screams "President Shot Dead." On the glass of the frame, Billy has written, "Killed by the N.W.O."—meaning the New World Order. Billy is friendly, unassuming. His mother works the register while he makes the sandwiches in back, listening to Alex Jones's radio show blaring out of the speakers.

Billy believes that "Obama should be tried for treason." But it's not personal. "He's a puppet in the New World Order. He picked up the ball where Bush left it. . . . As far as the Republican and Democratic Party, Parties, it's two sides of the same coin. They're all owned by the same bankers, whether it's the Rothschilds or the Morgans or the Rockefellers. . . . They put a black face on the New World Order because they know things are getting intense. They know people are starting to figure it out."

Like Alex Jones, Billy believes that 9/11 was an inside job. He says the planes hitting the towers were "remote controlled." What happened to the people on the planes, I ask. "What they do in black operations is incredible," Billy said. "I couldn't tell you what happened to the people on the planes." It wasn't bin Laden—"Al-Qaeda was formed by the CIA under the Carter Administration," he says.

Billy's bought into a topsy-turvy worldview where "the new definition for freedom is gonna be servitude." Obama's "job is to continue to destroy America for a world government. I mean it's so—it's so easy to understand. . . . It's sick. It's demented. But it's true."

But while Alex Jones is on the fright-wing fringe, Michael Savage reaches an audience of millions with his Hatriot-reinforcing predictions. "Martial law," he announced in 2009, "will be declared in this country over a pretext. I think the likelihood is very high that the gang that has taken over this country will declare . . . a pretext . . . the equivalent of the Reichstag fire [which helped the Nazis take over the German government] . . . to put in a form of martial law."[38]

Rush Limbaugh, along with other influential figures, adds fuel to the Hatriot fire with his hyperpartisan exhortations: "If we just sit idly by and let Obama get all this stuff done, we're cooked. Because this is not just standard, left-wing politics. This is radical, left-wing Marxist socialism—fascism, whatever you want to call it. This is designed to forever remake the United States and to destroy the prosperity-generating capitalist system and private sector."

When Glenn Beck declares, "There is a coup going on. There is a stealing of America . . . done through the guise of an election,"[39] he is reaffirming Hatriot fears. And when Beck announces that "the government under Bush and under Obama . . . [is] slowly but surely moving us away from our republic and into a system of fascism," he is singing straight from the Hatriot hymnal.

All this apocalyptic fearmongering has an impact on netroot "news" as well. In September 2009, the conservative magazine *Newsmax.com* (run by Clinton-era conspiracy entrepreneur and journalist Christopher Ruddy) had to pull down an online column from a regular contributor that imagined a "civilized" military coup "as a last resort to resolve the 'Obama problem.'" It was a rationale that echoed all the Hatriot themes and fears from the Oath Keepers on down:

Officers swear to "support and defend the Constitution of the United States against all enemies, foreign and domestic." Unlike enlisted personnel, they do not swear to obey the orders of the president of the United States.

They can see that Americans are increasingly alarmed that this nation, under President Barack Obama, may not even be recognizable as America by the 2012 election. . . .

Will the day come when patriotic general and flag officers sit down with the president, or with those who control him, and work out the national equivalent of a "family intervention," with some form of limited, shared responsibility?

Imagine a bloodless coup to restore and defend the Constitution through an interim administration that would do the serious business of governing and defending the nation. Skilled, military-trained, nation-builders would replace accountability-challenged, radical-left commissars.

Military intervention is what Obama's exponentially accelerating agenda for "fundamental change" toward a Marxist state is inviting upon America. A coup is not an ideal option, but Obama's radical ideal is not acceptable or reversible.[40]

In October, the idea of a coup was replaced by an online Hatriot call for revolution. A video anonymously posted on YouTube warned President Obama to "leave now and give us our country back." "If you stay," the message continued, "'We, The People' will systematically dismantle you, destroy you and reclaim what is rightfully ours . . . We are angry and we are ready to take back the rights of the people. We will fight and we will win . . . Dead line [sic] for your national response: October 15, 2009. Thank you to all patriots who support our cause . . . Be prepared for when the fateful day of the declaration of war is nationally announced."[41]

There is an understandable tendency to dismiss the danger of the lone Wingnut whose posts dot Hatriot websites. Extreme rhetoric and talk about armed resistance are not the same thing as action. But history shows us that it is most often the lone gunman who takes hate-filled teachings to their ultimate extension of outright violence.

Oklahoma City bomber Timothy McVeigh, for example, was not a dedicated member of any one militia group. He was a wannabe, an outcast who felt rejected even by the militiamen themselves. Likewise, the anarchist assassin of William McKinley, Leon Czolgosz, was not acting on the orders of an anarchist group. His fanaticism was so intense that he was thought to be a government agent and not welcomed into the anarchist circles of Chicago—not a generally discerning lot. The figure of the lone gunman was defined by the paranoid Marxist US marine who moved to Moscow and then re-defected, Lee Harvey Oswald. Even Eric Rudolph, the Atlanta Olympic bomber driven by anti-abortion and anti-gay beliefs, was influenced by indoctrination but acted alone. These figures were darkly inspired by the velocity of rhetoric around them.

The line between political fantasy and reality can blur for the unhinged. Hatriot fears can have deadly consequences, with a body count that piled up in the first six months of the Obama administration.

On April 4, three Pittsburgh police officers were shot and killed by Richard Andrew Poplawski, who was wearing body armor and wielding a semiautomatic weapon. Poplawski was a frequent visitor to Alex Jones's websites and posted on the white supremacist blog *Stormfront*, expressing fears that America was controlled by a cabal of Jews, that US soldiers would be used against American citizens and a ban on guns be imposed.[42]

On April 25, Joshua Cartwright, a Florida national guardsman, shot and killed two Florida sheriff's deputies as the officers attempted to arrest Cartwright on domestic violence charges. In the police report, Cartwright's wife said he "believed that the U.S. Government was conspiring against him. She said he had been severely disturbed that Barack Obama had been elected President."[43]

On May 31, Scott Roeder walked into a Wichita, Kansas, church and shot and killed Dr. George Tiller, who as part of his practice performed late-term abortions. Roeder was a member of the Posse Comitatus–descended Freemen movement in the 1990s, which asserted its members were "sovereign citizens" not subject to federal law but that African Americans were "14th amendment citizens." In 1996, Roeder had been pulled over and found to have a pound of gunpowder attached to a nine-volt battery and a switch, as well as blasting caps and bullets. The prosecutor in the case described him—accurately, as it turned out—as a "substantial threat to public safety."[44]

On June 10, James von Brunn, an eighty-eight-year-old neo-Nazi, walked into the United States Holocaust Memorial Museum in Washington, DC, killed a forty-year-old African American security guard, Officer Stephen Tyrone Johns, and wounded several others. Von Brunn had previously served six years in prison for attempting to kidnap members of the Federal Reserve at gunpoint. A note left in his car read, "You want my weapons, this is how you'll get them . . . the Holocaust is a lie . . . Obama was created by Jews. Obama does what his Jew owners tell him to. Jews captured America's money. Jews control the mass media."[45]

The common Hatriot strains behind all these killings are more chilling when you consider that President Obama received more death threats in the months after his election than any president on record[46]—and he received Secret Service protection earlier than any presidential candidate because of repeated threats to his life. Some of the plots have been serious, others half-baked, while chat-room comments about Obama's assassination are made almost offhand, such as an exchange on the draft-Palin site TeamSarah.com, where one poster named Heather described Election Day as the "most terrible" in history and then asked, "How long until obama is shot??????" To which a poster named Josie responded: "There are plenty of people that would like to see Obama end that way."[47]

So when you see militia groups recruiting at Tea Parties with signs that say "AK-47: Today's Pitchfork," or when a Washington, DC, man is found to have an M-16 rifle and two pistols that had been inscribed by a local gunsmith with the words "Christian Warrior" and "NoBama,"[48] it's worth being concerned.

There is a cost to the constant drumbeat that turns political opponents into personal enemies. All that's left is an unhinged soul who takes the hate as a call to heroism—the small but decisive step from being ready to die for a cause and being willing to kill for it. As one federal law enforcement agent, speaking anonymously of the Hatriots' rise, said: "All it's lacking is a spark. I think it's only a matter of time before you see threats and violence."[49]

11

THE KAMIKAZE CAUCUS

After the Wingnuts' long march from the political fringe to the corridors of congressional power, some responsible Republicans started to realize they had empowered radicals.

"Lemmings with Suicide Vests."[1] That's how California Republican congressman Devin Nunes described the hyperconservative kamikaze caucus as it prepared to rush off another fiscal cliff in the fall of 2013.

Our American experiment in self-government was starting to look like an exercise in self-sabotage. And partisan politics increasingly felt like a cult—ideological organizations pushing alternate sets of facts, demanding absolute loyalty, enforced by party purges. But this loopy parallel political universe has a real cost when it collides with the basic responsibilities of governing in the real world.

It had been a wild and unruly ride in the Obama era. Surfing the Tea Party wave in a low-turnout, high-intensity election, Republicans regained control of the House in 2010. But divided government—which previously produced everything from the national highway system to civil rights legislation to welfare reform—quickly degenerated into dysfunctional government. Bitter partisanship and the disproportionate influence of special interests made reasoning together seem all but impossible.

The 113th US Congress is the most polarized,[2] least productive,[3] and least popular in our history, with an approval rating in the single digits, prompting Senator John McCain to joke that support for Congress was down to "paid staffers and blood relatives."[4] Washington seems engaged in a war of attrition—not just between Republicans and Democrats, but an increasingly vicious civil war within the GOP between the Tea Party and what remains of the responsible center-right.

But it isn't just Washington politics that have been affected— there are economic costs for all Americans. In 2011, after months of ideologically fueled fights about whether the United States should raise the debt ceiling to pay its bills, the country's credit rating was downgraded for the first time in its history. Standard & Poor's explained the downgrade by saying, "The political brinkmanship of recent months highlights what we see as America's governance and policy making becoming less stable, less effective, and less predictable than what we previously believed."[5]

It was strange to see some avowed fiscal conservatives effectively cheer for default—as well as the rejection of a bipartisan grand bargain to rein in the deficit and the debt—but then it's always easier to be a demagogue on an issue than to deal with it. Perhaps most troubling was the way the self-inflicted near-disaster was quickly incorporated into the DC playbook. As the generally sober GOP Senate leader Mitch McConnell stated: "Some of our members may have thought the default issue was a hostage you might take a chance at shooting. Most of us didn't think that. What we did learn is this—it's a hostage that's worth ransoming."[6]

But slowly, a small cadre of Republicans started to realize that they had empowered a set of fifty or so radicals not interested in governing as much as grandstanding. For all the short-term political gains, they began to understand that extremes are ultimately their own side's worst enemy.

The first signs were evident even amid the conservative confetti of the 2010 elections. Despite riding a wave election where independent voters flipped from their sixteen-point support of President Obama in 2008 to a seventeen-point swing to the GOP in 2010, Republicans failed to take control of the Senate—the first time such a landslide momentum election had split the two houses since 1930. Wingnuts were the reason why.

In Delaware, Representative Mike Castle—a former governor and one of the most popular politicians in the state—lost a low-turnout closed GOP primary to a professional activist named Christine O'Donnell, who had previously lost two statewide races by landslides and never served in elected office. She was best known for being a colorful social-conservative activist who talked about her anti-masturbation policy and pre-evangelical flirtation with witchcraft on Bill Maher's late-night TV show. O'Donnell went from having five in-state donations to briefly becoming a Tea Party star and raising a boatload of national activist cash before losing to local Democrat Chris Coons, who almost certainly would have lost to Castle in November.

Senate majority leader Harry Reid faced a tough reelection in Nevada. But he drew a straight flush when Sharron Angle won the GOP Senate primary. Among her many howlers, Angle advised young girls who have been raped to take lemons and make lemonade, as a way of explaining her opposition to abortion even in cases of rape and incest.[7] She wanted to shut down the Department of Energy, the Department of Education, and the Environmental Protection Agency—and, of course, wanted the United States out of the United Nations. She opined about a fictitious imposition of Sharia law in Michigan and Tennessee. And even though her campaign was predicated on railing against big government, her family was largely supported by her husband's government pension. But the money quote of the campaign came when she warned, "I hope that's not where we are going, but if this Congress keeps going the way it is, people are really looking toward those Second Amendment remedies."[8] Unpopular in a home state with a 14 percent unemployment rate, Harry Reid still cruised to victory, even while his son Rory got crushed in the governor's race by a young Republican Hispanic pro-choice former judge named Brian Sandoval. In a sure sign that Angle was just too extreme, 20 percent of Sandoval's voters split their ticket to also vote for Harry Reid.

The broad outlines of this story were repeated in races from Colorado to Connecticut—even in Alaska, where Republican senator Lisa Murkowski won reelection as an independent write-in candidate after losing the Republican primary to her Sarah Palin–backed Tea Party challenger, Joe Miller.

Amid the resurgent Republican celebrations over massive gains in the House, it was easy to ignore inconvenient individual data points. But the allegedly libertarian-fueled fiscal-conservative crusade got lost in translation when it came to actual governing.

In the year after the Tea Party wave swept state legislatures, twenty-four states passed a record ninety-two restrictions[9] on abortion, including mandatory ultrasound legislation, waiting periods, insurance restrictions, and abortion bans after twenty weeks of pregnancy.

Taking on the gay civil rights movement also proved to be an unadvertised priority. When Republicans took control of the North Carolina state legislature, one of the first referendums they put on the ballot was a bid to ban same-sex marriage. It passed handily. In Iowa, three supreme court judges who ruled that same-sex marriage was constitutional found themselves removed from office. But even as Arizona Tea Party congressman Trent Franks declared that gay marriage "literally is a threat to our nation's survival" and RINO-hunting South Carolina senator Jim DeMint proclaimed his opposition to letting gays and lesbians teach in public schools,[10] a sea change in popular opinion on the subject of marriage equality made conservative culture warriors seem increasingly out of touch. Elections in three states have ratified the freedom to marry, and more than twenty federal judges declared various state bans on marriage equality unconstitutional by the outset of 2014.

Another hyperconservative hobbyhorse was hysteria around stopping the alleged threat of Islamic Sharia law being imposed in the United States. For reasons rooted in the US Constitution, this was always an essentially fear-fueled concern rather than one rooted in reality. Even sponsoring conservative legislators admitted they could not come up with a single example of a person trying to impose Sharia law in their states. But that didn't stop thirty-two state legislatures from trying to codify such assurances in state law between 2010 and 2012. The efforts proved successful in seven states: Arizona, Kansas, Louisiana, Oklahoma, South Dakota, Tennessee, and North Carolina.[11] Oklahoma's law was ultimately declared unconstitutional by a federal district court for infringing on Muslim citizens' rights.

But media attention was occupied by the fast-forward to the next presidential primary contest, which now unofficially kicks off just days after the midterm elections. When the GOP candidates started shuffling onto the national stage, the reality show primary began.

Mitt Romney was the tallest midget in the field. The handsome family man and former Massachusetts governor had tacked to the right in the 2008 primaries and seemed like the logical next choice to be the GOP nominee. But fate had made his signature accomplishment as governor—individual mandate-driven health-care reform—a massive liability at a time when the base viewed Obama's national version of the once-Republican-backed bill as a socialist government takeover of the economy that would end freedom as we know it and establish death panels. Romney's Mormon faith also made him suspect to some evangelicals. Voters in the base wanted an alternative to Mitt—and they were willing to look almost anywhere to find it.

The first beneficiary of the anybody-but-Mitt sweepstakes was Michele Bachmann. She pulled out a surprise victory at the closely watched (but electorally meaningless) summer Iowa Straw Poll, narrowly edging out libertarian grandfather-figure Ron Paul. Conservative populist passions briefly vaulted her to national prominence. But then she began to speak, warning that President Obama would be a "dictator" to raise the debt ceiling and accusing him of "economic Marxism." Bachmann's essential intemperance ensured that she was never going anywhere on the national stage or even in the Iowa caucuses. Ultimately, a series of campaign scandals led to multiple criminal complaints, a congressional ethics investigation, and her decision not to run for reelection in 2014.

Then came Rick Perry, a social conservative from central casting. George W. Bush's successor as governor of the Lone Star State, he had never lost an election and quickly vaulted to the front of the pack as a favorite of donors, activists, and evangelicals. He raised $15 million in a few weeks, before a series of debate stumbles made it clear that stringing sentences together on stage was a challenge for the tall Texan.

Next up was Herman Cain. The charismatic former CEO of Godfather's Pizza with no government experience briefly climbed to the top of the polls as he charmed conservatives with his oratorical skills and bumper-sticker economic plan known as "9-9-9." The Tea Party loved his outsider credentials and offered up his status as an African American conservative as proof that the movement was not motivated in any way by racial animus against President Obama. But a succession of sexual harassment claims hastened Cain's departure from the campaign, crowned with an exit speech that quoted the theme song from the film version of *Pokémon*.

Then it was Newt Gingrich's turn to mount the stage, and he was twice lucky: he had a brand name people remembered, and he had been absent from the spotlight just long enough that time had obscured his faults and exaggerated his glories. The thrice-married former speaker of the House and leader of the 1994 Republican Revolution was in many ways the most substantive candidate in this pygmy procession. Alternately described by onetime allies as "brilliant," "visionary," "arrogant," and "impulsive," Newt was the smartest man on stage and he knew it. But his high-minded historical references to Churchill and Reagan competed with rancid red-meat applause lines that accused President Obama of possessing a "Kenyan anti-colonial mindset" and running a "secular-socialist machine."[12]

There were still pleas from the faithful for Sarah Palin to get in and calls for New Jersey's first-term governor Chris Christie. Donald Trump even flirted with a presidential campaign solely built on calls for the president to release his birth certificate. About the only person in the race who couldn't seem to get a serious audition as the Romney alternative was the unfailingly civil Jon Huntsman. The former Utah governor and Obama's first-term China ambassador made the fatal mistake of seeming too centrist with tweets like this: "To be clear. I believe in evolution and trust scientists on global warming. Call me crazy."[13]

With the Iowa caucuses looming, Romney's unmatched organization was competing with a barrage of negative ads funded by Newt Gingrich's new sugar daddy, multi-billionaire Las Vegas casino magnate Sheldon Adelson, who pumped some $150 million into the 2012 election to defeat Barack Obama[14]—the equivalent of roughly $300 for an average American family.[15]

But the upset winner of the Iowa caucus was none of the above. Instead, former Pennsylvania senator Rick Santorum, a social conservative stalwart with a neocon foreign policy and a middle-class economic message, came out of obscurity to narrowly win the caucus by thirty-four votes. Santorum's rise was buoyed by the backing of a dedicated super PAC supported by the colorful conservative mega-donor Foster Friess. Playing the anti-elite card hard, Santorum threw out sound bites that resonated with the base but just as often alienated more moderate voters, as when he called President Obama "a snob" for saying "he wants everybody in America to go to college."[16] Likewise, he raised some eyebrows when he recounted how reading John F. Kennedy's legendary 1960 campaign speech on the separation of church and state made him "almost throw up." But Santorum ran a canny campaign, winning a hopscotch of eleven primaries and caucuses before dropping out and endorsing Romney.[17] And so in the end, Mitt withstood all the attacks and emerged as the GOP's 2012 nominee.

But even amid the campaign din, outbursts further down the food chain added to the appearance of a party where the fringe was blurring with the base.

In April, Tea Party congressman Allen West was asked by a constituent at a town hall, "What percentage of the American legislature do you think are card-carrying Marxists?" "That's a fair question," West replied. "I believe there's about 78 to 81 members of the Democratic Party that are members of the Communist Party."[18]

This echo of McCarthy barely registered on the outrage Richter scale. The numbers that Congressman West picked were apparently based on the members of the Congressional Progressive Caucus. The slippery-slope logic that lets a congressman conflate them with Communists is telling. As Richard Hofstadter wrote a few years after McCarthy, the fundamentalist "looks upon the world as an arena for conflict between absolute good and absolute evil, and accordingly it scorns compromises (who would compromise with Satan?) and can tolerate no ambiguities. It cannot find importance in trifling degrees of differences: liberals support measures that are for all practical purposes socialistic, and socialism is nothing more than a variant of Communism, which, as everyone knows, is atheism."[19]

In our time, slippery-slope logic is expressed along the same lines—right-wingers throw the liberal label on anyone who does not walk in lockstep with their beliefs—and then gallops down the line of association to blur the difference among liberals, socialists, and Communists, giving apocalyptic urgency to what are in many cases modest differences when seen with any sense of perspective.

There were also outbursts with more tangible electoral consequences. As in 2010, Tea Party Senate candidates had a tendency to self-destruct and deny their party gains as a result. In the Indiana primary, Tea-Vangelist state treasurer Richard

Mourdock beat Senator Richard Lugar, attacking Lugar's long-time record of bipartisanship by saying: "The time for collegiality is past . . . it's time for confrontation."

Mourdock blew himself up in the general election when he attempted to explain his opposition to abortion even in the case of rape by saying that when a woman becomes pregnant from a rape, "it is something that God intended." The ensuing backlash helped ensure that Democrat Joe Donnelly won the otherwise GOP-leaning seat.

Along the same tortured lines of logic, Missouri Senate candidate Todd Aiken declared that "if it's a legitimate rape, the female body has ways to try to shut that whole thing down"[20]—immediately provoking an outcry from left, right, and center—and lost his race in a state Mitt Romney won by almost ten points.

But the ugliest innovation of 2012 was in the unprecedented flood of money into the election—over $6 billion—much of it available thanks to the post–Citizens United era of super PACs, offering candidates plausible deniability for negative attacks. Undercutting the Supreme Court's promise of transparency, separate dark-money organizations abused tax-exempt 501(c)(4) status set aside for nonprofits dedicated to "social welfare" to hide donors' names.

According to the Center for Responsive Politics, spending from these dark-money groups passed $310 million—more than every other election cycle over the past twenty years combined. Just four groups—the Karl Rove–founded Crossroads GPS, the Koch brothers–backed Americans for Prosperity, American Future Fund, and the US Chamber of Commerce—accounted for more spending than all the other nondisclosing groups combined.

There was incessant ad talk about Obama's "War on Religion" and—from Democrats—about Republicans' "War on Women." For example, the Campaign for Family Values ran a super PAC–funded kitchen table ad in which the wife said, "Obama is trying to force gay marriage on this country—that's not the change I voted for."[21] Priorities USA, the biggest pro-Obama super PAC, released an ad that insinuated Romney's actions as head of Bain Capital destroyed a man's job, which then hastened his wife's death from cancer.[22]

The unrelenting negative air campaign was directly related to these stealth bombers. Some 88 percent of the television ads in the 2012 election were negative, and four-fifths of those negative ads were attacks on Democrats, according to the Wesleyan Media Project. After all, why would you spend dark money on positive ads? The whole point is plausible deniability.

About the only clear upside was for the political consultants who cashed in big-time in this partisan economy with hidden seven-figure salaries. The creation of a partisan super-PAC economy created a gold rush for consultants. Democratic consultant Hank Sheinkopf described it to me as "the greatest windfall that ever happened for political operatives in American history."

All of it conspired to create perhaps the most troubling aspect of our politics—the growing gap between narrative and facts. The result is not just division but a distortion that undermines our ability to recognize the same political reality.

"On the far right, [Obama] was denounced as an amalgam of Hitler, Chairman Mao and Huey Newton"—journalists John Heilemann and Mark Halperin memorably wrote in *Double Down*—"even as the left was disappointed to discover that he wasn't a combination of Ted Kennedy, Norman Thomas and John Lewis."[23]

But the problem went beyond perception and extended to an inability to agree on basic facts.

So a president who presided over a doubling of the stock market was attacked as being socialist and anti-business.

A health-care plan originally proposed by the conservative Heritage Foundation and championed by 1990s-era Republican senators as the "individual responsibility" alternative to HillaryCare was attacked as a socialist government takeover of one-sixth of the economy.

The president who ordered the killing of Osama bin Laden and the systematic targeting of al Qaeda leadership was called a secret Islamist-sympathizer.

And perhaps most significant, a legislative record that led nonpartisan political scientists at the respected *VoteView* blog to say, "President Obama is the most moderate Democratic president since the end of World War II," was instead credibly characterized as far-left liberal outlier.[24]

. This hyperpartisan reality-distortion field was powerful—so much so that on Election Night, the conservagencia had convinced themselves that victory was at hand, inspiring otherwise educated folks to ignore most polls in favor of feel-good tall tales about "Mitt-mentum" going into Election Day.

Among those caught up in the fever-swamp was Karl Rove, the architect of George W. Bush's two White House wins. On Election Night, he argued on air with Fox News's own pollsters about whether the election was over. Michael Barone, the otherwise respected editor of *The Almanac of American Politics*, predicted a Romney landslide, as did the dean of conservative columnists, George Will. And these were the adults at the table. Conspiracy entrepreneurs always peddle special knowledge, and days before the election, Dick Morris was still shilling on Fox, saying, "Romney will win this election by 5 to 10 points in the popular vote. And will carry more than 300 electoral votes."[25] A movement that prides itself on individualism ended up mired in groupthink.

In the end, Romney lost the popular vote resoundingly, securing just over two hundred electoral votes. President Obama won 332 electoral votes and every major swing state except North Carolina, on the way to becoming the first president since Dwight D. Eisenhower to surpass 51 percent of the vote in two elections. It was not close.

There were plenty of poll aggregators and statisticians (most notably FiveThirtyEight's Nate Silver) who correctly predicted the election outcome. So how did so many supposed professionals get it so spectacularly wrong?

One telling museum piece of the 2012 election was *Unskewed Polls*—the ironically named website where sample sizes of polls were adjusted to magically put Mitt in the lead during his dreary summer campaign. It was an extension of the insidious idea that mainstream media taints all stats and facts with their own unconscious liberal bias, so that only explicitly partisan news sources can be considered truly "fair and balanced."

Another factor is the intersection of groupthink and financial self-interest. The rise of partisan media has created incentives for some columnists, pundits, and pollsters to try to please ideological employers with pronouncements that resonate with the party faithful. After all, nothing gets clicks like confirmation bias.

This belief in their own convenient facts hurt Republicans as well as the republic. Blinded by the Tea Party landslide, the GOP confused the midterm electorate—narrow and ideologically intense—with the broader, more representative portion of the American public that votes in presidential contests. Trying

to apply the 2010 playbook to 2012 backfired badly. Occasionally unhinged anti-Obama intensity only alienated moderate
voters, who ended up supporting the president's reelection by a
sixteen-point margin.

The party's isolation was further amplified by the demographic fault lines now shaping our political landscape. Young
Americans, women under fifty, African Americans, and His-
panics overwhelmingly voted for Obama. White men and senior
citizens—now reaching into Reagan-era alumni—formed the
core of Mitt Romney's support.

The GOP's myopic misjudgment of the electorate read like an
inversion of the story about the Upper West Side liberal who,
after Richard Nixon's 1972 landslide, sniffed, "I only know one
person who voted for Nixon."[26] Closed socialization and a steady
diet of partisan media reinforced misguided gut instincts, and
feelings trumped facts.

A series of autopsies was unleashed in the wake of the GOP
defeat in 2012. The RNC declared its commitment to diversity and
reaching out to women and younger voters but pinned the problem on style as opposed to substance. Louisiana governor Bobby
Jindal declared that Republicans "must stop being the party of
stupid" but rejected any need to moderate their message, offering
a diagnosis of the problem but not a prescription to fix it.

Tea Party activists predictably declared that the problem was
that Mitt Romney was insufficiently conservative. But other Republicans believed that the GOP was becoming too extreme and
Congress fundamentally broken as a result. Maine's Republican
senator Olympia Snowe threw in the towel on her three-term
career, citing an "atmosphere of polarization and 'my way or the
highway' ideologies," and was replaced in the Senate by independent candidate Angus King.

THE KAMIKAZE CAUCUS** 255

A respected three-decade GOP congressional staffer named Mike Lofgren was less temperate in his description of the problem in a parting confessional essay on his way out the doors of the Capitol: "The Republican Party is becoming less and less like a traditional political party in a representative democracy and becoming more like an apocalyptic cult, or one of the intensely ideological authoritarian parties of 20th century Europe." Lofgren also pulled the curtain back on the cynical underlying strategy. "A couple of years ago, a Republican committee staff director told me candidly (and proudly) what the method was to all this obstruction and disruption. Should Republicans succeed in obstructing the Senate from doing its job, it would further lower Congress's generic favorability rating among the American people. By sabotaging the reputation of an institution of government, the party that is programmatically against government would come out the relative winner."[27]

Hopes that the hyperpartisan fever would break with President Obama's reelection proved naïve. The parallel political universe extended into the second term as 2012 ended with another dance up to the edge of the fiscal cliff, with Congress scrambling past the eleventh hour on New Year's Eve to pass an Obama-backed bill that kept the Bush tax cuts in place for 98 percent of Americans while returning the tax rate for the top 2 percent to what it had been in the 1990s. But 98 percent was not enough. The Tea Party caucus opposed the bill and the votes came from GOP leadership working with the vast majority of Democrats.

Likewise, a relief bill for Northeastern victims of Hurricane Sandy was initially blocked by House Republicans (many of whom had supported relief for their constituents after Hurricane Katrina devastated the Gulf Coast). This drew a quick condemnation from New Jersey Republican governor Chris

Christie, who blasted the "toxic internal politics of the House majority." "It's why the American people hate Congress," Christie fumed. "Unlike the people in Congress, we have actual responsibilities."[28]

The hyperpartisan conflicts continued. After a 2012 Christmastime slaughter at Sandy Hook Elementary School in Connecticut left twenty children dead, America reeled in horror and new urgency emerged around reinstating some gun-control registration. The assault weapons ban had been allowed to lapse a decade earlier, but a more modest measure was a proposal to close background check loopholes, which had the support of 91 percent of the American people—and 88 percent of gun-owning families.[29] But the bipartisan compromise bill, crafted by Republican senator Pat Toomey of Pennsylvania and Democratic senator Joe Manchin of West Virginia, ultimately failed to get sixty votes in the Senate. According to Senator Toomey, the problem was Obama's support for the legislation: "There were some on my side who did not want to be seen helping the president do something he wanted to get done, just because the president wanted to do it."[30]

Even the post-election decision of RINO-hunting South Carolina senator Jim DeMint to resign his office and take the helm of the Heritage Foundation (at a salary of over $1 million a year) did not promise to heal divisions in the strained Senate. Instead, it only focused outside efforts to intensify the GOP civil war.

And so there was a Heritage-backed attempt to force the president into defunding Obama Care, as the debt ceiling again loomed in October 2013. Tea Party freshman senators such as Ted Cruz and Mike Lee raised boatloads of activist cash with infomercials threatening to unseat fellow Republican incumbents, accusing them of being insufficiently conservative and therefore Obama collaborators. Cruz became a Tea Party celebrity because of his dogged efforts to undercut party leadership on anything resembling compromise and his propensity to question the loyalties of any dissenters—causing Senator John McCain to call Cruz & Co. "Wacko Birds." But fears over proposed primary challenges led to a collapse of common sense.

And so Republicans backed into a suicidal government shutdown strategy in an attempt to get President Obama to defund or delay his signature health-care reform law. This was always going to be a nonstarter because Democrats controlled the Senate as well as the White House. But Cruz and his kamikaze caucus built up their e-mail lists around this base-pleasing fantasy, without a real strategy for success.

Even a professional hyperpartisan like Grover Norquist of Americans for Tax Reform—who a decade before had bellowed, "The lefties, the takers, the coercive utopians are not stupid. They are evil. Evil!"[31]—felt compelled to criticize Ted Cruz, saying: "He pushed House Republicans into traffic and wandered away."[32]

Responsible Republicans with impeccable conservative credentials like California's Devin Nunes were getting nervous—there was no endgame in place. In an interview with the *Washington Post* on the eve of the shutdown, with a fiscal cliff looming, Congressman Nunes dropped the L-bomb: "Lemmings with suicide vests."

"They have to be more than just a lemming. Because jumping to your death is not enough," Nunes said. "You have this group saying somehow if you're not with them, you're with Obamcare. If you're not with their plan—exactly what they want to do, you're with Obamcare. It's getting a little old."[33]

But some people need to feel the thrill of unity that comes from holding hands in free fall before hitting the hard ground of reality.

And so a government shutdown kicked in, despite long-standing assurances to the contrary from GOP leadership. A minority of a minority was calling the shots through electoral extortion, threatening primary challenges to any Republican in a gerrymandered safe seat who did not do exactly as the clique demanded.

Kansas representative Tim Huelskamp summed up these sentiments neatly for the *New York Times* while pushing back on the prospect of a bipartisan compromise bill from the Senate: "We've got a name for it in the House: it's called the Senate surrender caucus . . . Anybody who would vote for that in the House as [a] Republican would virtually guarantee a primary challenger."[34]

Got that? A constructive concern about governing means being labeled a member of the "surrender caucus" by conservative populists who deal in bumper-sticker politics. And the threat is clear: we'll "virtually guarantee a primary challenger." The base alloy of Huelskamp's appeal wasn't principled courage; it was cowardice in the face of fear of losing an otherwise lifetime seat.

That anxiety was enforced at a critical moment by a press release from Heritage Action, the lobbyist wing of the once-venerable conservative think tank. Despite being exiled from the Republican Study Committee for, among other things, having an academic who believes that immigrants have lower IQs write its anti-immigration reform manifesto, the prospect of being labeled as insufficiently conservative in a "key vote" on its scorecard caused the gutless wonders on Capitol Hill to fold.

Some fiscal illiterates, fortified by drinking too much Kool-Aid, cheered the prospect of default. Case in point was

Representative Ted Yoho (R-FL), who defended debt-ceiling default by saying, "I think, personally, it would bring stability to the world markets."[35] Confronted by facts, he backtracked a bit, saying, "I need to be schooled, or somebody needs to convince me, why we need to raise the debt ceiling." But such prideful ignorance by key decision makers shows how responsibility has become a liability in the GOP.

Soon the mood shifted to punch-drunk defiance, summed up by Indiana Republican Marlin Stutzman, who told the *Washington Examiner,* "We're not going to be disrespected . . . We have to get something out of this. And I don't know what that even is."[36] Emotions were running high and logic had left the building.

After two weeks of a government shutdown and plummeting approval ratings for the congressional GOP especially, Republican Senate minority leader Mitch McConnell felt compelled to negotiate an end to the stalemate and abandon the hostage-taking strategy. In a significant concession to reality, he said: "I'm willing to work with the government we have, not the one I wish we had."[37]

Six years into the Obama administration, the overheated old accusations are still being hurled from conservative congressmen who call the president a socialist and a Communist and a would-be dictator. Conservative populist celebrities such as 1970s rocker Ted Nugent are called in to campaign for Republican candidates, despite (or perhaps because of) a record of red-meat statements, for instance, calling President Obama a "communist-nurtured subhuman mongrel."[38] Protests over privacy concerns and income inequality have fueled a resurgent liberal populism. Congress is more polarized than at any time in recent history, and the phenomenon political scientists call "partisan warfare" seems to have metastasized into the body politic, reinforcing the parallel political universe.

But as any good evangelical knows, you reap what you sow. And there is a cost to all this craziness. Months after the government shutdown, a Pew Survey found that a majority of Americans believed the GOP was "too extreme" (compared to just 39 percent who said the same about Democrats), and 65 percent said Republicans were "out of touch."[39] Meanwhile, public approval of the Tea Party fell to record lows because it was perceived to be a core part of the problem in Washington.

Attempted Tea Party primary purges escalated in 2014 even to senators with 90 percent conservative voting records, for example, Senate majority leader Mitch McConnell in Kentucky and John Cornyn in Texas. A handful of original Tea Party candidates even found themselves facing Tea Party challengers after two terms in office, almost always for the sin of insufficient obstructionism. The play-to-the-base Stockholm syndrome began wearing off. When a modest bipartisan budget deal was reflexively attacked by the cash-raising conservative activist groups, even Speaker John Boehner called bullshit: "They are using our members and they're using the American people for their own goals," he said. "This is ridiculous."[40]

12

CONCLUSION: HOW TO TAKE AMERICA BACK FROM THE LUNATIC FRINGE

We are allowing Wingnuts to hijack our politics. But it doesn't have to be this way. We can take America back from the lunatic fringe. The Wingnuts may have cable networks and netroots, but we have the numbers—the nonscreamers and the nonshouters, mainstream Main Street Americans who care more about solving common problems than obsessively attacking political opponents.

Wingnuts offer their fellow travelers the false comfort of rigid certainty in a changing world—dividing our country into good versus evil, us against them. Fundamentalism always has a powerful appeal for people who feel powerless, especially when it gets dressed up as an ideology or attaches itself to a party label. As Reinhold Niebuhr once explained: "Frantic orthodoxy is a method for obscuring doubt."

When you pull the curtain back on Wingnut politics, behind the all-or-nothing demands, the apocalyptic warnings, and the addiction to self-righteous anger, you'll see that fear is the motivating factor: fear of the other, fear wrapped up in the American flag, fear calling itself freedom.

The Wingnuts are recycling scripts that are decades old. But it is not the language of the Founding Fathers, as they like to believe. The Founding Fathers warned about the dangers of faction—Wingnuts enflame it. The Founding Fathers were focused on uniting the nation—Wingnuts try to divide it.

They are selling the same old snake oil that merchants of political paranoia have been pitching for most of American history.

The federal government has been accused of tyranny and trying to restrict states' rights since the debate to ratify the Constitution. It was the South's battle cry at the start of the Civil War, and it was the logic behind white resistance to Reconstruction and desegregation. It was the anxiety festering beneath militia explosions from Waco to the Oklahoma City bombing.

The specter of a sinister plot to create a one-world government goes back almost a century to fights over the League of Nations against the backdrop of the Bolshevik revolution. It was carried forward by the John Birch Society, which drew recruits with its talk of UN troops invading the United States through the Southern border with the approval of alleged Manchurian candidate and Soviet spy Dwight D. Eisenhower.

Days before John F. Kennedy's assassination, 5,000 flyers were distributed in downtown Dallas, featuring side-by-side photos of Kennedy in profile and face forward, like a mug shot. Below it read "WANTED FOR TREASON" with this list of charges:[1]

- Betraying the Constitution (which he swore to uphold): He is turning sovereignty of the U.S. over to the communist controlled United Nations: He is betraying our friends . . . and befriending our enemies.
- He has been WRONG on innumerable issues affecting the security of the U.S. (United Nations—Berlin Wall—missile removal—Cuba—weak deals—test ban treaty, etc.).
- He has given support and encouragement to the Communist-inspired racial riots.
- He has illegally invaded a sovereign State with federal troops.

- He has consistently appointed Anti-Christians to Federal office: Upholds the Supreme Court in its Anti-Christian rulings. Aliens and known Communists abound in federal offices.
- He has been caught in fantastic lies to the American people.

These accusations still echo from Wingnuts today. President Obama is accused of betraying the Constitution and turning national sovereignty over to the UN. He is accused of selling out allies in favor of talks with Iran and Russia while making our nation less safe. He is accused of giving support and encouragement to radical leftist groups and is seen by some as being the product not just of the civil rights era but of Communist influencers. From the Oath Keepers to the Tenthers, the specter of federal troops illegally invading sovereign states is raised. Obama is seen by some as anti-Christian, even Muslim, and accused of appointing radical secularists and Communists to federal office. And the Birthers see a sinister plot by Obama to hide his true identity as an illegal-alien Manchurian candidate.

Beneath it all is a fear that America is fragile and that our democracy can be undone in a few easy steps. These professed patriots do not seem to have faith in the strength of the American system they want to preserve. Their fervor is no longer isolated because of the Internet, and formerly fringe figures now have national reach. Political parties are held hostage by their most extreme voices, while the rise of partisan media pumps up political divisions. It's an old problem—"the best lack all conviction, while the worst are full of passionate intensity," as the poet William Butler Yeats once wrote—but it has taken on new urgency.

We're in danger of becoming numb to distortions and demagoguery in ways that ultimately damage the institutions of our democracy. Because any Republicans who think this cycle will stop with the next president are underestimating the ways that politics follow the lines of physics—every action creates an equal and opposite reaction. This will become the new normal. We need to stop this cycle of incitement before it destroys our ability to unite as a nation absent a disaster.

We cannot hope to change human nature. There will always be cranks and conspiracy theorists among us. But we don't have to accept the debasement of civil discourse or civic decline. We can take steps to ensure that the lunatic fringe remains on the fringe and stops bleeding into the base and then poisoning the mainstream.

First, we have the numbers on our side—more Americans identify as independents than as Democrats or Republicans, and more Americans are centrist than liberal or conservative. Americans are not deeply divided—our political parties, pundits, and activists are—and the explosive growth of independent voters is a direct reaction to this disconnect. If more Americans declare their independence from the extremes on both sides and organize across party lines, we can determine who wins elections and provide the balance of power in Congress—moving our nation not left or right, but forward.

Second, we need to change the rules of the game. The professional partisans have rigged the redistricting system to reelect incumbents by creating closed-primary safe seats that empower the extremes. It's an old trick that has gotten worse, reducing the number of genuinely competitive House seats to fewer than forty out of 435—giving Congress a 90 percent reelection rate despite a 9 percent approval rating. Not coincidentally, the number of ideologically overlapping moderates in the House of Representatives dropped from 344 in 1982 to just four in 2013.[2] And after winning the 2010 midterm elections, Republicans got to work drawing enough safe seats in swing states to give them something close to a lock on the House of Representatives for the next decade.

For example, in the 2012 elections, Democrats won 1.1 million more votes nationally in congressional races than Republicans, but the GOP kept control of the House of Representatives. Or, as the Cook Political Report summed it up, "House GOP Won 49 Percent of Votes, 54 Percent of Seats." In the swing state of Pennsylvania, the results were particularly stark: although Democrats won 83,000 more votes statewide, Republicans won thirteen House seats and Democrats only five.[3] Simple fairness and fidelity to the principle of one person, one vote should indicate that this is not an academic concern.

Likewise, closed partisan primaries are fundamentally unrepresentative. They're too easily hijacked by ideological activists and party hacks beholden to special interests. And because these local primaries are the gauntlet that candidates have to run, they lead directly to the culture of hyperpartisanship that now threatens to paralyze our capacity for effective self-government. Incentives drive outcomes, and our political incentive system is screwed up. If we enact nonpartisan redistricting reform to ensure competitive general elections with open primaries, it will have a calming effect on our contorted civic discourse. In California, an independent redistricting commission and top-two primary system was chosen by voters over the objections of party bosses. In the decade before the reforms were implemented, only one Golden State congressional seat—out of fifty-three—changed party hands. In the first election after the independent redistricting commission, fourteen incumbents were swept from office or declined to run for reelection. It's a strong step in the right direction. Reforming the rigged system of redistricting will empower the moderate majority rather than the Wingnut extremes. No single action would do more to heal the harsh but artificial polarization of American politics.

Third, we need to stand up against the extremes, playing offense not defense. And that's been a big part of the problem to date—the moderate majority of Americans has been bullied into intimidated silence. The Millennial Generation that was energized by the 2008 election is now perched on the precipice between apathy and engagement. Those voters have watched the way Washington works—a place where good people and good ideas are systematically destroyed—and some now believe that politics is not an effective way to solve problems. Many would rather be "slacktivists" engaging the world online, preferring to try to effect change through culture, not politics. The media play a role in this alienation, with play-to-the-base business models and a pervasive attitude where cynicism passes for wisdom. It's time to straighten our civic backbone and be the honest brokers in politics, punching both left and right as conscience and common sense dictate.

Taken together, this is a declaration of independence—a determination to view politics not simply in terms of right versus left, but right versus wrong. It means having a healthy skepticism and a sense of humor when confronted with ideological certainty. It means rejecting the reflexive defense of the indefensible when it comes from someone on your "team." Ironically, the parties have an interest in this as well—they cannot be held hostage by their most extreme wings and hope to win broad, durable mandates.

In the process, we can hold the extremes accountable while restoring a missing sense of perspective and balance to our politics. A lack of perspective is the telltale sign of the Wingnut. When we throw around such terms as "dictatorship" and "tyranny" in American politics to score partisan points, we debase ourselves and our history.

There are signs of hope on the horizon. The outrage industry is losing some of its luster. Right-wing talk radio is declining in popularity, as its audience ages out of existence and advertisers tire of the constant controversy. Rush Limbaugh is on the ropes. Keith Olbermann, Pat Buchanan, and Glenn Beck were fired from their respective perches on MSNBC and Fox News amid declining ratings as their shtick wore thin. Glenn Beck even briefly apologized for his role in the unhinged fever pitch of politics, saying, "I think I played a role, unfortunately, in helping tear the country apart."[4]

There's a final irony in the Wingnut Wars—everyone thinks they're fighting for freedom.

Conservatives see the threat of big government's taxing and spending as an assault not just on economic freedom but also on individual freedom. Liberals believe they are fighting for individual freedom in their struggle for civil rights and reproductive rights.

Partisans on each side think they are the true patriots. They all find a way to convince themselves that they are the inheritors and defenders of the American Revolution. And in an implicit acknowledgment of Americans' allergy to extremism, each side tries to paint its opponents as the real extremists. In this sense, at least, we are not all that far apart.

And so maybe a final word from the original Founding Father can help get us back on the same page. Wingnuts often try to pretend that there is nothing more American than a high-pitched, no-holds-barred ideological battle. But in his Farewell Address,

George Washington made it clear that he perceived no greater threat to the American experiment than a partisan demagogue who "agitates the community with ill-founded jealousies and false alarms, kindles the animosity of one part against another."[5]

Washington was the original independent. As a matter of principle, he belonged to no political party and warned against those who "serve to organize faction, to give it an artificial and extraordinary force; to put, in the place of the delegated will of the nation the will of a party." The resulting animosity and distrust between citizens "serves always to distract the public councils and enfeeble the public administration." And though Washington was enough of a realist to recognize that the rise of political parties was inevitable, he tried to tell future generations that "the common and continual mischiefs of the spirit of party are sufficient to make it the interest and duty of a wise people to discourage and restrain it."

After all, as Washington wrote, "the alternate domination of one faction over another, sharpened by the spirit of revenge, natural to party dissension, which in different ages and countries has perpetrated the most horrid enormities, is itself a frightful despotism."

George Washington warned us about the Wingnuts. We would be wise to take his advice.

ACKNOWLEDGMENTS

This book was initially written in three months, the first draft handed in two days before my wedding. So it should be no surprise that it is dedicated to my bride, Margaret, who showed superhuman support and patience during the process. She is beautiful and bright in every way—and four years later we are blessed to be the parents of a baby boy named Jack.

For this new edition of *Wingnuts,* I want to thank everyone on *The Daily Beast* team—especially Barry Diller, Rhona Murphy, Mike Dyer, Ben Zagorski, and our executive editor, Noah Shachtman; managing editor Katie Baker; deputy managing editor Jane Frye; and senior editor Justin Miller. It's an honor to work alongside great reporters like Mike Daly, Eli Lake, Josh Rogin, Eleanor Clift—and great columnists like P. J. O'Rourke, Patricia Murphy, Michelle Cottle, and Michael Tomasky—and many, many others. Together, we're taking *The Beast* to new heights and I'm proud to be editor in chief of such a great team doing great work.

Wingnuts was chosen to be the first book published by Beast Books, and I owe a deep debt of gratitude to Tina Brown for giving me this and many other opportunities, and to Harold Evans and my colleagues at *The Daily Beast* in 2009 and 2010 who helped me move the ball down the field at great speed. I am especially appreciative of Edward Felsenthal, Randall Lane, Rebecca Fox, Andrew Kirk, Christine Marra, and the team at Perseus for their work.

My research assistants were essential in getting the book done and documented on time, including Denver Nicks,

Stephen Brown, Ahmed Salim, and for the new edition, Malcolm Jones and—especially—Laura Ping. And special thanks go to my literary agent, Ed Victor. At CNN, the Wingnuts of the Week segment took off because of encouragement from Kiran Chetry, Janelle Rodriguez, John Roberts, Jamie Kraft, Karrah Kaplan, Alexis Ginsburg, Derek Dodge, and everyone at *American Morning*. In more recent years at CNN, it has been a real pleasure to work with Jeff Zucker, Ken Jautz, Amy Entelis, Wil Surratt, Erin Burnett (and the entire *OutFront* team), Mark Preston, Pete Hamby, Christine Romans, and Michelle Jaconi. Also, thanks to my fellow co-founders of No-Labels, a group of Democrats, Republicans, and independents dedicated to confronting hyperpartisanship and pursuing the politics of problem solving.

I want to thank my parents, John and Dianne Avlon—their love, support, and encouragement have always been invaluable. My in-laws, Andy and Jeanie Hoover, have been warm and welcoming (and Andy, just to be clear, you're not a Wingnut), as have my new brother- and sister-in-law, Alex and Margaret. I've been blessed with a wonderful family: my grandmother Toula Phillips, aunts Joan and Lexa, uncles Alex and David, my brother Reynolds, and cousin Alex Timbers. My godfather, Peter John, and godmother, Elaine, as well as my own godchildren, Alexandra Catlin, Catherine Vanderzee, and Benjamin, Flora, and Matilda Damon—and all our friends down in Charleston. I want to thank my best man, Jay Vanderzee, as well as my groomsmen Mike Jackson, George Catlin, Jesse Angelo, Owen Brennan, Eric DelBalso, Howard Gould, Jamie Schriebl, and Matt Lockwood. Special thanks also go out to Matt Pottinger (USMC), Rich Wager, the Policy Team: Dan Freedman, Jayson White, Jen Pollom, Chris Coffey, Jemma Futterman, and Marco DeSena; Bill Simon, Dave Maney, Dave Dunbar, Frank Barry,

Dick Dadey, Alan Dobrin, Peggy Noonan, Suzanne Robinson, and Erik Sorenson. Many people were generous with their interview time, including David Frum (who sparked the concept of white-minority politics), Joe Scarborough, Rich Lowry, Charles Johnson, Kathleen Parker, and Mark Potok of the Southern Poverty Legal Center, which is an invaluable resource. Let me add one final note to this new edition for our friend Michael Hastings, a great journalist who is very much missed.

NOTES

Editor's note: Since the first edition of *Wingnuts* in 2010, several cited blogs and right-wing websites have been taken off-line. We have updated links where available, but in some cases that was not possible, so the obsolete link has been left in place with the original year of access noted.

Preface

1. Richard Hofstadter, *The Paranoid Style in American Politics and Other Essays* (New York: Vintage Books, 1952, 2008), 3.

2. Jordan Fabian, "Poll: 45 Percent of Republicans Think Obama Born Out of the U.S.," *The Hill* (blog), April 21, 2011 (2:57 p.m.), http://thehill.com/blogs/blog-briefing-room/news/157167-poll-plurality-of-republicans-say-obama-born-outside-us.

3. Ben Smith, "More Than Half of Democrats Believe Bush Knew," *Politico* (blog), April 22, 2011 (10:56 a.m.), http://www.politico.com/blogs/bensmith/0411/More_than_half_of_Democrats_believed_Bush_knew.html.

4. Jonathan Swift, *Oxford Reference*, http://www.oxfordreference.com/view/10.1093/acref/9780191735240.001.0001/q-oro-00010553.

5. Daniel Patrick Moynihan, *Daniel Patrick Moynihan: A Portrait in Letters of an American Visionary*, ed. Steven R. Weisman (New York: PublicAffairs, 2010), 2.

6. "'Wingnuts' and President Obama," *Harris Polls*, March 24, 2010, http://www.harrisinteractive.com/NewsRoom/HarrisPolls/tabid/447/ctl/ReadCustom%20Default/mid/1508/ArticleId/223/Default.aspx.

7. Kyle Becker, "Forward: 61% Believe Obama Will Move America Towards Socialism," *Independent Journal Review*, December 18, 2012, https://www.ijreview.com/2012/12/25693-forward-61-believe-obama-will-move-america-towards-socialism/.

8. Derek Thompson, "55% of Likely Voters Think Obama Is a Socialist," *Atlantic*, July 9, 2010, http://www.theatlantic.com/business/archive/2010/07/poll-55-of-likely-voters-think-obama-is-a-socialist/59463/.

9. Tom Jensen, "Romney and the Birthers," *Public Policy Polling*, February 15, 2011, http://publicpolicypolling.blogspot.com/2011/02/romney-and-birthers.html.

10. Jim Williams, "Conspiracy Theory Poll Results," *Public Policy Polling,* April 2, 2013, http://www.publicpolicypolling.com/main/2013/04/conspiracy-theory-poll-results-.html.

11. Mark Potok, "The Year in Hate and Extremism," *Intelligence Report* 149 (Spring 2013), http://www.splcenter.org/home/2013/spring/the-year-in-hate-and-extremism.

12. H. L. Mencken, *Mencken Chrestomathy* (New York: Vintage Books, 1916, 1949), 407.

13. Cass R. Sunstein, *How to Humble a Wingnut and Other Lessons from Behavioral Economics* (Chicago Shorts) (Chicago: University of Chicago Press, 2013).

Chapter 1: Introducing the Wingnuts

1. Michael Savage, "Savage Says 'Obama Hates' and 'Is Raping America,'" April 21, 2009, *Media Matters for America*, accessed August 27, 2009, http://mediamatters.org/mmtv/200904210014.

2. Kyle Drennen, "MSNBC's Ed Schultz Erupts: 'Republicans Want to See You Dead!'" *NewsBusters* (blog), September 9, 2009 (14:54), http://www.newsbusters.org/blogs/kyle-drennen/2009/09/24/msnbcs-ed-shultz-erupts-republicans-want-see-you-dead.

3. "Oath Keepers Pledges to Prevent Dictatorship in the United States," *Las Vegas Review-Journal*, October 18, 2009, http://www.lvrj.com/news/oath-keepers-pledges-to-prevent-dictatorship-in-united-states-64690232.html.

4. Michael Sokolove, "Dick Armey Is Back on the Attack," *New York Times*, November 4, 2009, http://www.nytimes.com/2009/11/08/magazine/08Armey-t.html.

5. Glenn Beck, "Beck Claims Bush, McCain Were 'Progressive,' Adds That 'the Country May Not Survive Barack Obama," September 23, 2009, *Media Matters for America*, accessed September 25, 2009, http://mediamatters.org/mmtv/200909230021.

6. Mark Levin, "Levin on Hannity: Obama at War with American People," YouTube, August 7, 2009, accessed August 30, 2009, http://www.youtube.com/watch?v=h5qWFHzwAz8.

7. Rush Limbaugh, "Rush Limbaugh on Obama, Al-Qaeda, and the Race to 'Demolish America,'" *Huffington Post,* July 4, 2009 (6:12 a.m.), updated May 25, 2011 (2:25 p.m.), http://www.huffingtonpost.com/2009/06/03/rush-limbaugh-claims-obam_n_211162.html.

8. Jeff Zeleny and Jim Rutenberg, "Threats Against Obama Spiked Early," *New York Times,* December 5, 2009, http://www.nytimes.com/2009/12/06/us/06threat.html.

Chapter 2: A Brief History of Extremism in America

1. Richard Hofstadter, *The Paranoid Style in American Politics* (New York: Vintage Books, 1965), 3.

2. Eric Burns, *Infamous Scribblers: The Founding Fathers and the Rowdy Beginnings of American Journalism* (New York: PublicAffairs, 2006), 323.

3. A. J. Ayer, *Thomas Paine* (Chicago: University of Chicago Press, 1988), 162.

4. John Avlon, "The Mount Rushmore Fight Club: A History of Hating Presidents from Washington to Obama," *The Daily Beast* (blog), February 17, 2014, http://www.thedailybeast.com/articles/2014/02/17/the-mount-rushmore-fight-club-a-history-of-hating-presidents.html.

5. George Washington to Thomas Jefferson, July 6, 1796, http://founders.archives.gov/?q=Nero&s=1111311111&sa=&r=22&sr=.

6. U.S. Congress, Fifth Congress, *The Alien and Sedition Acts* (1798), http://www.ourdocuments.gov/print_friendly.php?flash=true&page=transcript&doc=16&title=Transcript+of+Alien+and+Sedition+Acts+(1798) (March 2, 2014).

7. P. L. Ford, ed., *The Writings of Thomas Jefferson*, vol. 8 (New York: Putnam, 1892–1899), 67.

8. Ed Crews, "Jefferson's Secret Bible," *University of Virginia Magazine* (Spring 2002), http://uvamagazine.org/articles/jefferson_bible.

9. Jerry W. Knudson, *In the News: American Journalists View Their Craft* (Wilmington, DE: Scholarly Resources, 2000), 27.

10. Avlon, "The Mount Rushmore Fight Club."

11. "Impeachment of Mr. Jefferson," *New York Bee,* September 7, 1802.

12. Arnold Forster and Benjamin Epstein, *The Trouble-Makers: The New Anti-Defamation League Report on Intolerance in the United States* (Garden City, NY: Country Life Press, 1952), 110.

13. Ibid.

14. Abraham Lincoln to Joshua Speed, August 24, 1855, http://www.abrahamlincolnonline.org/lincoln/speeches/speed.htm.

15. "Antebellum Southern Exceptionalism: A New Look at an Old Question," *Civil War History* 29 (3) (September 1983): 230–244, quoted on 244.

16. Don E. Fehrenbacher, "The Anti-Lincoln Tradition," *Journal of the Abraham Lincoln Association* 4 (1982): 6–28.

17. Avlon, "The Mount Rushmore Fight Club."

18. Fehrenbacher, "The Anti-Lincoln Tradition."

19. Ibid.

20. Robert Alan Goldberg, *Enemies Within: The Culture of Conspiracy in Modern America* (New Haven: Yale University Press, 2001), 15.

21. Forster and Epstein, *The Trouble-Makers,* 110.

22. Hiram W. Evans, "The Klan's Fight for Americanism," *North American Review* 223 (March 1926): 38–39.

23. Richard Hofstadter, *Anti-Intellectualism in American Life* (New York: Vintage Books, 1963), 124.

24. Kenneth Keulman, ed., *Critical Moments in Religious History* (Macon, GA: Mercer University Press, 1993), 146.

25. Walter LaFeber, Richard Polenberg, and Nancy Woloch, *The American*

Century: A History of the United States Since the 1890s, 7th ed. (Armonk, NY: M. E. Sharpe, Inc., 2013), 149.

26. Goldberg, *Enemies Within*, 17.

27. James P. Shenton, "Fascism and Father Coughlin," *Wisconsin Magazine of History* 44 (1) (Autumn 1960).

28. "FDR Was Called a Socialist and a Communist," *Politifact.com,* n.d., http://politifact.com/truth-o-meter/statements/2009/sep/22/barack-obama/obama-roosevelt-socialist-communist/.

29. Arthur M. Schlesinger Jr., *The Vital Center: The Politics of Freedom* (New Brunswick, NJ: Transaction, 1998), 37.

30. Senator Joseph McCarthy, "Speech Delivered by Sen. Joseph McCarthy Before the Senate on June 14, 1951," *Modern History Sourcebook: Senator Joseph McCarthy: The History of George Catlett Marshall, 1951,* June 14, 1951, http://www.fordham.edu/halsall/mod/1951mccarthy-marshall.html.

31. Hofstadter, *The Paranoid Style in American Politics,* 70.

32. Martha F. Lee, *Conspiracy Rising: Conspiracy Thinking and American Public Life* (Santa Barbara, CA: Praeger, 2011), 84.

33. Ibid., 80.

34. Goldberg, *Enemies Within,* 42.

35. Ibid., 44.

36. Ibid.

37. Albert J. Menendez, *The Religious Factor in the 1960 Presidential Election: An Analysis of the Kennedy Victory over Anti-Catholic Prejudice* (Jefferson, NC: McFarland, 2011), 22.

38. "Anti-Catholic Retiree Planned to Kill JFK," *Palm Beach Post.com,* n.d., http://www.historicpalmbeach.com/tag/kennedy/.

39. Robert F. Kennedy Jr., "Governor Palin's Reading List," *Huffington Post,* September 15, 2008, http://www.huffingtonpost.com/robert-f-kennedy-jr/governor-palins-reading-l_b_126478.html?page=32&show_comment_id=15725640#comment_15725640.

40. David Corn, "The Dark Side of 'I Have a Dream': The FBI's War on Martin Luther King," *Mother Jones,* August 28, 2013, http://www.motherjones.com/politics/2013/08/j-edgar-hoover-war-martin-luther-king.

41. Taylor Branch, *At Canaan's Edge: America in the King Years, 1965–1968* (New York: Simon & Schuster, 2006), lxxii.

42. Public Statement made by Governor George Wallace, May 8, 1963, in the *New York Times,* May 9, 1963.

43. Taylor Branch, *The King Years: Historic Moments in the Civil Rights Movement* (New York: Simon & Schuster, 2006), 163.

44. "The Road to Civil Rights: The Voting Rights Act of 1965," *Highway History: U.S. Department of Transportation,* n.d., http://www.fhwa.dot.gov/highwayhistory/road/s38.cfm.

45. Christopher Hewitt, *Political Violence and Terrorism in Modern America:*

A Chronology (Santa Barbara, CA: Praeger Security International, 2005), 28–90.

46. Hugh Hewitt, "Commentary on the Elections: The Seven Reasons Bush Will Win Big in Orange County; While Some Predict a Tight Race Locally, the President's Margin of Victory Here May Be What Wins Him the Election," *Los Angeles Times*, August 30, 1992, http://articles.latimes.com/1992–08–30/local/me -8365_1_orange-county.

47. Gwen Ifill, "The 1992 Campaign: Hillary Clinton Defends Her Conduct in Law Firm," *New York Times*, March 17, 1992, http://www.nytimes.com/1992/03/17 /us/the-1992-campaign-hillary-clinton-defends-her-conduct-in-law-firm.html.

48. Robin Toner, "The 1992 Campaign: Political Memo; Backlash for Hillary Clinton Puts Negative Image to Rout," *New York Times,* September 24, 1992, http:// www.nytimes.com/1992/09/24/us/1992-campaign-political-memo-backlash -for-hillary-clinton-puts-negative-image.html.

49. Ibid.

50. Dorthee Benz, "The Media Factory Behind the 'Hilary Factory,'" *Fair*, October 1, 1992, http://fair.org/extra-online-articles/the-media-factor-behind-the -hillary-factor/.

51. Anthony Lewis, "Abroad at Home: Tax-Exempt Politics?" *New York Times*, November 30, 1992, http://www.nytimes.com/1992/11/30/opinion/abroad-at-home -tax-exempt-politics.html.

52. Ibid.

53. Katharine Q. Seelye, "The 1994 Campaign: The Republicans; with Fiery Words, Gingrich Builds His Kingdom," *New York Times,* October 27, 1994, http:// www.nytimes.com/1994/10/27/us/the-1994-campaign-the-republicans-with -fiery-words-gingrich-builds-his-kingdom.html.

54. Ibid.

55. Ibid.

56. Joe Conason and Gene Lyons, *The Hunting of the President: The Ten-Year Campaign to Destroy Bill and Hillary Clinton* (New York: Thomas Dunne Books, 2000), 76.

57. Ibid.

58. R. W. Apple Jr., "The Capital Spotlight: Anguished Words from Dead Clinton Aide Make Washington Think About Its Values," *New York Times*, August 13, 1993, http://www.nytimes.com/1993/08/13/us/capital-spotlight-anguished-words -dead-clinton-aide-make-washington-think-about.html.

59. Anthony Lewis, "Abroad at Home: The Grassy Knoll," *New York Times*, August 5, 1994, http://www.nytimes.com/1994/08/05/opinion/abroad-at-home -the-grassy-knoll.html.

60. Conason and Lyons, *The Hunting of the President*, 129.

61. Byron York, "The Life and Death of the *American Spectator*," *Atlantic*, November 1, 2001, http://www.theatlantic.com/magazine/archive/2001/11 /the-life-and-death-of-the-american-spectator/302343/.

62. Conason and Lyons, *The Hunting of the President*, 140.

63. *The Clinton Chronicles,* documentary, directed by *Patrick Matrisciana* (1994: The United States, Citizens Video Press, 1994), video.

64. John Avlon, "Bill Clinton Is Back and Looking Good," *CNN Opinion,* August 21, 2010, http://www.cnn.com/2010/OPINION/04/20/avlon.bill.clilnton /index.html

65. *Washington Post,* December 4, 2003.

66. "2000 Official Presidential General Election Results," *Federal Elections Commission,* November 7, 2000, updated December 2001, http://www.fec.gov /pubrec/2000presgeresults.htm.

67. Meredith Aby and Kim DeFranco, "Tens of Thousands Say No to War," *Fight Back! News,* October 1, 2001, http://www.fightbacknews.org/2001fall /nowar.htm.

68. Ibid.

69. Delaware Dem, "Why We Hate George W. Bush," *Daily Kos* (blog), September 28, 2005, http://www.dailykos.com/story/2005/9/28/152665/-Why-We -Hate-George-W.-Bush.

70. Scott Conroy, "Anti-Bush Protests in NYC," *CBS News,* November 2, 2005, http://www.cbsnews.com/stories/2005/11/02/national/main1005030.shtml.

71. *Day to Day,* "Naomi Wolf Likens Bush to Hitler," *National Public Radio,* November 19, 2007, http://www.npr.org/templates/story/story.php ?storyId=16422285.

72. Keith Olbermann, "Keith Olbermann Calls George W. Bush a Fascist," online video clip, YouTube, February 15, 2008, http://www.youtube.com /watch?v=u19KHbTJEOk, accessed September 2, 2009.

73. Michael Janofsky, "The 2004 Campaign: Advertising; Bush-Hitler Ad Draws Criticism," *New York Times,* January 6, 2004, http://www.nytimes.com/2004/01 /06/us/the-2004-campaign-advertising-bush-hitler-ads-draw-criticism.html.

74. "Belafonte: Bush 'Greatest Terrorist in the World,'" *MSNBC,* January 8, 2006, http://www.msnbc.msn.com/id/10767465/.

75. Alex Fryer, "Sheehan Criticizes Bush, Doesn't Spare Democrats," *Seattle Times,* May 9, 2006, http://seattletimes.nwsource.com/html/localnews /2002981541_sheehan09.html.

76. *Breitbart TV,* http://www.breitbart.tv/?p=2973.

77. *Hannity and Colmes, Fox News,* September 26, 2005.

78. 2008 ANES (American National Election Studies) National Election Study.

79. See http://people-press.org/report/?pageid=1516.

80. William Safire, *Safire's New Political Dictionary* (New York: Random House, 1993), 453.

Chapter 3: The Rise of the Tea Party

1. "Santelli's Tea Party," *CNBC,* February 19, 2009, http://www.cnbc.com/id /15840232?video=1039849853.

2. Andy Roesgen, "Protestors Gather for Self-Styled Tea Party," myfoxchicago .com, February 27, 2009.

3. "100 Days of Bailouts and Making a Bad Situation Worse," U.S. Senate Republican Study Committee, April 29, 2009, http://www.docstoc.com/docs /5999316/100-Days-of-Bailouts-and-Making-a-Bad-Situation-Worse.

4. Dave Goldman, "House Passes $819 Billion Stimulus Bill," *CNN,* January 28, 2009, http://money.cnn.com/2009/01/28/news/economy/house_vote_wednesday /index.htm?postversion=2009012819.

5. Allahpundit, "House Passes $410 Billion Spending Bill as Obama Prepares $634 Billion Health Care Fund," *HotAir,* February 25, 2009, http://hotair.com /archives/2009/02/25/house-passes-410-billion-spending-bill-as-obama-prepares -634-billion-health-care-fund/.

6. Nate Silver, "Tea Party Nonpartisan Attendance Estimates: Now 300,000+," *FiveThirtyEight,* April 16, 2009, http://www.fivethirtyeight.com/2009/04/tea -party-nonpartisan-attendance.html.

7. Chris Good, "Lawmakers Will Face Tea Parties, and More, in August," *Atlantic,* July 30, 2009, http://politics.theatlantic.com/2009/07/lawmakers_will _face_tea_parties_and_more_in_august.php.

8. Lauren Auerbach, Rob Savillo, and Elbert Ventura, "On the House: Fox Airs 107 for Its Coverage of Tea Party Protests over 10 Days," *Media Matters for America,* April 17, 2009, http://mediamatters.org/research/200904170011.

9. Dennis Cauchon, "Tax Bills in 2009 at Lowest Level Since 1950," *USA To-day,* May 12, 2010, http://usatoday30.usatoday.com/money/perfi/taxes/2010-05-10 -taxes_N.htm?csp=hf.

10. Nate Silver, "Obama Has Cut Taxes for 98.6 Percent of Working House-holds," *FiveThirtyEight*, August 8, 2009, http://fivethirtyeight.com/features /obama-has-cut-taxes-for-98-6-percent-of-working-households/.

11. Paul Blumenthal, "Rep. Conyers: Don't Read the Bill," *The Sunlight Foundation,* July 27, 2009, https://sunlightfoundation.com/blog/2009/07/27 /rep-conyers-dont-read-the-bill/.

12. "Freshman Democratic Lawmaker 'Physically Assaulted at a Local Event' by Activists," *ThinkProgress* (blog), August 5, 2009 (2:25 p.m.), http://think progress.org/2009/08/05/freshman-dem-assaulted/.

13. Lee Fang, "Right-Wing Harassment Strategy Against Dems Detailed in Memo: 'Yell,' 'Stand Up and Shout Out,' 'Rattle Him,'" *ThinkProgress* (blog), July 31, 2009, http://thinkprogress.org/politics/2009/07/31/53761/recess-harassment -memo/.

14. Ibid.

15. Eric Kleefield, "Protestor in Connecticut: 'Treat' Dodd with Handful of Painkillers and Whiskey," *Talking Points Memo* (blog), August 4, 2009, http:// tpmdc.talkingpointsmemo.com/2009/08/protestor-in-connecticut-treat-dodd-with -handful-of-painkillers-and-whiskey.php.

16. "Rage Grows in America: Anti-Government Conspiracies," *Anti-Defamation*

League, November 2009, http://www.adl.org/special_reports/rage-grows-in
-America/Rage-Grows-In-America.pdf.

17. Associated Press, "McCaskill Admonishes Crowd at Health Care Forum,"
Columbia Missourian, August 11, 2009, http://www.columbiamissourian.com
/stories/2009/08/11/mccaskill-admonishes-crowd-forum/.

18. Sarah Palin, "Statement on the Current Health Care Debate," Facebook,
August 7, 2009, http://www.facebook.com/note.php?note_id=113851103434, accessed, September 2, 2009.

19. Brian Beutler, "Americans for Prosperity Compares Health Care Reform to
Holocaust, Tells Protesters to Put 'Fear of God' in Members of Congress," *Talking
Points Memo* (blog), August 7, 2009, http://tpmdc.talkingpointsmemo.com/2009
/08/americans-for-prosperity-compares-health-care-reform-to-holocaust-tells
-protesters-to-put-fear-of-go.php?ref=fpblg.

20. David Knowles, "John McCain Booed for Saying Obama Respects the Constitution," *Politics Daily,* August 25, 2009, http://www.politicsdaily.com/2009/08/25
/john-mccain-booed-for-saying-obama-respects-the-constitution/.

21. Stephanie Mencimer, "Tempest in the Tea Party," *Mother Jones,* December
30, 2009, http://motherjones.com/politics/2009/12/tempest-tea-party.

22. Jim Spellman, "Tea Party Movement Has Anger, No Dominant Leaders,"
CNN, September 12, 2009, http://www.cnn.com/2009/POLITICS/09/12/tea.party
.express/index.html.

23. Ibid.

24. Ibid.

25. Ben Frumin, "Finger Biting Victim Speaks—to a Reverent Neil Cavuto,"
Talking Points Memo (blog), September 3, 2009, http://talkingpointsmemo.com
/news/finger-biting-victim-speaks-to-a-reverent-neil-cavuto.

26. Eric Kleefeld, "Town Halls Turning into Town Brawls," *Talking Points
Memo* (blog), August 7, 2009, http://tpmdc.talkingpointsmemo.com/2009/08
/town-halls-turning-into-town-brawls.php.

27. "Man Who Got Finger Bitten Off at Town Hall Talks to Cavuto," YouTube,
September 3, 2009, http://www.youtube.com/watch?v=3fHSW4Txxz8, accessed
September 10, 2009.

28. Spellman, "Tea Party Movement Has Anger."

Chapter 4: Obama Derangement Syndrome

1. *Grassfire.org,* n.d., http://www.grassfire.org/111/about.htm.

2. John Amato, "FOX Website Commenter Wants to Assassinate Obama,"
Crooks and Liars, November 4, 2008, http://crooksandliars.com/john-amato/fox
-website-commenter-wants-assassinate.

3. Michael Eden, "Do Unto Obama As Liberals Did Unto Bush," *Free Republic* (blog), November 6, 2008 (8:17 p.m.), http://www.freerepublic.com/focus
/bloggers/2127465/posts.

4. Eve Conant, "Hate Groups Are Benefiting from Obama's Election," *Newsweek*, April 24, 2009, updated March 13, 2010, http://www.newsweek.com/id /195085.

5. See http://www.stormfront.org/forum/t542218/.

6. Ben Evans, "Georgia Congressman Warns of Obama Dictatorship," *Fox News*, November 10, 2008, http://www.foxnews.com/printer_friendly _wires/2008Nov10/0,4675,CongressmanObamaMarxist,00.html.

7. Associated Press, "Priest: No Communion for Obama Supporters," *NBC News*, November 13, 2008, http://www.msnbc.msn.com/id/27705755/.

8. "Obama Threats," *Fox News*, November 15, 2008.

9. David Edwards and Muriel Kane, "Idaho Students Chant 'Assassinate Obama' on School Bus: Report," *Raw Story*, November 12, 2008, http://rawstory .com/news/2008/Idaho_students_chant_assassinate_Obama_on_1112.html.

10. Joe Gandelman, "Arizona Pastor Repeats Wish for Barack Obama's Death," *TheModerateVoice*, August 31, 2009, http://themoderatevoice.com/44879 /arizona-pastor-repeats-wish-for-barack-obamas-death/.

11. Stephen Lemons, "Christopher Broughton's Pastor Steven Anderson Prays for President Barack Obama's Death," *Feathered Bastard* (blog), August 26, 2009 (1:30 p.m.), http://blogs.phoenixnewtimes.com/bastard/2009/08/tempe_pastor _steven_anderson_p.php.

12. Kyle Mantyla, "Drake: Tiller's Murder Answer to Prayers," *Right-Wing Watch* (blog), June 2, 2009, http://www.rightwingwatch.org/content /drake-tillers-murder-answer-prayer.

13. Brian Levy, "On CNN Headline News, Goldberg Compares Obama, FDR to Hitler," *Media Matters for America*, February 25, 2008, http://mediamatters .org/mmtv/200802250008; Glenn Beck, "Liberalism and Fascism," February 22, 2008, accessed June 3, 2009, http://transcripts.cnn.com/TRANSCRIPTS/0802/22/gb .01.html.

14. Lauren Auerbach, "Fox News Radio's Tom Sullivan Aired 'Side by Side Comparison' of Speeches by Hitler and Obama," *Media Matters for America*, February 13, 2008, http://mediamatters.org/research/200802130016?f=h_latest; *Tom Sullivan Show*, February 11, 2008, accessed June 8, 2009, http://mediamatters.org /research/2008/02/13/fox-news-radios-tom-sullivan-aired-side-by-side/142546.

15. Ben Armbruster, "Krauthammer Links Obama's Berlin Speech to Nazi Rallies," *ThinkProgress* (blog), July 29, 2008, http://thinkprogress.org/2008/07/29 /krauthammer-obama-nazis/; Brit Hume, *Fox News Special Report*, July 28, 2008.

16. Media Matters staff, "*Rocky* profile of Coffman Omitted Finding That Subordinate and 'Political Ally' Kopelman 'Does Appear to Have Violated State Statute,'" *Media Matters for America*, July 24, 2008, http://mediamatters.org /research/200807240001.

17. Andrew Walzer, "On *Hannity and Colmes*, Coulter Again Made Obama-Hitler Comparisons, Said Clinton 'Would Enjoy Torturing Detainees,'"

Media Matters for America, April 4, 2008, http://mediamatters.org/research
/200804040005; *Hannity and Colmes, Fox News*, April 3, 2008.

18. Anthony Man, "Republican Creator of Sign Likening Obama to Hitler
Defends His Work," *Broward Politics* (blog), October 18, 2008 (12:50 p.m.), http://
weblogs.sun-sentinel.com/news/politics/broward/blog/2008/10/republican_creator
_of_sign_lik_1.html.

19. Ibid.

20. *Breitbart*, n.d., http://www.breitbart.com/article.php?id=D94CDDM80&
show_article=1.

21. Rush Limbaugh, *The Rush Limbaugh Show*, August 10, 2009, http://www
.rushlimbaugh.com/daily/2009/08/10/white_house_threatens_rush_again.

22. John Harwood, "But Can Obama Make the Trains Run on Time?" *New
York Times*, April 19, 2009, http://www.nytimes.com/2009/04/20/us/politics/20
caucus.html.

23. Ali Frick, "Glenn Beck: I Was Wrong. We're Not Marching Toward Socialism, We're Marching Toward Fascism," *ThinkProgress* (blog), April 1, 2009,
http://thinkprogress.org/2009/04/01/beck-march-to-Fascism/.

24. Amanda Terkel, "Maryland GOP Group: 'Obama and Hitler Have a Great
Deal in Common,'" *ThinkProgress* (blog), June 23, 2009, http://thinkprogress.org
/2009/06/23/md-gop-obama-hitler/.

25. "Meet Pamela Pilger, the Crazy Lady Who Yelled Heil Hitler at a Jewish
Supporter of Health Care Reform," *Gawker*, August 8, 1008 (11:40 p.m.), http://
gawker.com/5340436/meet-pamela-pilger-the-crazy-lady-who-yelled-heil-hitler
-at-a-jewish-supporter-of-health-care-reform.

26. Steve Benen, "Don't Feed the Crazies," *Political Animal* (blog), December
11, 2009 (10:45 a.m.), http://www.washingtonmonthly.com/archives/individual
/2009_12/021407.php.

27. "Controversial Float Meant to Inspire Citizen Voices," *Mount Vernon News*,
September, 22, 2009, http://www.democraticunderground.com/discuss/duboard
.php?az=view_all&address=389x6608327.

28. Ibid.

29. Eric Kleefield, "Former Bush Official: Obama's Policies Are Like Hitler's and Peron's," *Talking Points Memo* (blog), September 17, 2009, http://
talkingpointsmemo.com/dc/former-bush-official-obama-s-policies-are-like
-hitler-s-and-peron-s.

30. Ibid.

31. Representative John Linder, "Progressivism? Not So Fast Folks," *Politico*, October 7, 2009, http://www.politico.com/news/stories/1009/27986.html
#ixzz0TJGDPKVR.

32. Lynn Thompson, "Hitler Poster Provokes Edmonds Incident," *Seattle Times*, September 17, 2009, http://seattletimes.nwsource.com/html/politics
/2009882084_gasparian16m.html.

33. J. R. Nyquist, "Bill Clinton Much More Than a 'Stealth' Communist: He Is an Illuminist," *The Cutting Edge* (blog), n.d., http://www.cuttingedge.org/news /n1315.cfm.

34. David Kupelian, "Yes, Barack Obama Really Is a Manchurian Candidate," *WorldNetDaily* (hereafter *WND*) *Commentary*, October 10, 2008, http://www .wnd.com/index.php?pageId=79411.

35. Kate Barrett, "Palin Invokes Socialism Charge Against Obama," *ABC News* (blog), October 20, 2008 (8:09 a.m.), http://blogs.abcnews.com/politicalradar /2008/10/palin-invokes-s.html.

36. Kelly Moeller, "Delay: Obama's a Marxist," *ABC News* (blog), June 6, 2008 (2:17 p.m.), http://blogs.abcnews.com/politicalpunch/2008/06/delay-obamas-a.html.

37. Amanda Terkel, "Lars Larson: Progressives Are 'Marxist'—But Don't Call Conservatives 'Fascist,'" *ThinkProgress* (blog), October 20, 2008, http://think progress.org/2008/10/20/marxist-fascist/.

38. Theo Lippman Jr., "Quayle Said of Reports That Ross Perot Has . . . ," *Baltimore Sun,* June 25, 1992, http://articles.baltimoresun.com/1992-06-25 /news/1992177016_1_spiro-agnew-ha-ha-ha-quayle.

39. Lisa Schiffren, "Obama's Political Origins," *National Review Online*, February 19, 2008, http://www.nationalreview.com/corner/159088/obamas-political -origins/lisa-schiffren.

40. Casey Gane-McCalla, "Top 10 Obama Player Haters of 2008," *Huffington Post*, December 21, 2008, http://www.huffingtonpost.com/casey-ganemccalla/top -10-obama-player-hater_b_152490.html_NoPara.

41. Andy Barr, "Whisper Campaign Persists Despite Election," *NBCChicago*, December 7, 2008, http://www.nbcchicago.com/news/archive/Whisper_campaign _persists_despite_election.html.

42. David Neiwert, "Beck: Obama Has Us on the Road Not Just to Socialism but Communism," *Crooks and Liars,* February 5, 2009, http://crooksandliars .com/david-neiwert/beck-obama-has-us-road-not-just-soci.

43. Drew Zahn, "Alan Keyes: Stop Obama or U.S. Will Cease to Exist," *WND,* February 21, 2009, http://www.wnd.com/2009/02/89612/.

44. Thomas Hargrove and Guido H. Stempel III, "Practically Everyone's Heard Toxic Rumors," Scripps Howard News Service, October 12, 2008, http:// www.deseretnews.com/article/705254718/Practically-everyones-heard-toxic -rumors.html?pg=all.

45. "Think Critically, Ditch the Chain Letter," *Charlotte Observer,* October 3, 2008, http://www.charlotteobserver.com/408/story/228317.html.

46. "Belief Watch: Is Obama the Antichrist?" *Newsweek,* November 14, 2008, http://www.newsweek.com/id/169192.

47. Ibid.

48. "Obama as Anti-Christ," March 2008, http://www.snopes.com/politics /obama/antichrist.asp.

49. Peggy Fletcher Stack, "Rapture' Distress About Wars and the World Economy Feed Apocalyptic Warnings," *Salt Lake Tribune*, October 31, 2008,

http://www.sltrib.com/faith/ci_10859898.

50. Amy Sullivan, "An Antichrist Obama in McCain Ad?" *Time*, August 8, 2008, http://www.time.com/time/nation/article/0,8599,1830590,00.html?iid=sphere-inline-sidebar.

51. Ibid.

52. Glenn Beck, "How the Liberal Media Works," *Glenn Beck*, March 4, 2008, http://www.glennbeck.com/content/articles/article/198/7060/.

53. *Salt Lake Tribune,* October 31, 2008.

54. "Belief Watch: Is Obama the Antichrist?" *Newsweek,* November 14, 2008.

55. Tom Jensen, "Extremism in New Jersey," *Public Policy Polling* (blog), September 16, 2009 (10:29 a.m.), http://publicpolicypolling.blogspot.com/2009/09/extremism-in-new-jersey.html.

56. Conspiracy Theory Poll Results, Public Policy Polling, April 2, 2013. http://www.publicpolicypolling.com/main/2013/04/conspiracy-theory-poll-results-.html

57. "Romney Ad: 'Obama Waging War on Religion,'" *Washington Post*, August 9, 2012.

Chapter 5: The Birth of White-Minority Politics

1. Noel Sheppard, "Garofolo: Tea Party Goers Are Racists Who Hate Black President," *NewsBusters* (blog), April 16, 2009 (22:56), http://newsbusters.org/blogs/noel-sheppard/2009/04/16/garofalo-tea-partiers-are-all-racists-who-hate-black-president.

2. Bureau of Labor Statistics, "Current Population Survey—November 2009."

3. Sam Roberts, "Projections Put Whites in Minority in U.S. by 2050," *New York Times,* December 17, 2009, http://www.nytimes.com/2009/12/18/us/18census.html?_r=0.

4. Richard Hofstadter, *The Paranoid Style in American Politics* (New York: Vintage Books, 1965, 2008), 23–24.

5. Greg Lewis, "The Friday Rush: Vive la Résistance!" *Media Matters for America,* December 11, 2009, http://mediamatters.org/columns/200912110041.

6. Michael Savage, "Savage Predicts 'a Revolution in This Country If This Keeps Up' Because 'the White Male . . . Has Nothing to Lose,'" *Savage Nation,* August 21, 2009, http://mediamatters.org/mmtv/200908210049.

7. Pat Buchanan, "Traditional Americans Are Losing Their Nation," *WND Commentary,* October 20, 2009, http://www.wnd.com/index.php?pageId=113463.

8. Patrick J. Buchanan, "It Can't Happen Here," *Human Events,* July 10, 2009, http://www.humanevents.com/article.php?id=32654.

9. Patrick J. Buchanan, "Is America Coming Apart?" *Patrick J. Buchanan Official Website* (blog), September 11, 2009 (10:26 a.m.), http://buchanan.org/blog/is-america-coming-apart-2159.

10. Ken Burns, *The Civil War*, documentary, directed by Ken Burns (1990; *The United States,* PBS, 2004), DVD.

11. Ad reprinted on http://www.professionalsoldiers.com/forums/showthread .php?t=24310&page=7.

12. Sarah Palin, "Palin's 'Pro-America Areas' Remark: Extended Version," *The Trail* (blog), October 17, 2008, http://voices.washingtonpost.com/44/2008/10/17 /palin_clarifies_her_pro-americ.html.

13. Michael Finnegan, "Obama Expresses Regret for Remarks," *Los Angeles Times*, April 13, 2008, http://articles.latimes.com/2008/apr/13/nation/na -obama13.

14. Andrew Malcolm, "John McCain Backer Dropped from Virginia Campaign Team Due to Racially Tinged Column," *Top of the Ticket* (blog), *Los Angeles Times*, October 7, 2008 (8:57 a.m.), http://latimesblogs.latimes.com/washington /2008/10/john-mccain-bac.html.

15. "Al-Jazeera Exposes Racism at Sarah Palin Rally in Ohio," *Yelp*, October 16, 2008, http://www.yelp.com/topic/los-angeles-al-jazeera-exposes-racism -at-sarah-palin-rally-in-ohio.

16. "Hatred at a Palin Rally in Johnstown, PA," YouTube, October 21, 2008 (2:51), http://www.youtube.com/watch?v=NtZWwgw_WY.

17. Andrew Malcolm, "John Moody of Fox News Goes out on a Political Limb—and Apparently Is Still on It," *Top of the Ticket* (blog), *Los Angeles Times*, October 25, 2008 (8:58 a.m.), http://latimesblogs.latimes.com/washington /2008/10/fox-news-execut.html.

18. "Election Polls," *New York Times*, November 5, 2008, http://elections.ny times.com/2008/results/president/exit-polls.html.

19. See http://www.nola.com/news/index.ssf/2008/11/obama_made_inroads _with_white.html.

20. Noah Kristula-Green, "Same Crazy, Louder Megaphone," February 24, 2010, *FrumForum* (blog), http://www.frumforum.com/same-extremists-louder -megaphones/.

21. Eric Foner, *Reconstruction: America's Unfinished Revolution, 1863–1877* (New York: HarperCollins, 1988, 2002), 198.

22. Ibid., 551.

23. John B. Judis, *William F. Buckley, Jr., Patron Saint of the Conservatives* (New York: Simon & Schuster, 2001), 138.

24. Foner, *Reconstruction*, 251.

25. "The Biography of Senator Strom Thurmond," The Strom Thurmond Institute, http://sti.clemson.edu/about-us-mainmenu-27/biography-mainmenu-126.

26. *National Review*, January 25, 1956.

27. Barry Goldwater, *The Conscience of a Conservative*, new edition (Princeton: Princeton University Press, 2007), 28.

28. John Cook, "GOP Tries to Claim the Ghost of Jackie Robinson," *Gawker*, October 13, 2009, http://gawker.com/5380714/gop-tries-to-claim-the-ghost-of -jackie-robinson.

29. Joseph A. Califano Jr., "It Took a Partnership," *Washington Post*, January 15, 2008, http://www.washingtonpost.com/wp-dyn/content/article/2008/01/14/AR 2008011402079.html.

30. Peter Applebome, "Impeachment Republicans, 130 Years Later; Dueling with the Heirs of Jeff Davis," *New York Times*, December 27, 1998, http://www .nytimes.com/1998/12/27/weekinreview/impeachment-republicans-130-years -later-dueling-with-the-heirs-of-jeff-davis.html.

31. "American Morning," *CNN*, July 10, 2009, http://transcripts.cnn.com /TRANSCRIPTS/0907/10/ltm.01.html.

32. *CNN*, July 10, 2009.

33. "Young GOP Chooses Hate," *The Daily Beast* (blog), July 11, 2009, http:// www.thedailybeast.com/articles/2009/07/11/young-gop-chooses-hate.html.

34. John Avlon, "New GOP 'Racist' Headache," *The Daily Beast* (blog), July 6, 2009, http://www.thedailybeast.com/articles/2009/07/06/new-gop-racist -headache.html.

35. See http://www.zoominfo.com/p/Audra-Sigler/1346137929.

36. *American Jewish Year Book* (New York: American Jewish Committee, 1967).

37. See http://newspaperrock.bluecorncomics.com/2013/01/thoughts-on -casino-jack-documentary.html.

38. *Leonardo's Note Book* (blog), November 2008, http://leonardosnotebook .blogspot.com/2008/11/on-airing-untoward-comments.html (as of 2010).

39. Janet Zink, "E-mail Flap Forces Tampa's Carol Carter to Resign Her Re-publican State Committeewoman Post," *Tampa Bay Times*, February 5, 2009, http://www.tampabay.com/news/localgovernment/article973693.ece.

40. Associated Press, "Mayor to Quit over Obama Watermelon E-Mail," *MSN*, February 27, 2009, http://www.msnbc.msn.com/id/29423045/.

41. "Rusty DePass, South Carolina GOP Activist, Says Escaped Gorilla Was Ancestor of Michelle Obama," *Huffington Post*, July 15, 2009, updated May 25, 2011, http://www.huffingtonpost.com/2009/06/14/rusty-depass-south-caroli _n_215439.html.

42. Rachel Weiner, "Historical Keepsake Photo: Tennessee GOP Staffer Emails Racist Obama 'Spook' Photo," *Huffington Post*, July 7, 2009, updated May 25, 2011, http://www.huffingtonpost.com/2009/06/16/tennessee-gop-staffer -ema_n_216085.html.

43. Zachary Roth, "Conservative Activist Forwards Racist Pic Showing Obama as Witch Doctor," *Talking Points Memo* (blog), July 23, 2009, http:// tpmmuckraker.talkingpointsmemo.com/2009/07/conservative_activist_forwards _racist_pic_showing.php.

44. David A. Graham, "More RNC Internet Follies: Racist Images on Fan Photo Page," *Newsweek* (blog), October, 26, 2009, http://www.newsweek.com/more -rnc-internet-follies-racist-images-fan-photo-page-212366.

45. Matt Woo, "Arlington Mayor Fires at Obama Online," *Commercial Appeal,* December 4, 2009, http://www.commercialappeal.com/news/2009/dec/04/mayor-fires-at-obama-online/.

46. John Avlon, "The GOP's Vote for Hate—and Suicide," *The Daily Beast* (blog), July 13, 2009, http://www.thedailybeast.com/articles/2009/07/10/the-gops-day-of-reckoning.html.

Chapter 6: Partisan Media: Polarizing for Profit

1. "Media Credibility," *Pew Research Center for the People and the Press,* August 17, 2008, http://www.people-press.org/2008/08/17/media-credibility/.

2. Ibid.

3. Cass R. Sunstein, *Going to Extremes* (New York: Oxford University Press, 2009), 4.

4. Richard Hofstadter, *The Paranoid Style in American Politics* (New York: Vintage Books, 1965, 2008), 29–30.

5. Interview with David Frum, October 15, 2009.

6. According to the radio ratings service Arbitron, nearly two-thirds of talk radio's listeners are over age fifty, and almost 90 percent are white.

7. Tim Mak, "Talk Radio Gets Angrier as Its Revenues Drop," *FrumForum* (blog), August 6, 2009 (3:42 p.m.), http://www.frumforum.com/talk-radio-gets-angrier-as-its-revenues-drop/.

8. Ibid.

9. Interview with Mark Potok, October 16, 2009.

10. Kenneth P. Vogel, "Right-Wing Talkers Go for the Gold," *Politico,* December 5, 2009, http://www.politico.com/news/stories/1209/30231.html.

11. Ibid.

12. Interview with David Frum, November 4, 2009.

13. David Corn, "The GOP's Ugly 2010 Campaign: Pushing the Obacalypse," *Politics Daily,* December 29, 2009, http://www.politicsdaily.com/2009/12/29/the-gops-ugly-2010-campaign-pushing-the-obacalypse/.

14. Glenn Beck, *The Real America* (New York: Pocket Books, 2005), 2.

15. *Glenn Beck,* http://www.glennbeck.com/content/tv/.

16. "Glenn Beck's Publisher Claims He's Making Bestseller History: True?" *Huffington Post,* March 18, 2010, http://www.huffingtonpost.com/2009/11/09/glenn-beck-publisher-clai_n_351184.html.

17. Brian Frederick, "Glenn Beck Now Setting the News Agenda for CNN as Well," *Media Matters for America* (blog), September 11, 2009 (5:23 p.m.), http://mediamatters.org/blog/200909110032.

18. Glenn Beck, "Glenn Beck Reveals the Plan," *Glenn Beck,* November 26, 2009, http://www.glennbeck.com/content/articles/article/198/33398/?ck=1.

19. Alexander Zaitchik, "The Making of Glenn Beck," *Salon,* September 21, 2009, http://www.salon.com/2009/09/21/glenn_beck/.

20. Beck, *The Real America*, 194.

21. Alexander Zaitchik, "Glenn Beck Becomes Damaged Goods," *Salon*, September 22, 2009, http://www.salon.com/news/feature/2009/09/22/glenn_beck_two/print.html.

22. Beck, *The Real America*, 53.

23. Alexander Zaitchik, "Glenn Beck Rises Again," *Salon,* September 23, 2009, http://www.salon.com/news/feature/2009/09/23/glenn_beck_three/.

24. "'Comrade' Beck Says 'the Destruction of the West Is Happening,'" *Media Matters for America,* March 4, 2009, http://mediamatters.org/mmtv/200903040029, accessed June 1, 2009, video.

25. Ibid.

26. "Beck: 'The Government Is a Heroin Pusher Using Smiley-Faced Fascism to Grow the Nanny State,'" *Media Matters for America,* March 31, 2009, http://mediamatters.org/mmtv/200903310037, accessed June 1, 2009, video.

27. "Teasing Tomorrow's Show, Beck Airs Photos of Hitler, Stalin, Lenin, Asks 'Is This Where We're Headed?'" *Media Matters for America,* April 2, 2009, http://mediamatters.org/mmtv/200904020037, accessed August 1, 2009, video.

28. "Beck: Healthcare 'System Is Going to Come Out the Other Side Dictorial [*sic*]—It's Going to Come Out a Fascist State,'" *Media Matters for America,* July 27, 2009, http://mediamatters.org/mmtv/200907270008, accessed August 1, 2009, video.

29. "Beck: Health Care Reform Is 'Good Old Socialism . . . Raping the Pocketbooks of the Rich to Give to the Poor,'" *Media Matters for America,* July 21, 2009, http://mediamatters.org/mmtv/200907210041, accessed August 1, 2009, video.

30. "Beck: 'The Health Care Bill Is Reparations; It's the Beginning of Reparations,'" *Media Matters for America,* July 22, 2009, http://mediamatters.org/mmtv/200907220015, accessed August 4, 2009, video.

31. "Discussing Gay Marriage Ruling in Iowa, Beck Says, 'I Believe This Case Is Actually About Going into Churches, and Going in and Attacking Those Churches and Saying, "You Can't Teach Anything Else,"'" *Media Matters for America,* April 13, 2009, http://mediamatters.org/mmtv/200904130030, accessed August 10, 2009, video.

32. "Beck Denies Responsibility for Pittsburgh Shooting, Adds That Obama 'Will Slowly but Surely Take Your Gun or Take Away Your Ability to Shoot a Gun, Carry a Gun,'" *Media Matters for America,* April 7, 2009, http://mediamatters.org/mmtv/200904070026, accessed August 10, 2009, video.

33. "Beck: 'Obama Has Exposed Himself as a Guy' with 'a Deep Seated Hatred for White People,'" *Media Matters for America,* July 28, 2009, http://mediamatters.org/mmtv/200907280008, accessed August 10, 2009, video.

34. "Responding to Krugman, Beck Claimed of FEMA Conspiracy Theories: 'Never Said Anything Like It,'" *Media Matters for America,* June 12, 2009, http://mediamatters.org/research/2009/06/12/responding-to-krugman-beck-claimed-of-fema-cons/151153, accessed August 10, 2009, video.

35. "Beck: 'There Is a Coup Going on . . . It Has Been Done Through the Guise of an Election,'" *Media Matters for America,* August 31, 2009, http://mediamatters .org/mmtv/200908310007, accessed September 3, 2009, video.

36. "Glenn Beck Stirring Up the Pot for the Big Revolt," *Stormfront* (blog), August 13, 2009 (1:27 a.m.–9:20 a.m.), http://www.stormfront.org/forum/show thread.php?s=5f77bb3973594fd6147d499bc9073207&p=7213067#post7213067, online forum.

37. "Glenn Beck Stirring Up the Pot for the Big Revolt," *Stormfront* (blog), August 13, 2009 (6:23 p.m.–7:13 p.m.), http://www.stormfront.org/forum/show thread.php?t=629488&page=13, online forum.

38. Michael Hiestand, "Despite Scorched Bridges, Olbermann Rejoins ESPN," *USA Today,* June 13, 2005, http://usatoday30.usatoday.com/sports/2005-06-13 -olbermann-espn_x.htm.

39. Keith Olbermann, "ESPN: Mea Culpa," *Salon,* November 18, 2002, http:// www.salon.com/news/sports/col/olbermann/2002/11/17/meaculpa/index.html.

40. Marvin Kitman, "Olbermann Rules," *Nation,* October 8, 2007, http:// www.thenation.com/doc/20071008/kitman.

41. "Keith Olbermann Does *The View:* Explains Why He Doesn't Vote, Says Sarah Palin Has TV Future," *Huffington Post,* November 10, 2008, updated December 11, 2008, http://www.huffingtonpost.com/2008/11/10/keith-olbermann -does-the_n_142749.html.

42. "Keith Olbermann Delivers One Hell of a Commentary on Rumsfeld," *Crooks and Liars* (blog), August 29, 2006, http://crooksandliars.com/2006/08/30 /keith-olbermann-delivers-one-hell-of-a-commentary-on-rumsfeld#comment-6.

43. Keith Olbermann, "Special Comment: Advertising Terrorism," *Countdown with Keith Olbermann* (9:40 p.m.), October 23, 2006, http://www.msnbc.msn .com/id/15392701/ns/msnbc_tv-countdown_with_keith_olbermann/page/2/, accessed August 15, 2008, video.

44. Keith Olbermann, "'Beginning of the End of America,'" *Countdown with Keith Olbermann,* October 19, 2006 (3:40 p.m.), http://www.msnbc.msn.com /id/15321167/, accessed August 15, 2008, video.

45. Keith Olbermann, "Special Comment: Condi Goes Too Far," *Countdown with Keith Olbermann, NBC News,* February 27, 2007, http://www.msnbc.msn .com/id/17351284/print/1/displaymode/1098/.

46. "ADL Letter to MSNBC," *National Defamation League,* July 28, 2006, http://www.adl.org/media_watch/tv/20060728-MSNBC.htm.

47. "ADL Letter to MSNBC," *Anti-Defamation League,* July 28, 2006, http:// archive.adl.org/media_watch/tv/20060728-msnbc.html#.U1W1cpUU9yo.

48. Keith Olbermann, *Countdown with Keith Olbermann,* April 7, 2009, http:// www.msnbc.msn.com/id/30109453/.

49. Keith Olbermann, "Olbermann: 'Ruined Senate Bill Unsupportable,'" *Countdown with Keith Olbermann,* December 16, 2009 (9:16 p.m.), http://www .msnbc.msn.com/id/34455168/, accessed December 17, 2009, video.

50. Keith Olbermann, *Countdown with Keith Olbermann,* December 14, 2009, http://www.msnbc.msn.com/id/34430893/ns/msnbc_tv-countdown _with_keith_olbermann/.

51. Noel Sheppard, "Olbermann: Scott Brown's a 'Homophobic, Racist, Teabagging Supporter of Violence Against Women,'" *NewsBusters* (blog), January 18, 2010, http://newsbusters.org/blogs/noel-sheppard/2010/01/18 /olbermann-scott-browns-irresponsible-homophobic-racist-teabagging-sup.

52. Brad Wilmouth, "Olbermann: 'Without 'Fascistic Hatred,' Malkin Is Just a 'Mashed Up' Bag of Meat with Lipstick,'" *NewsBusters* (blog), October 13, 2009 (20:53), http://newsbusters.org/blogs/brad-wilmouth/2009/10/13 /olbermann-without-fascistic-hatred-malkin-just-mashed-bag-meat-lipsti#ixzz ocMrII4Tc.

53. "Bush: MoveOn.org Ad on Petraeus 'Disgusting,'" *CNN,* September 18, 2007, http://www.cnn.com/2007/POLITICS/09/20/bush.petraeus/.

54. See http://www.dailykos.com/story/2013/12/17/1263546/-TDS-TCR-Screw -them.

55. Johanna Neuman, "Republicans Make Twitter Their Own," *Los Angeles Times,* August 20, 2009, http://articles.latimes.com/2009/aug/30/nation/na -ticket30.

56. Conservapedia: The Trustworthy Encyclopedia, http://www.conservapedia .com, accessed August 15, 2009.

57. See http://thecolbertreport.cc.com/videos/63ite2/the-word-truthiness.

58. Alexa: The Web Information Company, http://www.alexa.com/siteinfo /worldnetdaily.com, accessed June 4, 2009.

59. Aaron Klein, "Obama Worked Closely with Terrorist Bill Ayers," *WND,* September 23, 2008, http://www.wnd.com/index.php?pageId=76022.

60. Aaron Klein, "Hamas Terrorists Make 2008 U.S. Presidential Pick," *WND,* April 14, 2008, http://www.wnd.com/index.php?pageId=61631.

61. Ron Strom, "Obama's Church: More About Africa Than God?" *WND,* January 9, 2008, http://www.wnd.com/news/article.asp?ARTICLE_ID=59600.

62. Drew Zahn, "Next Step in H1N1Scare: Microchip Implants," *WND,* August 22, 2009, http://www.wnd.com/index.php?pageId=107588.

63. Janet Porter, "Unmistakable Evil," *WND,* August 11, 2009, http://www .wnd.com/index.php?fa=PAGE.view&pageId=106559.

64. "Sleaze Charge: 'I Took Drugs, Had Homo Sex with Obama,'" *WND,* February 17, 2008, http://www.wnd.com/index.php?fa=PAGE.view&pageId=56626.

65. Jack Wheeler, "How the Clintons Will Undo McCain," *WND,* February 4, 2008, http://www.wnd.com/news/article.asp?ARTICLE_ID=60020.

66. Joe Kovaks, "Blood Moon Eclipses: 2nd Coming in 2015?" *WND,* April 30, 2008, http://www.wnd.com/index.php?pageId=63076.

67. Bob Unruh, "Obama Ripped for Plan to Bring Back 'Inquisitions,'" *WND,* December 13, 2009, http://www.wnd.com/index.php?fa=PAGE .view&pageId=118710.

68. Jerome R. Corsi, "Does Obama Intend to Destroy Capitalism?" *WND*, December 14, 2009, http://www.wnd.com/index.php?fa=PAGE .view&pageId=118592.

69. Survival Seed Bank: Lets You Plant a Full Acre Crisis Garden! http:// www.survivalseedbank.com/, accessed July 9, 2009.

70. Joseph Farah, "Pray Obama Falls," *WND*, January 18, 2009, http://www .wnd.com/index.php?pageId=86469.

71. See http://www.faspe.info/journalism2013/?p=260.

72. Pew Research Center for the People and the Press, "Press Accuracy Rating Hits Two Decade Low," September 13, 2009, http://people-press.org/report/543/.

73. Howard Kurtz, "Administration Paid Commentator," *Washington Post*, January 8, 2006, http://www.washingtonpost.com/wp-dyn/articles/A56330 -2005Jan7.html.

74. "Press Accuracy Rating Hits Two Decade Low," Pew Center for People and the Press, September 13, 2009, http://www.people-press.org/2009/09/13 /press-accuracy-rating-hits-two-decade-low/; *Topic A with Tina Brown*, October 24, 2004.

75. Ali Frick, "Rep. Lamar Smith: 'The Greatest Threat to America Is a Liberal Media Bias,'" *ThinkProgress* (blog), June 4, 2009, http://thinkprogress .org/2009/06/04/smith-media-bias-threat/.

76. See http://www.people-press.org/2012/06/04/section-9-trends-in-party -affiliation/.

77. See http://www.timepolls.com/hppolls/archive/poll_results_417.html.

Chapter 7: Sarah Palin and the Limbaugh Brigades

1. Jeffrey M. Jones, "Huckabee, Romney, Palin See Most Republican Support for '12," *Gallup Politics*, November 5, 2009, http://www.gallup.com/poll/124097 /Huckabee-Romney-Palin-See-Most-Republican-Support-12.aspx.

2. Jonathan Martin, "McCain Lashes Out at Press over Palin," *Politico,* September 2, 2008, http://www.politico.com/news/stories/0908/13107.html.

3. Kate Phillips, "Palin: Obama Is 'Palling Around with Terrorists,'" *The Caucus,* October 4, 2008.

4. Juliet Eilperin, "Palin's 'Pro-American Areas' Remark: Extended Version," *The Trail* (blog), *Washington Post,* October 17, 2008, http://voices.washingtonpost .com/44/2008/10/17/palin_clarifies_her_pro-americ.html.

5. Scott Conroy, "Palin: Obama's Plan Is 'Experiment with Socialism,'" *CBS News* (blog), October 19, 2008, http://www.cbsnews.com/blogs/2008/10/19 /politics/fromtheroad/entry4531388.shtml.

6. Danny Shea, "David Brooks: Sarah Palin 'Represents a Fatal Cancer to the Republican Party,'" *Huffington Post,* November 8, 2008, updated May 25, 2011, http:// www.huffingtonpost.com/2008/10/08/david-brooks-sarah-palin_n_133001.html.

7. Alexander Mooney, "Palin Should Step Down, Conservative Commentator Says," *CNN*, September 26, 2008, http://politicalticker.blogs.cnn.com/2008/09/26/palin-should-step-down-conservative-commentator-says/comment-page-9/.

8. Dana Bash, Peter Hamby, and John King, "Palin's 'Going Rogue' McCain Aide Says," *CNN*, October 26, 2008, http://www.cnn.com/2008/POLITICS/10/25/palin.tension/index.html.

9. "Misconceptions of Obama Fuel Republican Campaign," *Al-Jazeera*, October 13, 2008.

10. Michael Cooper and Dalia Sussman, "Growing Doubts on Palin Take a Toll, Poll Says," *New York Times*, October 30 2008, http://www.nytimes.com/2008/10/31/us/politics/31poll.html?_r=2&scp=1&sq=palin%20%20poll&st=Search.

11. Rasmussen Reports, 2008, http://www.rasmussenreports.com/premium_content/econ_crosstabs/october_2008/crosstabs_fox_variety_october_31_november_1_2008 (as of 2010).

12. Massimo Calabresi, "Poll: Palin Less Popular with Women Voters Than Men," *Time*, October 2, 2008, http://www.time.com/time/politics/article/0,8599,1846443,00.html.

13. Geoffrey Dunn, "'Watermelon Roll': More Racism from 'Team Sarah,'" *Huffington Post*, December 21, 2008, http://www.huffingtonpost.com/geoffrey-dunn/watermelon-roll-more-rac_b_152743.html_NoPara.

14. Hannah Dreier, "Fox News Personalities Advance Palin's 'Death Panel' Claim," *Media Matters for America*, August 10, 2009, http://mediamatters.org/mobile/research/200908100054.

15. Dal Balz and Jon Cohen, "Palin Particularly Popular Among Fans of Limbaugh and Beck," *Washington Post*, November 30, 2009, http://www.washingtonpost.com/wp-dyn/content/article/2009/11/29/AR2009112902717.html.

16. Tom Jensen, "Who Do the Birthers Love?" *Public Policy Polling* (blog), August 21, 2009 (6:58 a.m.), http://publicpolicypolling.blogspot.com/2009/08/who-do-birthers-love.html.

17. Steve Benen, *Political Animal*, December 4, 2009, http://www.washingtonmonthly.com/archives/individual/2009_12/021287.php.

18. Rush Limbaugh, "Why Does Palin Scare You Libs?" *The Rush Limbaugh Show*, November 20, 2009, http://www.rushlimbaugh.com/home/daily/site_112009/content/01125110.guest.html, Web transcript, accessed November 21, 2009.

19. Tom Leonard, "US Talk Radio Host Rush Limbaugh Signs $400M Contract," *Telegraph*, July 2, 2008, http://www.telegraph.co.uk/news/worldnews/2236873/US-talk-radio-host-Rush-Limbaugh-signs-400m-contract.html.

20. Jon Ponder, "Median Age of Fox News Viewers Is 65—Average Dittohead Is a 67 Year Old Man," *Pensito Review*, May 5, 2009, http://www.pensitoreview.com/2009/05/05/average-age-of-fox-news-viewer-is-65/.

21. Frank Newport, "Limbaugh Well Liked by Many, but Not All, Republicans," *Gallup,* February 5, 2009, http://www.gallup.com/poll/114163/limbaugh-liked-not-republicans.aspx.

22. Rush Limbaugh, "Limbaugh: I Hope Obama Fails," *The Rush Limbaugh Show,* January 16, 2009, http://www.rushlimbaugh.com/home/daily/site_011609/content/01125113.guest.html.

23. Ben Armbruster, "Limbaugh Claims He's Being Told 'to Bend Over, Grab the Ankles' Because Obama's 'Father Was Black,'" ThinkProgress (blog), January 22, 2009, http://thinkprogress.org/politics/2009/01/22/35086/limbaugh-ankles-obama-black/.

24. Mike Allen and Jonathan Martin, "Emanuel: Rush Is the GOP's Brain," *Politico,* March 2, 2009, http://www.politico.com/news/stories/0309/19460.html.

25. Mike Allen, "Steele to Rush: I'm Sorry," *Politico,* March 2, 2009, http://www.politico.com/news/stories/0309/19517.html#ixzz0UiBZfSRx.

26. The University of Virginia, Center for Politics, n.d., http://www.centerforpolitics.org/crystalball/article.php?id=LJS2006031601 (as of 2010).

27. Sam Stein, "Michele Bachmann Channels McCarthy: Obama 'Very Anti-American,' Congressional Witch Hunt Needed," *Huffington Post,* November 17, 2008, http://www.huffingtonpost.com/2008/10/17/gop-rep-channels-mccarthy_n_135735.html.

28. Kevin Diaz, "Obama's Energy Cap-and-Trade Plan Has Bachmann Talking About a Revolution," *Star Tribune,* March 24, 2009, http://www.startribune.com/politics/national/house/41719957.html?elr=KArksLckD8EQDUoaEyqyP4O:DW3ckUiD3aPc:_Yyc:aUUsZ.

29. Steven Thomma, "Secret Camps and Guillotines? Groups Make Birthers Look Sane," *Truth to Power McClatchy DC,* August 28, 2009, http://www.mcclatchydc.com/100/story/74549.html.

30. Ernest Luning, "Bachmann: 'Slit Our Wrists, Be Blood Brothers' to Beat Health Care Reform," *Colorado Independent,* August 31, 2009, http://coloradoindependent.com/36840/bachmann-slit-our-wrists-be-blood-brothers'-to-beat-health-care-reform.

31. Eric Kleefeld, "Bachmann Blasts Obama's 'Economic Marxism,' Calls for 'Orderly Revolution' to Save Freedom," *Talking Points Memo* (blog), March 27, 3009, http://tpmdc.talkingpointsmemo.com/2009/03/bachmann-blasts-obamas-economic-marxism-calls-for-revolution-to-save-freedom.php.

32. Lee Fang, "Gohmert Trades Ideas with Conspiracy Theorist, Says Obama Health Plan Will 'Absolutely Kill Senior Citizens,'" *ThinkProgress* (blog), July 27, 2009, http://thinkprogress.org/2009/07/27/gohmert-conspiracies-alexjones/.

33. Christina Bellantoni, "Debating Hate Crimes, Gohmert Rambles on About Bestiality, Sex with Corpses, Voting for a Black Man," *Talking Points Memo* (blog), October 7, 2009, http://tpmdc.talkingpointsmemo.com/2009/10/debating-hate-crimes-gohmert-rambles-on-about-bestiality-sex-with-corpses-voting-for

-a-black-man.php?ref=mp.

34. Russ Mitchell, "King Announced Bid for Fourth Term," *Daily Reporter,* March 8, 2008, http://www.spencerdailyreporter.com/story/1316727.html.

35. Duke Reed, "At What Point Does Free Speech Become Hate Speech" *Daily Kos* (blog), May 9, 2006, http://www.dailykos.com/story /2006/05/09/208642/-At-what-point-does-free-speech-become-hate-speech.

36. Glenn Thrush, "Pelosi Critical of Baucus Bill," *Politico* (blog), September 17, 2009, http://www.politico.com/news/stories/0909/27266.html.

37. Jim Galloway, "Paul Broun: I Was the First to Call President Obama . . . Socialist," *Atlanta Journal-Constitution,* February 13, 2013, http://www .ajc.com/weblogs/political-insider/2013/feb/13/paul-broun-i-was-first-call -obama-socialist/.

38. "'Freedom Fighter' Paul Broun: Immigration Reform 'Disastrous for Anybody Who Is Freedom-Loving,'" *Right-Wing Watch,* February 24, 2014, http:// www.rightwingwatch.org/content/freedom-fighter-paul-broun-immigration -reform-disastrous-anybody-who-freedom-loving#sthash.rTXEDal6.dpuf.

39. See http://www.dailykos.com/story/2006/05/09/208642/-At-what-point -does-free-speech-become-hate-speech.

40. Glenn Thrush, "Franks: Obama Is 'Enemy of Humanity,'" *Politico,* September 30, 2009, http://www.politico.com/news/stories/0909/27725.html.

41. Amanda Hess, "Sorry, Alan Grayson: 'K Street Whore' Isn't Specific Enough," *The Sexist* (blog), *Washington City Paper,* October 28, 2009 (3:50 p.m.), http://www.washingtoncitypaper.com/blogs/sexist/2009/10/27/sorry-alan -grayson-k-street-whore-isnt-specific-enough/.

42. "Grayson Wants to Send Critic to Jail for Five Years," *The Orlando Sentinel* (blog), December 2009, http://archive.today/qfhke.

43. "GOP Rep. Trent Franks Calls Obama 'An Enemy of Humanity,' *Huffington Post,* November 29, 2009, http://www.huffingtonpost.com/2009/09/29/gop-rep -trent-franks-call_n_302713.html.

44. Brian Montopoli, "Conservatives Fight 'Homosexual Extremist Movement,'" *CBS News,* September 28, 2009, http://www.cbsnews.com/blogs/2009 /09/28/politics/politicalhotsheet/entry5346428.shtml.

45. David Weigel, "In Photos: How to Take Back America Conference," *Washington Independent,* September 28, 2009, http://washingtonindependent .com/61131/in-photos-the-how-to-take-back-america-conference.

46. Jo Mannies, "Nation Leaders at Conservative Conference Call for Tougher Talk Against Abortion and Gays," *St. Louis Beacon,* September 25, 2009, https:// www.stlbeacon.org/#!/list/.

47. David Weigel, "Bachmann in St. Louis: Defund the Left, Beware One-World Currency," *Washington Independent,* September 26, 2009, http:// washingtonindependent.com/61037/bachmann-in-st-louis-defund-the-left -beware-one-world-currency.

48. *CBS News,* September 28, 2009.

49. Jim O'Neill, "Taking Back America," *Canada Free Press,* September 26, 2009, http://canadafreepress.com/index.php/article/15130.

50. "Mass Resistance's Brian Camenker Speaks at National 'How to Take Back America' Conference in St. Louis," *Mass Resistance,* October 2, 2009, http://www.massresistance.org/docs/gen/09c/StLouis_conference/index.html.

51. Jonathan Martin, "Romney Rouses Values Voters," *Politico* (blog), September 19, 2009, http://www.politico.com/news/stories/0909/27342_Page2.html#ixzzoTU0UH2VD.

52. Eric Kleefeld, "The Values Voter Summit: A Celebration of the 'Religious Right,'" *Talking Points Memo,* September 21, 2009, http://tpmdc.talkingpointsmemo.com/2009/09/the-values-voter-summit-a-celebration-of-the-religious-right.php#more.

53. "Polling the Tea Party," *New York Times,* April 14, 2010, http://www.nytimes.com/interactive/2010/04/14/us/politics/20100414-tea-party-poll-graphic.html?_r=1&#tab=4.

Chapter 8: RINOs and DINOs: Hunting for Heretics

1. *CNN,* November 2008.

2. John Avlon, "Specter's Shocking Defection," *The Daily Beast* (blog), April 28, 2009, http://www.thedailybeast.com/articles/2009/04/28/specters-shocking-defection.html

3. Faiz Shakir, "Gingrich Expresses Concern with Identifying Beck and Limbaugh as Leaders of the GOP," *ThinkProgress* (blog), October 26, 2009, http://thinkprogress.org/2009/10/26/gingrich-beck-limbaugh/.

4. "Newt Gingrich—'King of the RINOS,'" *Examiner.com,* October 27, 2009, http://www.examiner.com/article/newt-gingrich-king-of-the-rinos.

5. Adam Nagourney, "G.O.P. Considers 'Purity' Resolution for Candidates," *The Caucus* (blog), November 23, 2009 (1:32 p.m.), http://thecaucus.blogs.nytimes.com/2009/11/23/gop-considers-purity-resolution-for-candidates/.

6. *American Spectator,* http://search.opinionarchives.com/Summary/AmericanSpectator/V35I6P32-1.htm.

7. Bob MacGuffie, "Right Principles—Rocking the Town Halls—Best Practices," http://thinkprogress.org/wp-content/uploads/2009/07/townhallactionmemo.pdf.

8. Clive Webb, *Massive Resistance: Southern Opposition to the Second Reconstruction* (New York: Oxford University Press, 2005), 22.

9. Harry Overstreet and Bonaro Overstreet, *The Strange Tactics of Extremism* (New York: W. W. Norton, 1964), 27.

10. *Calbuzz,* http://www.calbuzz.com/tag/ken-khachigian/.

11. Robin Toner, "Conservatives Savor Their Role as Insiders at the White

House," *New York Times*, March 19, 2001, http://www.nytimes.com/2001/03/19/us/conservatives-savor-their-role-as-insiders-at-the-white-house.html.

12. Office of the Inspector General, "An Investigation of Allegations of Politicized Hiring by Monica Goodling and Other Staff in the Office of Attorney General," July 2008, www.justice.gov/oig/special/s0807/chapter3.htm.

13. John Avlon, "How I Got Interrogated by the Bushies," *The Daily Beast* (blog), January 15, 2001, http://www.thedailybeast.com/articles/2009/01/15/how-i-got-interrogated-by-the-bushies.html.

14. Christopher Buckley, "Sorry, Dad, I'm Voting for Obama," *The Daily Beast* (blog), October 10, 2008, http://www.thedailybeast.com/articles/2008/10/10/the-conservative-case-for-obama.html.

15. David Frum, "Why Rush Is Wrong," *Newsweek,* March 6, 2009, updated March 3, 2012, http://www.newsweek.com/id/188279.

16. Interview with Charles Johnson, October 14, 2009.

17. Kathleen Parker, "Palin Problem," *National Review Online,* September 26, 2008, http://www.nationalreview.com/articles/225784/palin-problem/kathleen-parker.

18. Interview with Kathleen Parker, October 14, 2009.

19. Buckley, "Sorry, Dad, I'm Voting for Obama."

20. "Address of Governor Ronald Reagan to California Republican Assembly," Lafayette Hotel, Long Beach, April 1, 1967.

21. "Conservatives Seek Test for RNC Funds," *Washington Times,* November 24, 2009, http://www.washingtontimes.com/news/2009/nov/24/conservatives-seek-reagan-litmus-test-for-rnc-fund/.

22. Janie Lorber, "Cheney's Model Republican: More Limbaugh, Less Powell, *New York Times,* May 11, 2009, http://www.nytimes.com/2009/05/11/us/politics/11cheney.html.

23. Andrew Marshall, "From Lunatic to Luminary," *Independent,* May 31, 1998, http://www.independent.co.uk/news/from-lunatic-to-luminary-1156281.html.

24. "Barry Goldwater Dead at 89," *CNN,* May 29, 1998, http://www.cnn.com/ALLPOLITICS/1998/05/29/goldwater.obit/.

25. Robin Toner, "For 'Don't Ask, Don't Tell,' Split on Party Lines," *New York Times,* June 8, 2007, http://www.nytimes.com/2007/06/08/us/politics/08gays.html.

26. "Corporations, Political Spending, and the Supreme Court," *PBS* (blog), January 29, 2010 (3:09 p.m.), http://www.pbs.org/moyers/journal/blog/2010/01/corporations_political_spendin.html.

27. John P. Avlon, "Would Goldwater Leave?" *New York Sun,* April 7, 2006, http://www.nysun.com/opinion/would-goldwater-leave/30647/.

28. "Even the Gipper," *Politifact.com,* January 10, 2008, http://www.politifact.com/truth-o-meter/statements/2008/jan/11/mike-huckabee/even-the-gipper/.

29. Jonathan Alter, "Reagan vs. the New Right," *Newsweek*, September 18, 1983.

30. Hedrick Smith, "Reagan Loyalists Are Wondering About Their Champion's Loyalty," *New York Times*, November 20, 1980.

31. "Beck Attacks Graham for Saying GOP Should Reach Out to 'Different Constituencies,' McCain for Idolizing TR," *Media Matters for America*, October 22, 2009, http://mediamatters.org/mmtv/200910220038.

32. Andy Barr, "Mike Huckabee: Big Tent Will Kill GOP," *Politico* (blog), http://www.politico.com/news/stories/1209/30393.html, accessed October 25, 2009, video.

33. See http://www.rightprinciples.com/rino1.html (as of 2010).

34. Eric Kleefeld, "Perkins: At This Rate, GOP Will Become Big, *Empty* Tent," *Talking Points Memo,* March 12, 2009, http://tpmdc.talkingpointsmemo.com/2009/03/perkins-at-this-rate-gop-will-become-big-empty-tent.php.

35. Interview with Joe Scarborough, October 30, 2009.

36. Interview with Rich Lowry, October 20, 2009.

37. See http://videocafe.crooksandliars.com/node/31259/print (as of 2010).

38. "Obama Fact Sheet," *World Can't Wait,* January 18, 2008, http://www.worldcantwait.net/index.php?option=com_content&view=article&id=5330:obama-fact-sheet&catid=117:homepage&Itemid=289.

39. Ibid.

40. See http://www.warcriminalswatch.org/images/stories/pdfs/obamatorture%2017x22-wcw.pdf.

41. Heather, "Ed Schultz: Right Now Mr. President Your Base Thinks You're Nothing But a Sellout," *Crooks and Liars,* December 17, 2009, http://crooksandliars.com/heather/ed-schultz-right-now-mr-president-your-base.

42. Ibid.

43. "Howard Dean Is Perfectly Positioned to Primary Obama in 2012, *Firedoglake* (blog), December 17, 2009 (8:49 p.m.), http://seminal.firedoglake.com/diary/19581.

44. "Liberals Hope to Push Obama Left," *CBS News*, December 1, 2008, http://www.cbsnews.com/stories/2008/12/01/politics/main4641170.shtml?source=related_story.

45. Jordan Fabian, "Frank: President Obama Is Wrong to Be 'Post-Partisan' in Face of GOP Opposition," *The Hill* (blog), October 5, 2009 (3:27 p.m.), http://thehill.com/blogs/blog-briefing-room/news/61611-frank-obama-wrong-to-be-post-partisan.

46. Tilting Yard, "Bipartisanship Is a Silly Beltway Obsession," *Wall Street Journal,* February 18, 2009, http://online.wsj.com/article/SB123491659161904365.html.

47. Alex Fryer, "Sheehan Criticizes Bush, Doesn't Spare Democrats," *Seattle Times,* May 9, 2006, http://seattletimes.nwsource.com/html/localnews/2002981541_sheehan09.html.

48. Byron York, "Cindy Sheehan Heads to the Vineyard—Will Anyone Cover the Story? (Protesting Obama!!)," *Washington Examiner,* August 17, 2009, http://

www.freerepublic.com/focus/f-news/2319084/posts.

49. Valeria Criscione, "Nobel Prize Winner Obama Will Face Afghan War Opponents in Oslo," *Christian Science Monitor,* December 10, 2009, http://www .csmonitor.com/World/Europe/2009/1210/p06s01-woeu.html.

50. "Ted Rall: It's Increasingly Evident That Obama Should Resign," *State Journal-Register,* May 29, 2009, http://www.sj-r.com/opinions/x124603932/Ted -Rall-It-s-increasingly-evident-that-Obama-should-resign.

51. Lauren Kornreich, "MoveOn.org Targets Democrats on Public Option," *CNN* (blog), September 30, 2009 (3:32 p.m.), http://politicalticker.blogs.cnn .com/2009/09/30/moveon-org-targets-democrats-on-public-option/.

52. See http://www.dailykos.com/story/2009/11/10/803004/-New-PCCC-Ads -Hit-Blue-Dog-Betrayal.

53. See http://voices.washingtonpost.com/ezra-klein/2009/12/joe_lieberman _lets_not_make_a.html.

54. Victor Navasky, "Lieberman's Betrayal: That's No Way for a Jew to Act, Senator," *Tablet,* December 23, 2009, http://www.tabletmag.com/jewish-news-and -politics/22857/liebermans-betrayal.

55. "Social Security History," *Social Security Administration,* n.d., http:// www.ssa.gov/history/tally.html.

56. See http://www.ssa.gov/history/tally65.html.

57. "1996 Welfare Amendments," *Social Security Administration,* n.d., http:// www.ssa.gov/history/tally1996.html, accessed August 18, 2009.

58. Frank Newport, "Approval of Congress Falls 21%, Driven by Democrats," *Gallup Politics,* October 6, 2009, http://www.gallup.com/poll/123491/Approval -Congress-Falls-21-Driven-Democrats.aspx.

59. Lydia Saad, "In U.S., Majority Now Says Obama Policies 'Mostly Liberal,'" *Gallup Politics,* November 4, 2009, http://www.gallup.com/poll/124094/Majority -Say-Obama-Policies-Mostly-Liberal.aspx.

Chapter 9: The Big Lie: Birthers and Truthers

1. David Weigel, "Rep. Mike Castle Fends Off the Birthers," *Washington Independent,* July 20, 2009, http://washingtonindependent.com/51736/rep-mike -castle-fends-off-the-birthers.

2. Lisa Wangsness, "Obama Fighting False E-Mail Rumors in South Carolina," *Boston.com,* January 26, 2008, http://www.boston.com/news/nation /articles/2008/01/26/obama_fighting_false_e_mail_rumors_in_south_carolina/.

3. David Weigel, "Poll: One-Third of Tennesseans Think Obama Is Muslim or Foreign Born," *Washington Independent,* October 14, 2009, http://washington independent.com/63817/poll-one-third-of-tennesseans-think-obama -is-muslim-or-foreign-born.

4. See http://pumaparty.com/vb/puma-talking-points-media-relations/18349 -write-your-local-areas-newspapers-ask-if-obama-legal.html (as of 2010).

5. "Born in the USA," *FactCheck.org,* posted on August 21, 2008, updated on November 1, 2008, April 27, 2011, http://www.factcheck.org/2008/08/born-in -the-usa/.

6. See http://pumaparty.com/forum/viewtopic.php?f=4&t=185&p=924.

7. "Concerning President Bush's Texas Air National Guard Service," *Report of the Independent Review Panel Dick Thornburgh and Louis D. Boccardi,* September 8, 2004, http://wwwimage.cbsnews.com/htdocs/pdf/complete_report/CBS_Report.pdf.

8. Interview with Linda Starr, December 30, 2009.

9. Interview with Philip Berg, December 9, 2009.

10. "Rage Grows in America: Government Conspiracies," *Anti-Defamation League,* n.d., http://www.adl.org/special_reports/rage-grows-in-America/birther -movement.asp.

11. Max Blumenthal, "Queen of the Birthers," *The Daily Beast* (blog), July 30, 2009, http://www.thedailybeast.com/blogs-and-stories/2009-07-30/queen -of-the-birthers/.

12. Chelsea Schilling, "Meet the Fierce Blonde Behind Obama Eligibility Law-suits," *WND,* April 12, 2009, http://www.wnd.com/index.php?pageId=94377.

13. Blumenthal, "Queen of the Birthers."

14. Dr. Conspiracy, "Dr. Orly Taitz," *Obama Conspiracy Theories,* January 8, 2009, http://www.obamaconspiracy.org/2009/01/dr-orly-taitz/.

15. Alex Koppleman, "Lou Dobbs Embraces the Birthers," *Salon,* July 22, 2009, http://www.salon.com/politics/war_room/feature/2009/07/22/dobbs/.

16. Lee Fang, "Rep. Neugebauer: 'I Don't Know' If Obama Is a Citizen," *Think-Progress,* June 23, 2009, http://thinkprogress.org/2009/06/23/gop-birther-bill/.

17. Steve Benen, "The Birthers," *Washington Monthly,* March 2, 2009, http:// www.washingtonmonthly.com/archives/individual/2009_03/017108.php.

18. *Orlytaitz.com,* accessed July 9, 2009, http://www.orlytaitz.com.

19. Liza Mundy, "Burden of Proof on Obama's Origins," *Washington Post,* October 6, 2009, http://www.washingtonpost.com/wp-dyn/content/article/2009 /10/05/AR2009100503819_pf.html.

20. Glenn Thrush, "58 Percent of GOP Not Sure/Doubt Obama Born in US," *Politico* (blog), July 31, 2009 (8:14 a.m.), http://www.politico.com/blogs/glenn thrush/0709/58_of_GOP_not_suredont_beleive_Obama_born_in_US.html ?showall.

21. "Rep. McKinney Accuses Bush of Profiting from 9/11," *Fox News,* April 12, 2002, http://www.foxnews.com/story/2002/04/12/rep-mckinney-accuses -bush-profiting-from-11/.

22. See http://97.74.65.51/readArticle.aspx?ARTID=10051 (as of 2010).

23. Charles Ryder, "Scenes from a Protest, Part 2," online video clip, You-Tube, January 28, 2008 (5:27 p.m.), http://www.youtube.com/watch?v =k3wxkvsQvtQ&eurl=, accessed June 1, 2009.

24. David Weigel, "The Awful Truth About 9/11," *reason.com* (blog), June 19, 2007 (1:31 p.m.), http://reason.com/blog/2007/06/19/the-awful-truth-about-9-11.

25. Paul Joseph Watson, "Charlie Sheen Requests Meeting with Obama over 9/11 Cover-Up," *Infowars.com,* September 8, 2009, http://www.infowars.com /charlie-sheen-requests-meeting-with-obama-over-911-cover-up/.

26. Andrew Malcolm, "Breaking: Charlie Sheen Demands Obama Meeting in 9/11 Cover-Up," *The Los Angeles Times* (blog), September 9, 2009 (7:40 a.m.), http:// latimesblogs.latimes.com/washington/2009/09/obama-charlie-sheen-911.html.

Chapter 10: The Hatriots: Armed and Dangerous

1. Jeff Zeleny and Jim Rutenberg, "Threats Against Obama Spiked Early," *New York Times,* December 5, 2009, http://www.nytimes.com/2009/12/06/us /06threat.html.

2. "Declaration of Orders We Will Not Obey," *Oath Keepers,* March 3, 2009, http://oathkeepers.org/oath/2009/03/03/declaration-of-orders-we-will-not-obey/.

3. Larry Keller, "Evidence Grows of Far-Right Militia Resurgence," Intelligence Report, no. 135 (Fall 2009): 1, http://www.splcenter.org/intel/intelreport /article.jsp?aid=1092.

4. Mark Potok, "The Year in Hate and Extremism," Intelligence Report no. 149, *Southern Poverty Law Center* (Spring 2013), http://www .splcenter.org/home/2013/spring/the-year-in-hate-and-extremism.

5. Mark Potok, "Exploring the Death of Matthew Shepard," Intelligence Report no. 92, *Southern Poverty Law Center* (Fall 1998): 1, http://www.splcenter .org/news/item.jsp?aid=392.

6. *ThreePercenter.org,* accessed June 8, 2009, http://www.threepercenter.org /page.php?al=about.

7. See http://www.theamericanresistancemovement.com/forums.php?a =vtopic&t=27 (as of 2010).

8. Mike Vanderboegh, *Sipsey Street Irregulars* (blog), November 25, 2009 (5:12 a.m.), http://sipseystreetirregulars.blogspot.com/2009/11/individual-mandate -you-can-believe-in.html.

9. Mike Vanderboegh, *Sipsey Street Irregulars* (blog), December 10, 2009 (3:28 p.m.), http://sipseystreetirregulars.blogspot.com/2009/12/fatal-errors-and-big -die-off.html.

10. James C. McKinley Jr., "Texas Governor's Secession Talk Stirs Furor," *New York Times,* April 17, 2009, http://www.nytimes.com/2009/04/18/us/politics /18texas.html.

11. Jason Linkins, "Glenn Beck: Secession or Suicide," *Huffington Post*, May 17, 2009, updated May 25, 2011 (5:40), http://www.huffingtonpost.com/2009/04/16 /glenn-beck-secession-or-s_n_187779.html, video, accessed June 5, 2009.

12. *Huffington Post,* May 17, 2009.

13. Jennifer Harper, "Voight: Is Obama Creating a Civil War in America?" *Washington Times,* August 21, 2009, http://www.washingtontimes.com/news /2009/aug/21/inside-the-beltway-68484451/.

14. Kyle Mantyla, "Dobson's Lament: Obama Is No Reagan," *Right Wing Watch,* October 7, 2009, http://www.rightwingwatch.org/content/dobsons -lament-obama-no-reagan.

15. George Joyce, "After Obama Fails," *American Thinker,* June 18, 2009, http://www.americanthinker.com/2009/06/after_obama_fails.html.

16. James Verini, "Stopping the Next McVeigh," *The Daily Beast* (blog), November 11, 2009, http://www.thedailybeast.com/articles/2009/11/07/stopping -the-next-mcveigh.html.

17. Charles Johnson, "Hot Air Comments of the Day," *Little Green Footballs* (blog), October 13, 2009, http://littlegreenfootballs.com/article/34899_Hot_Air _Comments_of_the_Day.

18. Ibid., October 27, 2009, http://littlegreenfootballs.com/article/35021_Hot _Air_Comments_of_the_Day.

19. See http://legiscan.com/GA/research/SR327/2013.

20. Jay Bookman, "Georgia Senate Threatens Dismantling the USA," *ajc .com* (blog), April 16, 2009 (7:02 a.m.), http://blogs.ajc.com/jay-bookman -blog/2009/04/16/georgia-senate-threatens-dismantling-of-usa/.

21. *League of the South: Servant Leadership, State Sovereignty, and Southern Independence,* accessed June 8, 2009, http://dixienet.org/New%20Site/index.shtml.

22. Harry Overstreet and Bonaro Overstreet, *The Strange Tactics of Extremism* (New York: W. W. Norton, 1964), 218.

23. Alan J. Stein and David Wilma, "FBI Arrests Right-Wing Minutemen on January 26, 1968, for Conspiring to Blow Up Redmond City Hall and Rob Four Banks," *HistoryLink.org,* July 5, 1999, http://www.historylink.org/index .cfm?DisplayPage=output.cfm&file_id=1464.

24. T. J. Greaney, "Minuteman Outlasted Notoriety, Died with Regrets," *Columbia Daily Tribune,* August 6, 2009, updated January 23, 2013, http://www.columbiatribune.com/news/2009/aug/06/minuteman-outlasted -notoriety-died-with-regrets/.

25. *American Jewish Year Book,* 1967.

26. See http://www.textfiles.com/conspiracy/walker.txt (as of 2010).

27. "General Walker Faces Sex Charges, Right-Wing Figure Accused in Dallas of Lewdness," *New York Times,* http://select.nytimes.com/gst/abstract .html?res=F50B1FFE3F5A167493CBA9178CD85F428785F9.

28. "Eisenhower Says Officers Should Stay Out of Politics," *New York Times,* November 24, 1961.

29. John F. Kennedy, "Conspiracy Theories Speech, November 18, 2961," *PBS,* n.d., http://www.pbs.org/wgbh/amex/presidents/35_kennedy/psources /ps_conspir.html.

30. "Sovereign Citizens Movement," *Anti-Defamation League,* n.d., http://www .adl.org/Learn/Ext_US/SCM.asp?LEARN_Cat=Extremism&LEARN_SubCat =Extremism_in_America&xpicked=4&item=sov.

31. "5 Are Convicted of Threats Against I.R.S. Agents," *New York Times,* October 4, 1987.

32. See http://www.splcenter.org/blog/2010/02/18/irs-long-a-target-of-anti government-extremists/ (as of 2010).

33. "Aryan Financial 'Whiz' Pleads to Ripping Off Investors," Intelligence Report no. 113, *Southern Poverty Law Center* (Spring 2004), http://www.splcenter .org/news/item.jsp?aid=383.

34. Christopher Hewitt, *Political Violence and Terrorism in Modern America: A Chronology* (Santa Barbara, CA: Praeger Security International, 2005), 28–90.

35. Peggy Noonan, "Keeping America Safe from Ranters," *Wall Street Journal,* October 2, 2009, http://online.wsj.com/article/SB1000142405274870447150457 4447621545728370.html.

36. Lee Fang, "Gohmert Trades Ideas with Conspiracy Theorist, Says Obama Health Plan Will 'Absolutely Kill Senior Citizens,'" *ThinkProgress* (blog), July 27, 2009, http://thinkprogress.org/2009/07/27/gohmert-conspiracies-alexjones/.

37. Interview with Billy Glassberg, October 2009.

38. "Rage Grows in America: Anti-Government Conspiracies," *Anti-Defamation League,* November 2009, http://www.adl.org/special_reports/rage-grows-in -America/Rage-Grows-In-America.pdf.

39. "Beck: 'There Is a Coup Going On . . . It Has Been Done Through the Guise of an Election,'" *Media Matters for America,* August 31, 2009, http://mediamatters .org/mmtv/200908310007, accessed September 3, 2009, video.

40. Terry Krepel, "Newsmax Columnist: Military Coup 'to Resolve the Obama Problem Is Not Unrealistic,'" *Media Matters for America,* September 29, 2009 (5:57 p.m.), http://mediamatters.org/blog/200909290042.

41. Rob Waters, "'Leave or Else,' YouTube Video Warns Obama," *Southern Poverty Law Center* (blog), October 7, 2009 (10:11 a.m.), http://www.splcenter.org /blog/2009/10/07/leave-or-else-youtube-video-warns-obama/.

42. Dennis B. Roddy, "Suspect in Officers' Shooting Was into Conspiracy Theories," *Pittsburgh Post Gazette,* April 5, 2009, http://www.post-gazette.com /local/city/2009/04/05/Suspect-in-officers-shooting-was-into-conspiracy-theories /stories/200904050116.

43. Arthur Delaney, "Joshua Cartwright: Another Deadly Gunman 'Severely Disturbed' by Obama's Election," *Huffington Post,* May 28, 2009, http://www .huffingtonpost.com/2009/04/27/joshua-cartwright-cop-kil_n_191929.html.

44. Drew Griffin, Randi Kaye, Kathleen Johnston, Paul Vercammen, Ashley Fantz, and Matt Smith, "Clinic Worker Chased Off Suspect Before Doctor's Slaying," *CNN,* June 1, 2009, http://www.cnn.com/2009/CRIME/06/01/kansas.doctor .killed.charges/index.html.

45. "Obama 'Created by Jews,' Museum Killing Suspect Wrote," *CNN,* June 11, 2009, http://www.cnn.com/2009/CRIME/06/11/museum.shooting.suspect.two/.

46. *New York Times,* December 5, 2009.

47. Geoffrey Dunn, "'Watermelon Roll': More Racism from 'Team Sarah,'" *Huffington Post*, December 21, 2008, http://www.huffingtonpost.com/geoffrey-dunn/watermelon-roll-more-rac_b_152743.html_NoPara.

48. Potok, "Exploring the Death of Matthew Shepard."

49. Eileen Sullivan, "Officials See Rise in Militia Groups Across US," *Huffington Post*, August 12, 2009, http://www.huffingtonpost.com/2009/08/12/officials-see-rise-in-mil_n_257128.html.

Chapter 11: The Kamikaze Caucus

1. Rosalind S. Hildebrand, "Nunes Calls Fellow House Republicans 'Lemmings with Suicide Vests,'" *Washington Post*, September 30, 2013, http://www.washingtonpost.com/blogs/post-politics/wp/2013/09/30/nunes-calls-fellow-house-republicans-lemmings-with-suicide-vests/.

2. Chris Cillizza, "How Congress Became the Most Polarized and Unproductive It's Ever Been," *Washington Post* (blog), February 3, 2014, http://www.washingtonpost.com/blogs/the-fix/wp/2014/02/03/how-congress-became-the-most-polarized-and-unproductive-its-ever-been/.

3. Ibid.

4. John McCain, Twitter, October 26, 2011 (4:43 p.m.), https://twitter.com/SenJohnMcCain.

5. Alastair Jamieson, "Standard and Poor's Statement: US Credit Rating Could Be Cut Even Further," *Telegraph*, August 6, 2011, http://www.telegraph.co.uk/finance/financialcrisis/8685668/Standard-and-Poors-statement-US-credit-rating-could-be-cut-even-further.html.

6. Jonathan Chait, "Hostage Taking Not Like Regular Negotiating," *New York Magazine*, January 11, 2013, http://nymag.com/daily/intelligencer/2013/01/hostage-taking-not-like-regular-negotiating.html.

7. Sam Stein, "Sharron Angle's Advice for Rape Victims Considering Abortion: Turn Lemons into Lemonade," *Huffington Post*, July 8, 2010, http://www.huffingtonpost.com/2010/07/08/sharron-angles-advice-for_n_639294.html.

8. Greg Sargent, "Sharron Angle Floated Possibility of Armed Insurrection," *Washington Post* (blog), June 15, 2010, http://voices.washingtonpost.com/plum-line/2010/06/sharron_angle_floated_possibil.html.

9. "States Enact Record Numbers of Abortion Restrictions in 2011," The Guttmacher Institute, January 5, 2012. http://www.guttmacher.org/media/inthenews/2012/01/05/endofyear.html

10. Steve Benen, "Congressman: Gay Marriage 'a Threat to the Nation's Survival,'" *Washington Monthly* (blog), October 28, 2011, http://www.washingtonmonthly.com/political-animal/2011_10/congressman_gay_marriage_a_thr033151.php. Rachel Weiner, "Jim DeMint Criticized for Comments on Gay and Sexually Active Single Teachers," *Washington Post*, October 6, 2010, http://voices.washingtonpost.com/44/2010/10/jim-demint-criticized-for-comm.html.

11. Michael Kirkland, "Islamic Law in U.S. Courts," United Press International, May 19, 2013, http://www.upi.com/Top_News/US/2013/05/19/Islamic-law-in-US-courts/UPI-64481368948600/.

12. Newt Gingrich, "How America Became a 'Secular-Socialist Machine,'" *Washington Post*, April 23, 2010, www.washingtonpost.com/wp-dyn/content/article/2010/04/22/AR2010042204207.html.

13. Jon Huntsman, Twitter, August 18, 2011 (10:57 a.m.), https://twitter.com/JonHuntsman/status/104250677051654144.

14. Peter H. Stone, "Sheldon Adelson Spent Far More on Campaign Than Previously Known," *Huffington Post*, December 3, 2012, http://www.huffingtonpost.com/2012/12/03/sheldon-adelson-2012-election_n_2223589.html.

15. Seth Cline, "Sheldon Adelson Spent $150 Million on Election," *US News*, December 3, 2012, http://www.usnews.com/news/articles/2012/12/03/sheldon-adelson-ended-up-spending-150-million.

16. Felicia Sonmez, "Santorum: 'Obama Is "a Snob" Because He Wants "Everybody in America to Go to College,"'" *Washington Post*, February 25, 2012, http://www.washingtonpost.com/blogs/post-politics/post/santorum-obama-is-a-snob-because-he-wants-everybody-in-america-to-go-to-college/2012/02/25/gIQATJffaR_blog.html.

17. Paul Johnson, "When Church Met State: A New Romantic Comedy from Rick Santorum," *Huffington Post*, February 29, 2012, http://www.huffingtonpost.com/pauljohnson/rick-santorum-church-state_b_1308690.html.

18. Darius Dixon, "Allen West: 80 Communists in the House," *Politico* (blog), April 11, 2012, http://www.politico.com/news/stories/0412/75025.html.

19. Richard Hofstadter, *Anti-Intellectualism in American Life* (New York: Vintage Books, 1963), 135.

20. John Eligon and Michael Schwirtz, "Senate Candidate Provokes Ire with 'Legitimate Rape' Comment," *New York Times*, August 19, 2012, http://www.nytimes.com/2012/08/20/us/politics/todd-akin-provokes-ire-with-legitimate-rape-comment.html?_r=0.

21. Hunter Walker, "Pro-Romney Super PAC Launches Anti–Gay Marriage Ad to Snag Southern Swing State Votes," *New York Observer*, September 4, 2012, http://observer.com/2012/09/super-pac-targets-obama-with-gay-marriage-scare-campaign/.

22. Brianna Keiler, "Ad Linking Mitt Romney to Woman's Death Continues to Dog Obama Campaign," *CNN*, August 9, 2012, http://whitehouse.blogs.cnn.com/2012/08/09/ad-linking-mitt-romney-to-womans-death-continues-to-dog-obama-campaign/.

23. John Heilemann and Mark Halperin, *Double Down: Game Change 2012* (New York: Penguin Press, 2013), 13.

24. *Voteview*, "An Update on Political Polarization (Through 2011)—Part III: The Presidential Square Wave," *Voteview* (blog), February 3, 2012, http://voteview.com/blog/?p=317.

25. Dick Morris, "Romney Will Win in a 'Landslide,'" *The O'Reilly Factor,* October 31, 2012.

26. From a speech by Pauline Kael, delivered to Modern Language Association on December 28, 1978, and cited by *New York Times.*

27. Mike Lofgren, "Goodbye to All That: Reflections of a GOP Operative Who Left the Cult," *Truth-Out.org,* September 3, 2011.

28. Ryu Spaeth, "Watch: Chris Christie Slams the GOP over Sandy Aid," *Week,* January 2, 2013, http://theweek.com/article/index/238341/watch-chris-christie -slams-the-gop-over-sandy-aid.

29. Emily Swanson, "Background Checks Beat Apple Pie, Baseball, Kittens in America's Hearts: Poll," *Huffington Post,* April 13, 2013, http://www.huffingtonpost .com/2013/04/13/background-checks-poll_n_3070954.html.

30. Greg Sargent, "Pat Toomey Confirms: Obama Is Right About GOP," *Washington Post,* May 1, 2013, http://www.washingtonpost.com/blogs/plum-line /wp/2013/05/01/pat-toomey-confirms-it-obama-is-right-about-gop/.

31. Paul Waldman, *Fraud: The Strategy Behind the Bush Lies and Why the Media Didn't Tell You* (Naperville, IL: Sourcebooks, 2004), 266.

32. Ezra Klein, "Grover Norquist on Ted Cruz: 'He Pushed House Republicans into Traffic and Wandered Away,'" *Washington Post,* October 2, 2013, http:// www.washingtonpost.com/blogs/wonkblog/wp/2013/10/02/grover-norquist-ted -cruz-pushed-house-republicans-into-traffic-and-wandered-away/.

33. Hildebrand, "Nunes Calls Fellow House Republicans 'Lemmings with Suicide Vests.'"

34. Michael D. Shear and Jeremy W. Peters, "Senators Near Fiscal Deal, but the House Is Uncertain," *New York Times,* October 14, 2013, http://www.ny times.com/2013/10/15/us/politics/seeking-deal-to-avert-default-lawmakers-to -meet-obama.html.

35. David A. Fahrenthold, "For Rep. Ted Yoho, Government Shutdown Is 'the Tremor Before the Tsunami,'" *Washington Post,* October 4, 2013.

36. Jonathan Capehart, "Stutzman, Obama, and Disrespect," *Washington Post,* October 3, 2013, http://www.washingtonpost.com/blogs/post-partisan/wp/2013 /10/03/stutzman-obama-and-disrespect.

37. Tom Kludt, "McConnell: I'll 'Work with the Government We Have—Not the One I Wish We Had,'" *Talking Points Memo* (blog), October 11, 2013, http:// talkingpointsmemo.com/livewire/mcconnell-i-ll-work-with-the-government -we-have-not-the-one-i-wish-we-had.

38. Morgan Whittaker, "Ted Nugent Calls Obama 'Subhuman Mongrel,'" *MSNBC,* January 22, 2014, http://www.msnbc.com/politicsnation/ted-nugent -calls-obama-subhuman-mongrel.

39. "GOP Seen as Principled, but Out of Touch and Too Extreme," *Pew Research Center for the People and the Press,* February 26, 2013.

40. Jenny Beth Martin, "John Boehner's Betrayal," *New York Times*, December 19, 2013, http://www.nytimes.com/2013/12/20/opinion/john-boehners-betrayal .html.

Conclusion: How to Take America Back from the Lunatic Fringe

1. Peter Pringle, "'We're Heading into Nut Country': President Kennedy Said This to an Aide . . . ," *Independent*, November 20, 1993, http://www.independent .co.uk/life-style/were-heading-into-nut-country-president-kennedy-said-this -to-an-aide-as-he-began-his-fatal-visit-to-texas-thirty-years-ago-here-peter -pringle-evokes-dallas-as-it-was-then-a-hostile-place-which-cared-very-little -for-the-dream-that-died-there-1505387.html.

2. Chris Cillizza, "The Ideological Middle Is Dead in Congress. Really Dead," *Washington Post*, April 10, 2014, http://www.washingtonpost.com/blogs/the-fix/wp /2014/04/10/the-ideological-middle-is-dead-in-congress-really-dead/?la.

3. Dave Weigel, "How Ridiculous Gerrymanders Saved the House Republican Majority," *Slate.com*, November 7, 2012, http://www.slate.com/blogs/weigel /2012/11/07/how_ridiculous_gerrymanders_saved_the_house_republican _majority.html.

4. Conor Friedersdorf, "Glenn Beck: I Played a Role . . . in Helping Tear the Country Apart," *Atlantic*, January 24, 2014, http://www.theatlantic.com/politics /archive/2014/01/glenn-beck-i-played-a-role-in-helping-tear-the-country-apart /283304/.

5. George Washington, "Washington's Farewell Address, 1796," *The Avalon Project*, accessed July 20, 2009, http://avalon.law.yale.edu/18th_century/washing .asp.

BIBLIOGRAPHY

Conason, Joe, and Gene Lyons. *The Hunting of the President: The Ten-Year Campaign to Destroy Bill and Hillary Clinton*. New York: Thomas Dunne Books, 2000.

Edwards, Mickey. *The Parties Versus the People*. New Haven: Yale University Press, 2012.

Fiorina, Morris, Samuel J. Abrams, and Jeremy C. Pope. *Culture War? The Myth of a Polarized America*. London: Longman, 2010.

Foster, Arnold, and Benjamin Epstein. *The Trouble-Makers: The New Anti-Defamation League Report on Intolerance in the United States*. Garden City, NY: Country Life Press, 1952.

Goldberg, Robert Alan. *Enemies Within: The Culture of Conspiracy in Modern America*. New Haven: Yale University Press, 2001.

Haidt, Jonathan. *The Righteous Mind*. New York: Pantheon Books, 2012.

Hofstader, Richard. *Anti-Intellectualism in American Life*. New York: Alfred A. Knopf, 1962.

———. *The Paranoid Style in American Politics and Other Essays*. New York: Vintage Books, 1952, 2008.

Mann, Thomas E., and Norman J. Ornstein. *It's Even Worse Than It Looks: How the American Constitutional System Collided with the New Politics of Extremism*. New York: Basic Books, 2012.

Overstreet, Harry, and Bonaro Overstreet. *The Strange Tactics of Extremism*. New York: W. W. Norton, 1964.

Schlesinger, Arthur, Jr. *The Disuniting of America: Reflections on a Multicultural Society*. New York: W. W. Norton, 1998.

Sunstein, Cass R. *Conspiracy Theories and Other Dangerous Ideas*. New York: Simon & Schuster, 2014.

———. *Going to Extremes: How Like Minds Unite and Divide*. New York: Oxford University Press, 2011.

———. *How to Humble a Wingnut and Other Lessons in Behavioral Economics*. Chicago: Chicago Shorts, 2013.

INDEX

John Avlon is an author, columnist, and editor-in-chief of *The Daily Beast*. A CNN contributor, he won the National Society of Newspaper Columnists' Award for Best Online Column in 2012. He is the author of *Independent Nation* and co-edited two volumes of *Deadline Artists: America's Greatest Newspaper Columnists*. President Bill Clinton praised the first edition of *Wingnuts*, saying it "offers a clear and comprehensive review of the forces on the outer edges of the political spectrum that shape and distort our political debate. Shedding more heat than light, they drive frustrated, alienated citizens away from the reasoned discourse that can produce real solutions to our problems."